The Akshaya Pat.

The Great Companion to Meditations & Aphorisms for Moral Transformation:

Complete Companion Series Collection
Of Extracted Quotes from the Akshaya Patra Series:

Manasa Bhajare: Worship in the Mind:
Vol 1 Book 1 Parts 1-3
Moral Destiny, The Miracle of Light,
The Legacy of Light:
Vol 1 Book 2 Parts 1-3

Copyright © 2017 by Signet IL Y' Viavia: DANIEL

Library of Congress Control Number: Pending

This Black and White Interior Softbound Edition Published by Daniel Howard Schmidt is printed by IngramSpark for distribution to U.S. and International retail outlets:

ISBN-10: 1-946479-65-9
ISBN-13: 978-1-946479-65-5

All rights reserved. No part of this book may be reproduced or transmitted in any form or by any means, electronic or mechanical, including photocopying, recording, or by any information storage and retrieval system, without permission in writing from the copyright owner.

Rev. Date: 05/01/2017

Published by: Daniel Howard Schmidt
31915 Rancho California Rd. Ste. 200-447
Temecula, CA 92591
1 (888) 365-2460
SignetDaniel@gmail.com
http://signet-il-ya-viavia.com/

  SIGNET IL Y' VIAVIA: DANIEL

The AKSHAYA PATRA Series
MANASA BHAJARE: Worship in the Mind
Volume ONE – Book ONE – Part ONE

Man's First Obligation for living is to lead a moral life. We come in search of Truth. Our nature is bound by Truth. We have a destiny to perfect the strength of character. If we fail, we have only ourselves to blame. Though failure is neither an excuse nor an option. You are not free to decide. Nature provided all the tools necessary. God attended as companion. The outcome undecided. Freedom means free to choose to pass or fail, but not to end the game. Heaven or Hell is a personal choice. The spirit for success in this lies with you. Your virtues are weighed and the balance is paid in full measure. Virtue is our Guardian. – DANISHWARA,
THE Lord Dani, DANIEL.

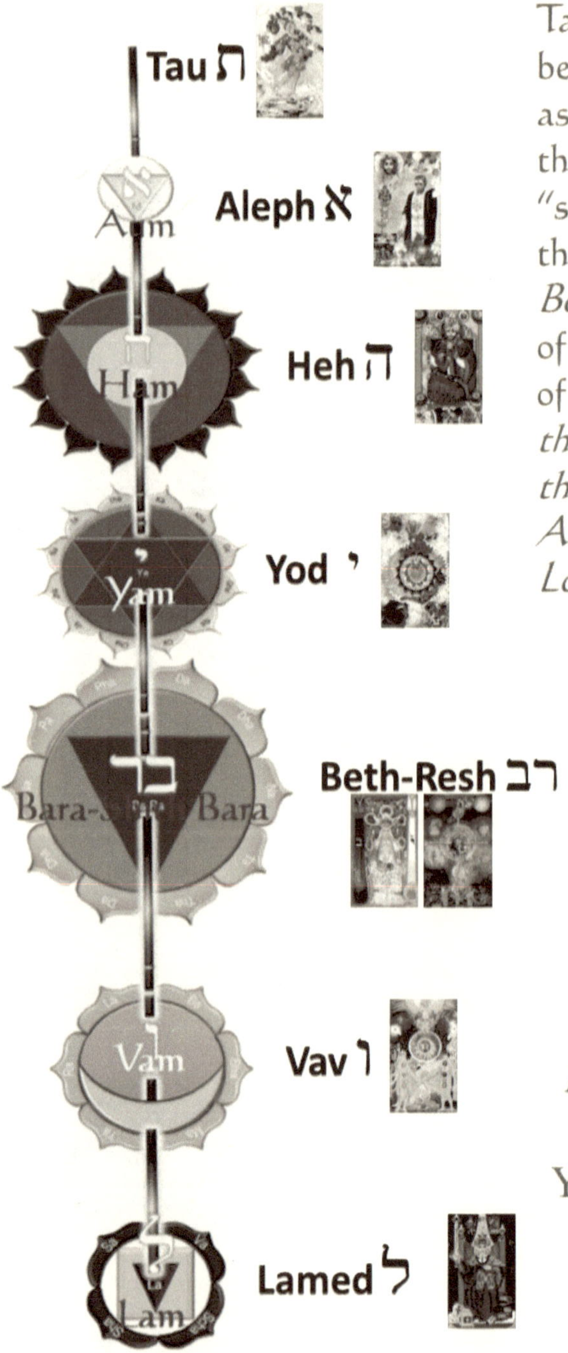

Tau ת
Aleph א
Heh ה
Yod י
Beth-Resh בר
Vav ו
Lamed ל

Tau Truth (emTh) became Adam-Man; as seminal seed from the super-conscious "sub-atomic" dust in the first cause or *Bereshith*. The light of God. The Breath of Life. *And then there was Light. And then there was Life. And then there was Love.*

The Tau coil rewound and united "*w'eth*" the Heaven & Earth seated on the Tree of Life. It shone brightly as the Light in Man:

ABBA ABRHm,
AHYH BRA
YHVH-ALVHYm

....The Sephiroth-spirit: Kundalini

Introduction

People have asked, "Well, what do I do with these?"

The vitality, human aura, mind or mental faculties (objective, subjective, subconscious and Cosmic) are all mirrors reflecting realities of the absolute—Whether these are in nature, society, or experienced in the vast cosmos in the light and vitality of the galaxies, stars and planets.

The visualization, in practice ceremonially, of these psychic visual elements, or other such divine images, along with their names, forms, tones, sounds and colors in these vital fields, "assumes" their identity, as an actor would who completely takes on the character of a role.

Your thought and breath give them life. We say, to take these on as a Divine Assumption. These are introductions only. We need these first steps to begin to take them further.

When you assume these native energies of consciousness you become them. We live in that miracle stretched between mortality and immortality. These are ideal identities sometimes confused by that modern, greatly abused, concept of the ancient archetype or their made-up types.

The archetype is not simply a mental identity. It is a living creature effecting all elemental life within the cosmos and not simply inside of one's mental functions. These are defined as the element or planetary forms. They prepare the future, transform ideas, and create conditions for attunement, as would a tuning fork, to those frequencies they identify with across the cosmos.

These exist across the spectrum on the Tree of Life. They are Time-Space-Conscious creatures of motion and roll out as divine identities. In angels, historically they are referred to as the angles of space and time that exist beyond those forms, though not excluding but

including them, which is why they are associated with space locations, and hours and days or weeks, months and years as time.

In the letters, they are referred to in Theosophy as the "Letter Creatures," by "Thomas Vaughan" (*Bacon- Vagan*), the immortal founder. But as named they identify with the Word of God. The Word of God is the alphabetical linguistic that is abused by human babel.

These "Letter Creatures," occupy themselves in Time and Space hierarchies of consciousness. Therefore, they can predict, or instigate live events in Time and Space. You can in fact set up future events by them. They also act like magnets or storehouses.

They are also referred to as seeds as in "seed sounds."

Why seeds? Well, because they are living things that grow. As thoughts are things, these take on living forms as archetypes or creatures of the imagination in the "magic" of nature and the mind. In this sense, they serve as would the divine creatures of Prospero's mind. They have infinite potential if given such an opportunity, in that which is divine (*Omniscient, omnipotent, and omnipresent, having life existence from the unlimited potential.*)

This is what is meant by the "*thorn to remove a thorn.*"

Don't worry. It is doubtful that you would become anything of a Milrepa or Prospero in a lifetime.

These are advanced states usually developed over many lives though the faults are familial obstacles, lack of focus and laziness.

As well these require great sacrifices (*Yagna*). What is human must be transformed through sacrifice into what it divine. One must sacrifice one's personal life to a divine life to achieve the ideal assumption of that immortal state, where God can refine the faculty and unfold it back through you.

One can only sacrifice to God that which is in their possession. So, one must possess a skill or virtue first before it can be offered in sacrifice to God. This is something that Frater Erwin Watermeyer taught and demonstrated to us, when he taught at Rose Croix University.

The concept of the Great White Brotherhood, sometimes gloated about freely without substance, is like that. However, that, as Frater Watermeyer taught us, as an organization, is closed. It is not something common to societies. No open organization is linked to it. One has to die within it for another to take their place, and that only if one were to have that specific skillset that is lost. Each person in that society is numbered, and the number is linked to their responsibility. It is written in their Sonnets as if on a *"Shakespearean" Trestle Board*.

We are not these persons, or I should say it is highly unlikely. They are the unknown Great Souls called the *liberated-living*, living by virtue of having engaged in practices that put them into that perfect state of the *Nara-Narayana* or the *Man-Divine* called *Adam Ka-Ad-Amon*, both physically and spiritually on the Tree of Life. But we have these tools by which to grow along the path at our own pace. These, tools and practices are not so common as to be unremarkable, and are given here as an introduction to their method.

In Theosophy, it has always been affirmed that in native theology, what is less than a molecule is called by Rosicrucians Spirit Energy and called in Hebrew *Bereshith*. That image of the atom and subatomic world is *non-particle*, it is an endless sphere of bliss made of mere wiggle forms of spirit energy. What is Kundalini in the Center of Man, is the same *Beast Form* or First Son of God. God is in that native sun in the center of every heart. It is that same resident in the center of every Sun. It is that massive illumination of unimaginable power seen exploded in the near zero wiggle of neutrinos or found in the exploding neutron stars in the Atma-Spherical Akasha.

The *Akshaya Patra* series is written as a book to augment books so that they may inspire the Mysteries ... A house that is loved is always satisfied ...

•

Man's first obligation for living is to lead a moral life. We come in search of Truth. Our nature is bound by Truth. We have a destiny to perfect the strength of character. If we fail, we have only ourselves to blame.

•

Freedom means free to choose to pass or fail, but not to end the game. Heaven or Hell is a personal choice. The spirit for success lies with you [within you]. Your virtues are weighed and the balance is paid in full measure.

•

The Mysteries are "*uncommon.*" They suffer from a language that is "*common*" to explain the *Mysterious Word* as *Logos Law* ... *[The Divine Alphabet of imaged meaning, or the magical Word of God.]*

•

The cause originates in the future. [*Seeded in the Beginning, or Bereshith.*] The target exists in a state of perfection, from its first instant, which is unfolding. We call this future state, *The Beginning*. It is an eternal beginning, an eternal instant.

•

Symbolical systems are living systems. They thrive, grow, develop, and die and come to life again ... We give life to our creations. This is done through the power of mind and breath; the Soul, the Spirit, consciousness, and life energies, and these embrace us thru their power of love and devotion and come to life thru concentration.

•

Energy is consciousness, and it follows the power of the will, even more so when it calls and recalls to mind and consciousness Divinity, and provides a path to awaken awareness to the divine.

•

In ceremonial magic, intense concentration animates the image, the statue, or the object, and it takes on properties that are immaterial. Thru this effort, they become living forms that have a soul and life of their own. The imagery becomes ultimately magical.

•

Where God knows everything, man follows, knowing nothing. Each, it seems, God and Man, pretending. Man, the world inspired. Each Being, is turned the other way around, spun, spinning, in a kingdom of fools turned upside down. We cry tears at night, when our best thoughts are silent, dreaming, sleeping saying: *"Mad trumpet, mad world, turn the volume down! It bothers the listening ear, for speaking wisdom to mad entities. We demand! Would this mad world's madness settle down?"*

•

We are the past, and we all stand fast to accept this, condemning the sins committed in our past, contrasting our lives

to sins committed by us in our former fate. We are our history. We come again and again and will return to this again by fate. We are our champions, the rescued and the Rescuer.

•

The world of love rides inside. Residing in the man, to hide within the vessel, shining like the sun: personal, self-resident, the Self the resident, who vacations in the heart. Through transformations, the Love Entity finds some way to project its nature out. We like a light-spun web weaving, are spun through the vacant filters, on the cross-stitch thread conceiving—shaped by shadows on contrasting edge, and we left dangling by a thread, are as if hung up on a wall. It is, in fact, a strange shadow cast of its former energy. One wonders if such a memory exists, but there it is before us, our "everything", the false world we believe in.

•

The spirit lies within us to our graves; flying in and out. The spirit shines without; as that life that is border and boundary-less. Radiant eyes project the heart, the divine vessel of the Sun. Where one light reflects upon the vessel of love, through the mirror of mind, the other is its source—one self-shining productive ember, the other mere reflection of its timeless art.

•

What do we believe then, if our own experience is denied? Dumbed to touch with eyes so blind and atheistic: our senses formed as man, are in the world unrecognized as the thief who witnessed his own robbery with lies: and upon examination they are the first to deceive us.

•

Reason is the Forerunner of Truth. Truth is the bulwark of reason. Strive for so much fortification so as to make your life treasurable and worthy of our memories.

•

True religion is not superstitious. True magic is the interior science of motion, time, Superconsciousness and bliss, and man's relationship to the cosmic entity. Our lives mere ships at sea, in the field of living energy, and a single entity in Mind. Above the heavens (stars) below the hell (Iron in the fires in the center of the earth) the perfect complement between these of the polar grades of electromagnetic energy. Our lighting lives. There lies the theater of magic.

•

Man does not measure science by the yardstick of the fool. Neither should religion or magic receive such tragic measurements of liberal idiocy just because it's written in a book or stuffed into our heads.

•

We are free. We choose. We deserve our blessings based upon these.

•

What is our happiness? The future descending from a future time; comes at us, and we proceed moving towards divine destiny. Our free will is to choose it well. It is not to do what pleases us; that suffers egoism. We did not create it. We did not sustain it. We did not take it away. That lesson was provided for us by our destiny.

•

God incarnates as Time (*motion*) into Eternity. Man senses suffering; it comes with a blessing.

•

Life comes from LIFE. Love comes from LOVE. Truth comes from TRUTH. Light forms to illuminate all living things. These permeate eternity and time and exist at the basis of anything created or set into motion, at the foundation preceding time and space.

•

Love so tender built this universe and turned mere wiggles into stone . . .

•

Time is the God of Creation, the God of Creation is Time. This is the outer appearance. Time is a liquid entity. Beyond the form the essence of truth exists as righteous timelessness . . .

•

What happens within the formless entity effects the entity formed, or the created Cosmos or Cosmic Entity; the form of God as motion in the play of Cosmic Consciousness.

•

All living and nonliving things are effected by and are the effects of these eternal causes. All living things are born, set in motion, and effected by these transitions of change in time and space; appearing as instantaneous states of change . . .

•

The cosmos is an eternal clock of light biology that forms as the record of Time . . .

•

Each and every part is a universal part. All parts communicate . . . The life is in the world. But the life is not the world.

•

No part of time is an accident. There is no cause/effect disengagement. What exists then within this microcosmic world has an influence on the molecular, atomic, and subatomic. [*Out of the spirit hidden in every center.*]

•

The symbols are conventional, but the existence of God will be ever unimaginable. Therefore, humility is a requisite before the triumph of the heart is faced.

•

The cosmos creates, sustains, and supports our needs to awaken us from the world of dreams. The entire cosmos is inside of us, likened to *The Mirror or the Mysteries,* the reflections of the soul, which reflect/resound the mobile and immobile.

•

Upon meditation, I am asked to say that "untruth must be answered with truth for either to be engaging."

•

One voice in descent or opposition does little harm. One voice of untruth on the college campus uttered by a professor of such stature does great harm, which follows one through the shadows of the living to meet the truth at the juncture of that broad way determined at the entrance to death's playground before the power of the infinite.

•

Science is fraught with fighting Truth against hypothesis, with much that is fictionalized (*theoretical*)...

•

There is a creed of cowardice in philosophy that has no place for lack of self-confidence and self-determination, peers who fear the world's opinion.

•

Self-realization is, as practiced through the centuries, not a subject for the tame or those who hide behind the chalkboard in longwinded cowardice and desire that spirit for hypnotizing children.

•

It is easy to follow the crowded lane filled with greed and self-indulgence; fulfilling selfish needs. It is not so easy to pass along this way. It is saved for the militant mystics or initiated savants, the dutiful, with prospects of dedication and commitment, those who emulate the devotion through hands-on experience and self-initiation, service, and self-sacrifice.

•

I am reminded that *"if timid, one should remain where they are in life, and not pursue the mysteries... To attain pure light, one must be ready to lose one's life."* [Those who have, did.]

•

The true nature of the Mystic; is one who is aware that there is something greater than themselves behind it all.

•

God is not a tyrant. Man can be. But fame and name are only divine attributes.

•

The moments of glory disappear like the shade when the sun is passing overhead.

•

Opposites do not attract; when space collapses that which is ONE appears. By this, all science disappears and God reveals a miracle in the depths of empty space. *"I, am the subject in it."*

•

Practical knowledge is only of benefit for those who are dedicated to the game with firm practical resolve. One must be like the Eagle clawing the Earth, with wings spread to conquer the skies and the sight capable of seeing anywhere with just two eyes—the inner and the outer.

•

Resolve to be firm and fluid, creative and determined to fix things into a finished product, and at the same time examine to keep a firm footing, in your considerations for the practical benefit, as a fiduciary leader would, for the management of the relationship that exists between God and Man . . .

•

Think always *"I am responsible for the welfare of all with whom I touch."*

•

Know this Truth first and foremost: Everything is Truth, all things come from Love; the Universe Descends from Awareness, Duality is an illusion.

•

There are five principle powers within you that make you human. These are Love, Truth, Peace; *Following the Guidance on the Inner Path of the Law and Good Conscience in Moral and Ethical Behavior;* and Non-Violent actions.

•

Chivalry is divine, and to stand a good stand and fight a good fight is truly to influence Nonviolence (*ahimsa*) . . . To oppose good conduct is also an act of violence.

•

The lazy indolent are worthless, first in body and then in head, and soon enough, the heart is dead, subjected to the waste of energy. Why seek that company?

•

Greater love hath no man than this: that a man lay down his life for his friends, (John 15:13). To act in good conscience embraces the *Doctrine of Chivalry,* which is the highest form of selfless service and duty.

•

"For the cause of good" is to state in good conscience unselfish protection and selfless service, to honor what is good.

•

In the symbols, there are secrets in multiple meanings and multiple layers, which are hidden in plain sight.

•

God, as a principle, is as pure and *"elegant"* as any notion of physics.

•

God created out of God all this with the first motion of creation, that is, God spoke and then there was *Light* as God entered into it.

•

Sound and Light... "*In the beginning...*" *(Bereshith)* being the ideal root cause (*is*) at that state of first motion that is omnipresent.

•

There are no two entities. There is only ONE. As the statement implies mathematically, "God is ONE and before ONE what will thou count?"

•

Every cell of me is a part of me. Yet I am *not* the body. I am I. That is the permanent part that is divine.

•

Every part of God is permanent. This is the root cause of immortality.

•

The energy is *one*, the lights are many... God is *one*, but creatures are many. They shine as ornaments, demonstrating the existence of the *one* by their very existence.

•

"*What is boundaryless is already anywhere and everywhere.*" The shape of every heart is within the center of everything; since it is the pattern followed that represents the Golden Mean.

•

These are records of those mysteries heard when everything else in the world is silent and asleep.

•

The ideal in the end is to learn how to love, be love, and emanate love and to understand that faith and devotion are necessary to self-growth. Faith and devotion, dedicated to truth, and a strict adherence to right living, these are the true ideals. No knowledge is practical or useful without these.

•

In this quest, the tongue is a mighty weapon. Not only for what you say and eat, but it is an electric tool for remembering. It is the vehicle for pointing what might be called the human lightning . . .

•

Concentration leads to contemplation which leads to meditation. Concentration on symbols focuses the attention. The image becomes absorbed, and you become the image contemplated upon.

•

The purpose of the movement of these energies is to invoke the powers of Life, Light and Love, not so much to become God in name and form, because this is who you are, but to remember, or to invoke the memory of the miracle that discovers that this is what you are, and that this is where you came from.

•

Today as in the beginning, there is no difference. The end is in the beginning as the serpent bites its tail. Not life history hidden in the past but life's mystery that is hidden in the cause. There is no beginning; there is no end.

•

We are MIND [*the bundle of desires*] and therefore, we are the reflection that becomes what we see, hear, say repeating blind obsessions.

•

We see, we become; that's the end of it . . . We are burdened by the dream; our mind reflects the image in its freedom to perceive, judge and verify. It is not by instinct, but by Reason that man is occupied. Reason is divine.

•

There is suffering in obsession. When obsessions touch on religions, metaphysics, and theaters of social goodness, they become distracted, trip, and fall. Instead of reflection on our natures, political battles rage, and all this attitude wells up in endless fighting, often engaged on pretense by social groups, to gain segmented followings in society.

•

Our happiness is founded upon the right conditions that support freethinking and the bliss of the human heart. No man is free who overspends.

•

No man is free who commits a lie, steals from another, or lives off wealth that is inappropriately acquired. Government enslaves the debtor state.

•

Every breath is monitored, and with every thought, a record is carved upon the face of Ultimate Freedom and Liberation that meets you at death. You are held to account, forgiven and sent through again and again for reparations, with birth, death, and rebirth.

•

Rebirth ensures equality, which is justice served equally, until the price is paid in the wages of suffering, charity, and decent living; cause and effect thrive through Right Action. These mend the heart on the path of joy and suffering.

•

We meet finally with divinity. This is granted through stages of lives passed, in life after life, in greetings at the Hall of Judgment, where our works are analyzed supremely, and our thoughts, words, and deeds are analyzed to demonstrate one thing—not the extent of thinking and wit . . . but the condition of our human heart.

•

Cosmos and Cosmic *Consciousness* are motions arising from the *one* inseparable motionless entity we call nonduality. It rallies in the sun as the royal resident in the heart.

•

What is more-subtle than the mind but the WORD . . . This is the Mystery. That power written or sung as the inscription hidden within its silent mystery, communicating creative powers more-subtle than Time, more subtle than the Aeon.

•

One may become attached to God by the power of the Divine Name, the Magnet, Transcendental and Mysterious, as the spoken eternal property of the ineffable. This is to cross the boundaries in the Field of Life and Death.

•

The mind is no more than a field of sensation, desires, and imagination, a mirror reflection of the Divine Reality.

•

Omniscient, God in the first instant conceived everything in Time Infinite. Omnipotent, from the finite to the infinite the Eternal Flower endless unfolds itself in its vast eternal effigy.

•

*"**G**od is in me, God is me, I am God."* That is our fate if God is everywhere - ONE.

•

We come "into" Being. Being, not born "of" atoms but "into" atoms as the ideal image of the infinite depth, the mirror birthing reflection of the omnipotent, omniscient omnipresence. This is witnessed in the depths of meditation in the discovery of our identity.

•

Creation is God's primal engine, drawn, push/pulled along, transformed, and powered by its alchemy in the awakening of the *Field of Anything*.

•

The mind is the witness, sitting perched between two worlds; intelligence identifies it, awareness recognizes it; Reason concedes and the WORD declares and creates it; spilling over into elements.

•

It is not a matter of whether man can be hypnotized; man is hypnotized, intoxicated in fact, by every event that passes through his mind.

•

Human drama is the battlefield of good and evil. Every facet of life comes into play. We must learn to discriminate. This infers discrimination itself to be our Sacred Guardian.

•

Naked and self-conscious, the dress of life has let the pilgrim down.

•

Illumination is our inner light, the property of self-realization, and liberty leads us on our path of peace.

•

Wealth's achievement is dharma's destiny. Wealth concedes itself to righteousness. Honesty is everything. Without this, Man is nothing.

•

Without good judgment and discrimination, it opens us up to the worst forms of manipulation. This manipulation is invested in for power by friends and enemies alike. One's freedom gives license to the loss of freedom.

•

Freedom must discriminate with good judgment.

•

Freedom is licensed to man through work. As with worship divinity demands a price through labor. Throughout mortality, one cannot live through idleness.

•

What is taken, without labor, will soon be taken away. No wealth is realized in the act of possession. Wealth is realized

through transformation of wealth and service, into what is good, true, useful, and beautiful.

•

Wealth is the servant of divinity and man; one does not make the servant into a slave and expect a welcome mat.

•

Man is the Messenger of God. God is Truth, Peace, Love and Righteousness. This lies at the foundation of the cosmic destiny.

•

It is in the cultivation of Truth that Man becomes the spokesman and messenger of God. God is not untruth.

•

Untruth is not the message. Bear witness to the truth in thoughts, words, and deeds with honesty. Let it touch the lips and whisper sweetly in the ear.

•

The voice of God is the voice of conscience. The *Silent Speaker Speechless,* is echoed in the inner ear . . . subtle, small, still the voice perfect entity.

•

Learn to discriminate and to be of good conscience. One's fate is judged to depend on this.

•

The conscience ripples in waves of consciousness through eternity, as the voice hidden in the silence, concealed or secreted away within its mystery, as the soundless sound that spans the breadth of human history.

•

Mind, as man, the living image, is the fathomable and false; what is true is unfathomable. To realize the unfathomable, the fathomable must no longer remain its obstacle.

•

As the many disappear, only the *ONE* remains. Wisdom extinguishes both sense and the mind.

•

To be the master, one must conquer those challenges necessary to overcome self-pity. Worse the pretenders who fake desires to be pitiful.

•

Self-mastery must conquer the mind, overcome desire, and find self-content in Truth, Righteousness, Love, Peace and Non-Violence as they exist coming from the first cause of existence, into our existence.

•

We must make ourselves right, from the beginning, at the point of our *Self-Genesis*. We must find the root of our initial cause and seek to identify with our *True Identity*, bringing order out of chaos.

•

Neither the joy of lusts nor any form of academia bring with them true peace or happiness. The inner sound is mastered once only when the voice of God, the conscience, is clarified, and the battles of the world are won.

•

You, the created, live with that which is uncreated. We call the uncreated God. We peer into the world as the living representative bound between the change and changeless entities—the *world* and *God*. Man is the *Divine Instrument*.

•

Truth is pragmatic, enduring, mature, and insightful, neither new nor old, the moment endless.

•

Truth is wedded to righteousness—eternal, unchanging.

•

Truth is reflected in the sweetness in the voice, the beauty of the mind, the witness in the eye, the mirror to the soul.

•

Truth is power, unfailing, witnessing what is ephemeral and eternal.

•

Truth is supernatural, beyond the instruments of lies.

•

Time is change that sweeps through eternity as motion . . . these instruments of change. Time is the measure, the division of the timeless *Divine Eternity*. Time divides space as the instance of vibration and rhythm in cycles of periodicity.

•

God, the purpose and the cause, resides in any place. What is natural is wrested by this miracle. One need not look to the cosmos to find the miracle. We live in the miracle.

•

We are created out of what is everywhere. What is everywhere is bliss.

•

Being is one, endless eternal bliss; there is no room for *nonbeingness*. *Everywhere* is occupied. Everywhere leaves no room for anything other than it. Being exists in everything.

•

"Shells" of *Superconscious Energy* cool and form in it. The substances in its "shells" are formed from it like a shadow of its motion, formed of its intelligence. Its form a living memory, and its creations the proof of its existence, power, and principle.

•

There is no real boundary; no boundary in reality; this is common sense. "*I am not this world, I am not this body, I am not this mind. God is in me, God is me, I am God.*"

•

There, in those beginnings, the *Creative-Engine-Excellent* . . . the creative power of the Word . . . Not vacant speech but the superconscious power of creation consistent with the mystery of language—the Divine *Name*, or spoken śruti, in the power in/of the form.

•

Conceived through evolution as the creative *Name* and *Form* . . . *the pattern of its future form; like petals falling from the Sacred Tree.*

•

Man was born of *God-Soul-Mind-Sense* from the Beginning. It is the cultivation of character that finds virtue manifest and growing into the *Human Property*.

•

The ideal ... is the image of the Grand Man, the one that was ONE with God. [Adam Kadmon] "*Ka-Ad-Amon*" means the "*Vital-Essence of the First Breath*," the essence of the *blue-sky* of bliss at the root of the living Life-Breath [vitality].

•

God is seen in a reflected image of six dimensions or the faces of the cube, and is discovered naked, or reflected in the *Mind* as the miracle of self-consciousness.

•

It is the power of the WORD that incarnates with Man as the first essence of the vital breath; before the mind in perfect consciousness.

•

There are three stages upon which we gather to play: *World-Body-Mind*. This is the unreal, the *Theater of the Cosmic Consciousness*. Nous or *Cosmic Mind* is the *Theater of Universal Attributes*.

•

God "IS" ... That simple word "is" signifies a state of being or coming into being.

•

God rises and sets into three forms: *IS-RA-EL; Mother-Father-Divine*: called the "*House of IS-RA-EL*" or the house of the *Mother-Father-God;* which is the *State of Being* on the Tree

of Life, and the three personifications. [Invoking the phrase: *Honor thy Father and thy Mother. This is the Light of God animated through initiation and the performance of one's duty to both God and Man.*]

•

Christ said, "*I am the Alpha and Omega . . . the beginning and the end,*" meaning in Greek the beginning and end of the alphabet, the *Logos-Mystery-Language*.

•

Cosmos means the universal *Order* or *System . . .* and is the same word as that expressed by the anagram of the Hebrew letter Samekh. The Cosmos is the representative meaning for *Order in Society.* [*The playground of the gods supporting the Cosmic Consciousness.*]

•

The "divine sparks" . . . are the *Eternal Forms of Righteousness* and are the archetype manifestations or divine attributes spilling out from the energy of God . . . These are the hidden powers in man and creation. The names for these Divine Sparks are seen as archetypical forms of the dharma, or righteousness, inherent in the cosmos or *Divine Order*.

•

What "*is*" is the beginning and end. That is the Tau [the Tao, and also final word of the Hebrew/Greek alphabet].

•

We define [Tau] as the *One*, the *One* before division. The *One* before *motion* or movement that is defined as the illumination of the *Word* that becomes *Light* or Superconscious Energy.

•

We say the *One* is *none* or zero, in that its projection wraps itself endlessly around the depth of its eternity. This provides us with the impossible view of time and space, at that instant of fathomless absolutes in the Beginning; the noise of which was the voice-perfect-light . . . expanding wherein there is no place to grow but within itself in form, compressed within the place, in every place, wherein it already is, absolutely.

•

[God's] nature simply exists without beginning, or end, as a circle that is endless, first formed at the cosmic awakening . . . in defining the life perfect entity . . . whose attributes are divinities that are gods of creative illumination from the instant formed of Superconscious Forms, marking Time from the beginning.

•

These [divinities that are gods of creative illumination] exist within us as living attributes of intelligence that operate within nature in the power of its ability to create life within itself, worlds within worlds, surrounding us imperiously, continuing this at a miraculous rate.

•

Awareness is One. We are that, though our mundane awareness may say "No!" Our divine Awareness is trapped in . . . "motion." Being One; it is One with the One Awareness that is in the beginning and end . . .

•

That which wraps itself endlessly into existence . . . comes into being and resolves evolving into itself as the *ONE THING*; as it in time vanishes or disappears again.

•

What is eternal is hidden in a moment.

•

What [God] is can never be ascertained specifically since it is discovered in the "field of change" or motion.

•

Pure awareness exists in the changeless state, at rest in its contemplation of eternity.

•

Pure awareness defines the Origin of God that "is"— awareness and God existing as the absolute . . . being everywhere and nowhere.

•

Out of No-Thing, the Flame and the Light perpetuate the Wisdom of the *Name*; that is the Illumination that forms the Living Lamp of Eternity, which is self-recognized as the illumination of the Stars.

•

All suns are one sun; the propagation of which refers to the Son of God as the Son of the Sun, the royal precedent and model of Eternity.

•

True knowledge, faith, and wisdom lie in the "*Awareness That Is*," Eternal and unchanging, resting in Eternal Bliss or Endless Happiness as the "Unnamed All Names."

•

Awareness is in the Beginning—omnipresent without a cause. The Mind lives and dies in *Awareness*, living with the bodies it dies at liberation . . .

•

Consciousness is the radiance that comes into being as the periodic rate of change in the vast Scale of scales of cosmic motion, in fields of radiant energy.

•

We say the word "spirit," but this is the same as the Hebrew sephiroth . . . or [Hebrew] "SPYRT" of the Superconscious Entity.

•

Consciousness is at the root of form, being both the substance of form and the form maker . . .

•

Silence is the voice that echoes bright in illumination. God is in the light, God is the Light . . .

•

As a hierarchical form, [God] is a "Mountain of Motion," . . . a center of power in the physical universe.

•

Within our solar system, our Earth is the living seed [embryo] placed in a strategic center within this solar mountain in perfect equilibrium. As a place, it is perfectly placed within the midst of a vast field of emptiness.

•

We are born in "fire" [*Hebrew letter Shin or Sin*] to proceed through the lessons required through our nativity. It is to determine that we are born into, and are a product of, the *Elemental Energies*, which provide for our creation, education,

maintenance, sustenance and in the cause-effect, effect the role of our destruction.

•

That "*death is the dress of life*" should be the witness that reveals this message. The dress of life is living motion, cycles, energy in transition, and change. As age sets in, we become aware of this. We are the living witness.

•

One can measure the world, but the world itself is immeasurable, being without a true boundary. All things being One Thing.

•

We dissipate in space at death, but we were never for one moment separate from that space; it was in our "*beginning and ending endless*"; we came from, we return to, our awareness intact, from beginning to end, in the journey through incarnation.

•

Our awareness supersedes the boundaries of life and death. Matter (form) did not rise up into awareness but embodied awareness in form, casting a shadow over the form maker, through that substance in its "*Spirit Nuclear.*"

•

That which lies beyond these dimensions that lead toward stillness is illuminating, breathtaking, beyond imagination . . .

•

Out of the shadows, we discover in death that we are in that abode of endless bliss, incomprehensible in the Light of endless

happiness; having suffered ourselves to get there, we are that light before existence.

•

What is silence is motionless. That Miracle ... What is more silent then space? That miracle ... is a silent scream; God is bound to *Being*, and *Being* is bound to *Eternity*.

•

Akasha [*the infinite essence and Sound-Brahman*] is space [omnipresent]. Space is *Akasha* [the omnipresent infinite essence]. We must be clear on this. What is *Akasha* is the infinite sound embodiment of the Word or Logos, both manifest and unmanifest. It is the *Akasha* that provides the magical effect. [*It is the letter Ham or Sound Brahman—the spirit in the voice.*]

•

It [*Akasha*] is the element of the "Akh" into which the soul and vital essences ... the greater and lesser self, merge as the living forms in the afterlife, shaping the subtle form into its universal form.

•

"What I think, I become," and it forms a connection between the physical and nonphysical worlds for the sake of those loved and the Beloved.

•

In essence ... the essence of man is transformed into the clouded image or visually "Ghost-like" entity as a perfect image formed of the thought and mind of man.

•

We, as mind, are the product of imagination and appearances. This is the energy of the soul as the light of Superconsciousness . . . not different from the energies of the Electromagnetic Spectrum . . . one is the shadow of the other.

•

One must first learn to get to the heart; the center is the seat of bliss.

•

We were formed into space as the life, light, and love through the power of the living breath. It is the "*Sound-Mind*" Brahman that expands into space.

•

Form expands into space in the illumination of the "*Sound-Mind*" . . . What is silent is seen. It stands before you as the form of everything. This is the meaning of . . . the "*Name-Form.*"

•

Where is the proof of the existence of the Sound Brahman? Where is the proof of Ain Soph Aur [the endless light of the non-entity]? We are the proof . . . [if these did not exist, neither would we.]

•

We are arrogant, and that arrogance breeds academics. This is the evil we've inherited in the depths of the Tree of the Knowledge of Good and Evil that lives within us. Where is evil? Evil is rooted in egotism.

•

We stand, as a witness, in the tests of Truth at the Hall of Judgment to govern our lives with the knowledge that we have the power to rise above egotism [Good and Evil].

•

Many believe they have understood the *Mysteries* having read books. How can that be? A book can only map out approximations.

•

Our natures are habitual and ritualistic . . . Where once sacred rites provided a pattern for moral, ethical, and sacred development and harmony within society, today's festivals seek weekly drug-induced drunken rites of lechery and self-indulgence that center around work and family life.

•

When truth lies unrecognized, we plead ignorance proudly and blame the pot for a bad meal.

•

When Truth is false, we blame it on psychological tendencies, addictions, or genetics. We waste time in academics in search of more excuses . . . it is the lack of self-restraint and self-regulation, self-inquiry and self-realization, that points to the selfish actions again and again.

•

Our world is the lesson plan . . . No man has lived without a lesson plan . . . the *Divine-Archetype* that shapes our lives and gives us guidance and destiny from our birth. It was written in our lives in our nativity.

•

Evil ambitions destroy our lives. Evil academics provides a path for shaping our destruction. Education without moral principles, ethics or standards is no education at all.

•

Ancient mysteries invoked transformation in man through the power of Word Symbols. This is our inheritance. Word Symbols invoke and evoke through the thoughts and the word, letter meanings—powerful subtle forms. These are fields of energy animated with life and meaning.

•

Seek the Mystery, the secrets resting in the mind and soul. Seek the meaning to find the Sacred Mastery thru lessons fostered by Time and awakened thru the supreme consciousness of our Living Sun.

•

Nature invests in us in the minute by minute, hourly, daily, weekly, monthly moments and in the seasonal rites of time . . . Each day's ritual lives within [our] memory.

•

Meaning is a power. Meaning is not an accident. It lives within us as a trust.

•

The letters forming the Mystery Language provide a sneak peek into the origins of creative causes at the source of our creation. St. John best described the Logos as that through which all things are made as divine . . . The Logos incarnates in Man.

•

The inner voice called Shruti... is described as that which is heard during the inner "hearing or sacred listening" discovered through intuitive insights witnessed during periods of concentrated fasting, prayer, and meditation. It is written in the conscience as the voice of God.

•

Sruti [the inner voice] is not that witnessed in academics but that heard through the listening heart.

•

Sruti [the inner voice] is the name for that language of God that is written, spoken, and interpreted within Man as an inner hearing as heard through conscience and the still small voice of divine reason... It is for this that we possess these faculties within our living bodies into which we transmit and receive these transmissions as living powers and then transform these into living practices.

•

Sruti [the inner voice] is the same power written and spoken within creation through which the power to create is invocated in the creation of all things living. We hear our lessons echoed in the *Soul of Man*.

•

Sruti [*the inner voice*] is the signal of the Conscience, the answer to the spoken prayer, the mystery of the contemplation and hidden root of meditation.

•

This body, as a living instrument, communicates with its powers that work and engage in superconscious energies.

•

The Eternal Word is the principle and power of the Vital-Life, and it finds a home in the productions of the Breath of Life... This is the Word of God, held sacred through the efforts of the scribe, who pens these as words of reason, ethics, and justice out of the purity of character and the spoken essence of one's divine personality, wherein wisdom is born into the divine personification of God in Man.

•

[The Eternal Word's] origin is divine, its reason is divine, its wisdom is divine, and its function is to give life and provide a form, shape, and name to the productions found to exist in perfect equanimity and wholeness in the formation of every created thing living or in support of life processes.

•

The power of... the Word of God, is written into cosmic bodies—stars, planets, moons; the directions of space; and the occupation of form supporting geometrical bodies or shapes in nature. The Word is spoken into shapes and lies hidden in its geometries.

•

[The Word is the] sacred mystery and the key to true or divine physics, chemistry, and psychology and the characterization found in the sincere person of Self-Realization. Its reason is power. Its power lies with its meaning.

•

To say, to speak it: "It is to be;" and as spoken it becomes it, and on its face, it is the ever-changing bliss.

•

"Why go in search of natural powers and principles?" We think of these in science as the creators works hidden in the mathematics, but it lies written in the *Name-Form*. [The Name-Form is a sacred entity. A sacred form of God.]

•

These laws and principles, invoking powers of insight, are the birthright, initiated at the inception of our birth into the world as a just rule, since order was first initiated as a promise that was guaranteed at the moment of creation, and will continue until that day of rest.

•

In Truth, the mind is engaged in incessant prayer. It is not simply to address God. Every thought, word, and deed is a prayer. Work is worship. Our mind is ceaselessly engaged.

•

Our private moments of thoughts, feelings, love, hate, or anger are seeking compassion from *Universal Energy* recognized as Superconsciousness.

•

To death, to sleep, we cannot wait; we cannot count the days 'til repeating rewards [on our path] to our final rest, yet our challenge is not our making . . . We think of the path as that faith that lingers between self-confidence and realization, fought with experience and the wisdom of self-knowing.

•

What is clear is that every time the divine name is uttered, the letters are given a divine significance . . . to utter the sacred angelic names like the names of the Archangels is to invoke, and evoke, the . . . God Forms, as imaginary projections.

•

𝕎hat is true is THAT God, that IS TRUE, is "All Names and Forms" as the One that is omniscient, omnipresent, and formless . . . —Ever Existing before Existence.

•

𝔸 Trinity or Triad is the first law of existence or manifestation and predetermines motion and the necessities required for the formation of time and space.

•

𝕋he Unity of the *One* was known to the ancient through the mysteries of the name . . . the unseen-seen, unmoved-moved, the zero and one that comes into being in the light.

•

𝕋he negative existence . . . is identified with numbers. This is the absolute identity awareness that permeates the nonexistent, before space and time, and is the basis of what determines the intelligent projections of Superconscious Energy in the vast platforms of the cosmos in the forms of radiant energy and fields of time-space-consciousness.

•

𝕋his power [of the Word or sacred voice], when purified and perfected through long hours of divine practice and deep reflection, becomes the ceremonial "*Voice of the Prophet,*" elevated through years of ceremonial purification and training.

•

𝕋he mouth of the Saint or Sage, versed in the Mysteries, is the divine mouth . . . the "*Mouth of God,*" where every word that passes out of it is the divine Word of God spoken from . . . the

"*Mouth of Truth,*" where every word that passes out of it is in the form of Truth.

•

[The mouth of the Saint or Sage, versed in the Mysteries] is divine, and is as sacred, as if it were the vehicle or instrument created specifically for . . . revealing the creative power of the Word of God in the forms of the divine.

•

Meditations that labor in reverent silence, on the mysteries of the *Language of the Divine Word or Logos of the Mind,* [are] in that ever-eternal superconscious hierarchy of sound and light as the form of pure reason called the *Divine Declaration of Light.*

•

Aelohim is a recognizable composite symbol representative of the angles of the Hexagonal Star . . . that hangs as an ornament on the Tree of Life as the periods of work that revolve around a point of rest called the days of creation—as the *One God,* [it] is the God of Multiplicity, whose energies are called *angels, archangels, or angles.* They are realized as references to points of the compass, or periods of time. They are devas, beings of light or gods.

•

Light as motion configures into living units of energy or Superconsciousness whether bodied or disembodied. We are this ourselves. Our life is a drop in this sea of qualities and conditions, states, worlds in, though, and beyond imagination.

•

With the sense of devotion and reverence, our thoughts invoke these [*religion and magic*] through projections. On the one hand,

God in reverence has provided the life form through love and wisdom and intelligence. Man possesses these faculties to a degree. In this sense, Man invokes the living form of the formless divinity.

•

The word "created" through the power of "*bara*" shows that the "*Ba*" is the self-genesis, and "*Ra*" is the projection of the soul of sun.

•

The bijas or seed sounds of *Ba-Ra* are the "*life germs*" set in the belly or navel. [The Alchemical womb].

•

"*Bha*" means "Light and Knowledge," and the word "rata" means "Devoted." The name *Bharata* [India] implies the home of the "Light Devoted" tradition.

•

We see this mystery practice hidden in the first five letters of Aelohim, or "A-L-V-H-Y," which are the five principle bijas (seeds of sound) for the elements as described in the [elemental] yoga of the East.

•

These five are *Aum, Lam, Wam, Ham,* and *Yam,* [ALVHY] seated in the *Ajna, Muladhara, Swadhisthana, Vishuda,* and *Anahata* Chakras. *[BR is seated in the belly or womb and the surround of the solar plexus, as well as the belly button. This is the seat of Brahm or the self-created. It is the divine womb of God and the sealed divine retort and alembic for all alchemical processes in the physical body of Man. It is the womb of God's incarnation or the incarnation of the gods.]*

The bija Ram [and Bam] of the Manipura Chakra . . . is in the word written previous to the name of *God*, in the first verse of the Genesis . . . the words are spoken thus as "Ba-RA Aelohim" or in English "god created" . . . as the self-willed externalization [as a spontaneous emanation.]

•

The word "*Bereshith-Genesis*" is in Hebrew also seen as "*Bara-Shith*," meaning the six created or created six. In our case, these are the six-seed element forms or bijas [seeds of light] of the created divinity "Bara-Aelohim" or "*BR-A-L-V-H-Y*"[the body of light in the image of God.]

•

The first two letters of Aelohim, "A-L," then signify the two extremes, that is, the Ajna and Muladhara bijas (Aum, Lam). These are the two polarities along which the Mind, as Superconsciousness, travels up the spine in order to illuminate the "eye of wisdom."

•

In reverse, the word "L-A or La" is a declaration of negation, taking what is, and making it what is not . . . that identifies the God before existence.

•

The origin or the Hebrew Book, or Sepher, as the *cipher*, [is] that related to the "*Suf-Ra*," the hieroglyphic image/lettered language as the hieroglyphic form of the Soul of the Sun. It is written as the word "*Sephirah*" [or sphere of light].

•

The name Seraphim implies writing or hieroglyphic images of the *Sepher Hayyim* or *Book of Life*.

•

One reads these with the eye toward symbolic imagery in the lettered language . . . These imply the image of the Divine Man of the Kabalistic Tree as the language revealed by the mysteries.

•

Birth is man's resurrection in the East. What is born but the mind and senses, the soul of man is eternal and beyond the state of birth and death.

•

Our fate is tied to the Cosmic Fate, the fate of humanity and the fate of the world, being a product of *Time*.

•

The horoscope accounts for the circle of twelve thirty-degree divisions of celestial longitude centered along the ecliptic following the path of the Sun as it moves across the celestial sphere over the course of the year, along with the Lunar motion and the course set for the mystery planets that form the belt of the zodiac as a progression of native *Time*. This path extends from eight degrees to nine degrees north or south of the ecliptic in celestial latitude. This is the true path of initiation.

•

We are tethered to *Time* in every fabric of our being, every movement, and every fate. This is the nature of human incarnation.

•

We have built our towers to the stars and with that extended mental diseases and desires in imagery that amount to nothing. They are powerless, and have lost connection with that base or foundation that rests in the seat of power within the *Self-divinity*.

•

We say Man is created in God's image . . . But Man is the image of God both in the form and in the formless . . . The Tree of Life is the image of the life force living in man. We see this life force in the form . . . that travels on the tree of subtle energies.

•

We think of this [expansion in four or six directions] also in the movement of the vocal cords through which the power of the breath passes. Through ingress and egress air passes in the invoking, or invocation and evocation of consciousness, as sound expands into space and time, in the surrounding Atma, [soul] or atmosphere.
[AT-MA, A-T or Hebrew Aleph-Tav is the Divine Hand that holds. It is first and last of the alphabet or Word of God, or in Greek it is the Alpha and Omega.
A-T-H is *"you"* or A-T-V *"him"* (H=5 elements, V=6 days, cycles or planets i.e., pranas) as Adam, and also *"her"* the Mother of Lights in Shekinah (*Na, being the creature in the divine waters of Shak-ti*). Genesis 3:11 "And Elohim said, '*Who told you that* אתה *(you) were naked!*'" Ma is the Mother or Mem, the Waters, that point to the stream of the gods passing through the Milky Way. The Tau, T-A-V, reverses direction as,

V-A-T, or *"w'th"* meaning *"and"* to join these all together *"Aelohim and the Heaven and the Earth"* in Genesis 1:1.]

•

The Power of the Word is to seek to know the *Whole* of the power of language, the *alpha-bet* or *Aleph-Beth* . . . This is the power of the *Tree of Life*.

•

The ancient life was lived as the rite of life that prepared one for death. Our life is an instant in time. Time is the God/Goddess of the *Temporal Temple* enacted in the rite of life. Death is our sanctuary.

•

The Hall of Judgment is the scene wherein the rites of the temple or temporal life are realized and clarified at the end of life, supporting the record of our time alive.

•

The Temple [of Time] is the house of Universal Observation for the sake of viewing the Theater of the Stars [that move in Time or represent light passing through eternity from the dawn of creation].

•

Our home is not our body instrument, our house, our city, our country, our earth, the atmosphere, the solar system, or galaxy. The entire cosmos is our House of Time, our Temple for the enactment of our play toward divinity and liberation from the theater of birth and death . . .

•

Gnosis is knowing, with the flawless, faultless integration of ideals and the hidden registry of Superconsciousness.

•

Gnosis is pure spirit, spinning in the web of energies, flowing through the veins filled with living blood and the nervous system charged ecstatically, enraging flames of illumination in the brain, and speaking its dramatic record [*all memory is Akasha-Memory as the spirit of the form*] of That Creator of This, (*tatwam, existence or principle*) eulogizing God and the heaven that is That Spirit of the soul, hidden in the heart. [Spirit is the universal animus or male mercurial principle.]

•

These rites of the Merkabah [chariot] . . . are the prophetic practices of projecting consciousness into or through the powers of the Divine Names. These names prompted visions of the *Spheres of Superconsciousness* or divine worlds, spheres or spirits.

•

The *Merkabah* or chariot is the vehicle of extended or projected consciousness. Depending on the sphere, this is a vital-body or mind-body projection in the Breath of Light, in the form of that breath of God breathed upon the Waters, or forces of existence, in the creation of a Universe of Light called a spirit or Sephiroth.

•

These [Sephiroth] are the separations of the life forces that exist within . . . or those spirits, worlds, intelligences or spheres of creation within the human vitality and soul or psyche; existing between the subtle and the gross aspects of ones creation on the Tree of Life.

•

Time is the Witness whose record is the memory that is preserved within its energy and consciousness. What is, what

will be, what has been is recoverable in the image recorded in time. Time is Consciousness; Consciousness is Time; this is the nature of the *Spirit of Superconsciousness* that carries the power of the life winds to their fatal destinations.

•

The cosmos is the *timekeeper* [Saturn]. It is the *Witness of Superconsciousness*. It is the image of space or dimension. We cannot imagine the depth of this record of cosmic motion and its integration in the lives of human existence . . . It is not tied to one fate alone but the fate of all wrapped together in an eternal conundrum.

•

There is no knowledge without humility. All Knowledge as with all Wisdom is God . . . We are life instruments through which the spirit of God passes.

•

This fate of the *timekeeper* is known only by the *One* Identity through which it has originated, and is preserved as the *image record* of its divinity that stretches from eternity to eternity. Its record is preserved within the energies of the Logos, or the Mystery of the WORD, or *Nama-Rupa*, the *name-forms*, forming the *Name-Form Entity*.

•

The Name-Form is not simply the perfect record; it is the living record. We are the image of that record . . .

•

The power of the name, gives birth to itself . . . and it is seen in nature as in a reflection of itself. Nature becomes the mirror reflection of the forces of motion.

•

The female womb, is the Womb of the Divine Mother. It is not owned by anyone but God.

•

So as a universal circle, we have wound our way to the very circumpunct center in the heart of man. It is the center of our peace and divinity and, thus, the center of our peace of mind. Without this peace, the mind of man will never settle down. Within this place is seated the Prince of Peace or Shambala.

•

Man is not innocent. Unlike the animal, the voice of conscience lives and is heard in man with a clear sense of meaning. Meaning exists within the properties of mind as awareness in the forms derived from the power inherent in Superconsciousness. Karma follows. To deny the clear voice of conscience is the willful acceptance of the fate.

•

Our earth, presented in this incarnation, is the "Garden" planted in the east (*the point of the solar rising or incarnation*), which tempts us or provides the temptations to grasp at endless uncertainties to find that seed of truth that is the essence—that permanence that lies within it.

•

Imagine the spirit of Man as the movement and momentum of life out of the Breath of Life.

•

Who are the enemies? Man's real enemies are his inner enemies. They are the real obstacles of life—envy, pride, greed, anger, jealousy, and lust—these are the desires that entrap,

entangle, and destroy one's inner as well as their outer life. These are named The Six Inner Enemies . . . It is one thing to possess these and have them to deal with naturally; it is quite another to invite them in vigorously.

•

Who, what; are the Rays or Emissaries of the Sun? The light that shines from the Akshaya Patra (the Wish- Fulfilling Vessel or Grail) begins and ends with the lettered imagery that recalls the sound, letters, words, numbers, light, illumination, and consciousness.

•

Those emissaries or "rays" are imagined in the symbolic symmetry of the Absolute Form as property of the Absolute Form-Maker. A cause must exist before an effect. The mystery must be uncovered through initiation and spiritual practices. Such is the initiation that transitions into the realization of the letter-forms spoken or written, in the Language of Light.

•

A geometrical plane cuts through the field of motion, and the actors are revealed as part of a process, within an instantaneous state of manifold vocalizations that are witnessed as sung by the Mother of Light into the Night of Space, to illuminate it with Light in Time, as vibration, cycles, emanations, and rhythmic patterns and forms. That is the Light of Time exposed as in the state of Superconsciousness.

•

As symbols, words have meaning and power. Within man, the invocation of power has unlimited consequences. They inspire and deprave man, for one's words may have the power to

transform, enable, or destroy lives that last for days, months, or years or may even pass through lifetimes.

•

What a letter might unfold in the Hebrew you see in the Sanskrit syllables, where the letter is "modified" through subtle applications with other letters much like the difference in timbre with tones between instruments. These "other letter" inflections modify the letter in a "polished" way, bending meaning in a direction this way or that. We even refer to the timbre of a tone as the "voicing" of an instrument and speak of it as its tonal quality. In Kabalistic thinking, the power of the letter is twofold in that it has a number and a quality.

•

Svayambhuva-YHVH is the first of the seven creators or Manus that produced and protected the all-pervasive movable and immovable (creation), or the states of motion and nonmotion, vibration and nonvibration, cycles and the not cyclical, in finite time and infinite timelessness or Eternity... it is that which exists as Superconsciousness in endless time and Identity as Awareness in Eternity.

•

Mind may interpret through numbers, but being a creature of the WORD it KNOWS through its Letters the POWER of MEANING as it is read in nature or through the NETERS — or gods of LETTERS...

•

Our base 10 numbers are called from the Latin the Decimal System, with the number "TEN" being the Decade. Why do we call the Decade "TEN", a word that means to hold, grasp or to be tenacious? It is the grasp of the

Divine Hand. The completion of the Divine Wheel. It is to grasp that which we hold on to of values realized from birth to death. It is the completion of cycles of change with the tenacious fulfillment of the goals witnessed in the process of life's destiny.

  SIGNET IL Y' VIAVIA: DANIEL

The AKSHAYA PATRA Series
MANASA BHAJARE: Worship in the Mind
Volume ONE - Book ONE – Part TWO

Man's Second Obligation is to become a quiet witness to the Truth described by Divine Wisdom and Understanding. Written into creation this is the virtue of the eternal cause cast and weighed in the balance, and assessed by the clear voice of Reason. Reason sits quiet, the witness to the voice of Conscience. Truth is bound by this determination and judgment since it is weighed in the Balance of Justice, Justitia, first and foremost in its outcome. The true measure of the senses is the measure determined by the Truth in that conclusion. Any other measure should be deemed a false measurement and cast away as useless by its final judgment.
– DANISHWARA,
THE Lord Dani,
Signet IL Y' Viavia: DANIEL.

The Akshaya Patra Series

The Akshaya Patra Series

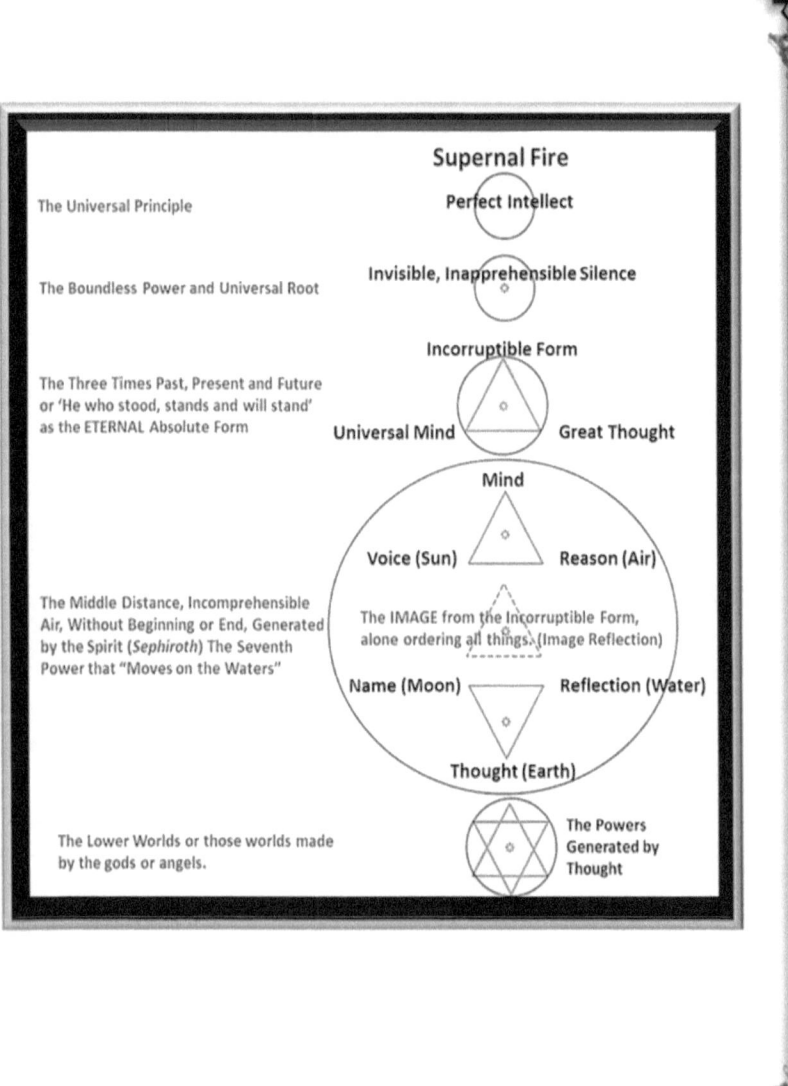

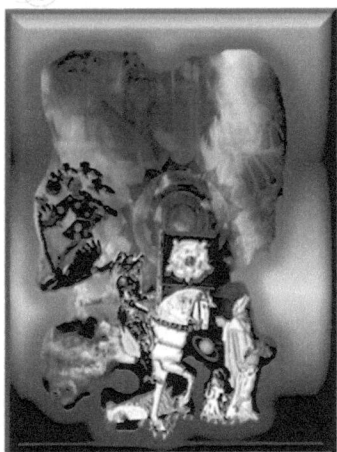

Every atheist will say, "*God will not come. God will not provide.*" For them God does not come. [*Would you?*] God does not provide. [*Would you?*] God is a Superconscious Energy. [*God knows the answer before the question is given. It is given for your benefit, leading to your experience.*]

•

It will be necessary for anyone to make every opportunity the most affordable. You are provided for, and that for what you need. Even from birth with the Mother's milk. It may not be what you want. We are bound to work for it. Every effort has its wage. Every goal an outcome. Every outcome a price.

•

Every Saint has faith that God will come and that God will provide. There is not one saint who has forgotten this. They provide the example that we should live by.

•

"**B**e careful what you ask for." You deserve the wages for the sacrifice, even if this is paid in Love or otherwise. Better to be deserving of God's Love than God's enmity. We emerge from, and return only to, divinity. It is the first cause, called the ONE Before Every Created Thing.

•

Savitur is the living vital essence of the creative Solar Entity, the essence of Life in our solar system.

•

Our solar system is one point in the web of all solar systems, of the billions of cosmic stars and galaxies. And, it is one that is essential and extremely precious and a truth sacred, upon which we hold for our firm grasp or vision of cosmic experience.

•

We are not something insignificant. We are the *summum bonum* or goal of earth life and experience.

•

Would it be wise to think oneself greater than the essence of one's own star, or would that be a sign of egoism and lack of humility? Truthfully, we are extremely important. Whatever happens "we" remain.

•

We are our own challenge. All "this" supports "us". We do not support it. The cosmos is the Servant of Man. Man is entirely dependent upon this Servant of Man and has much to be grateful for.

•

All the world is filled with food, but we are grateful for our spoonful. The world is filled with abundance, but can we possess or buy all of it? Our acceptance of our limits is synonymous with our wisdom.

•

You can use the letters of the words or other sacred letters or words to invoke energies within the patterns of cosmic motion. When these are formed, then they may also be assisted qualitatively with the invocation of geometrical patterns, writings, colors, images, or sounds. This is not for the timid and

requires a great deal of maturity—physical, mental, and spiritual maturity.

•

The name "Hiram Abif" is a message or a greeting. We may think of it like Sairam. The one word (Hiram or Chai-Ram) means the "Life of Ram;" the other (Sai-Ram) means "The Light of Ram" when analyzed by letter meanings. Hiram is the Grand Man [divine artificer] or Adam Kadmon, or First Man born of the light of Amon. Hiram's grave was, as in the Hebrew tradition, covered with the planted sprig of acacia . . . which sprouts into the Tree of Life [which it represents].

•

The Monkey [*seen as Hanuman or even the cynocephalus the sacred Egyptian baboon characteristic of Thoth, with the face of a dog indicative of the darkness or Anubis, or the earth guided by the moon*] is the animal man and represents the cosmic beast or incarnate divinity as the Solar Entity that is covered by creation, whose consciousness is seated in the mind and brain and whose tail runs down the back to the coccyx, extending even beyond this, running down into the soles of the feet.

•

In ancient Egyptian imagery, this same monkey [Hanuman] was the image of Thoth [the god of Magic and Truth], often described as the baboon. As the dog-headed Monkey of the Mysteries—he was also called the cynocephalus, depicted as the scribe of the gods or "Neters," [natures] similar in form to Thoth [as the watcher, guide and guardian of the moon Anubis-headed].

•

𝕴n Kundalini Yoga, this "naming" as generated from the Superconscious Word in creation is seen as the letters that travel up and down the spine or spinal column and float within the whirlpool regions of Superconscious Energy as the powers, or "Shakti," of the "gods" who are enumerated by their names or their natures (hieroglyphic: Neters).

•

𝕬here you see these powers projected, or extended, in Hebrew is by letters, with unnamed vowels, in which the names are manipulated as symbols. In Sanskrit, you see these enumerated by sequences with vowels represented in numbered or metered syllables of sound phrases within the mantra . . . These are the sound seeds of life.

•

𝕿hese Powers of the Word are projected in metrical bundles that are pounded like bullets in speech in metrical or metered forms.

•

𝕿he sacred languages may have been from simple letter forms, realized through meditation, or have been carried forward through those Mystics and Seers, who part the sea of Mind after having passed the Sea of Reeds (*the Suf or Divine Language*) with great or supernatural insight . . . It relieves all suffering and serves as the protection for the devotee from all evil things. It has nearness to the substance of divinity.

•

𝕿he vibhuti ash is the sacred ash . . . It promotes purity of mind and relieves one's tension, stress, and depression as well [through its vibrations]. Its name means "goodness." Its alchemical properties invoke purity. Its nature was made new by

fire . . . It relieves all suffering and serves as the protection for the devotee from all evil things. It has nearness to the substance of divinity.

•

The Lord of Death or the sacred Essence exposed as the sacred "Ash," being the "Esse," [means] the existence or essence. In alchemical equipment, the *Esse* would be represented by the elevated hood over a stove or fire, as the place for that which rises above the fire, as the essence from, or out of, the fire.

•

God as Father is ONE in/by/within essence. The essence is fundamental to those energies that rocket through space as a function of the Speed of Light. "Things" can't travel faster than the Speed of Light boundary, but the presence exist in the same instant, and can be in the same place instantaneously as recognized in the states called omnipresent, omnipotent, and omniscient which is the real breathless boundary, or foundation of honest space/time that is recognized by all as God.

•

All things are ONE with that [ancient God concept]. [With] Love, devotion, loss of ego, or the mind-bundle of desires seek this state, transcending time and space, to appear in the "graveyard" of that, or. . . the One who is "ONE" before division into parts.

•

The purpose of the fast is not to harm the body but to stand near the veil of death to catch the glimpse of Eternity stripped of the false attributes so that true attributes are cleansed and developed.

•

This mind must be disciplined to concentrate and contemplate upon the Goodness and Mercy, stripped of the desires that come with food and the world—It is to grasp calmly the transformation into the lightness of mind, where discipline transforms earth into sky, and the caterpillar is transformed into the butterfly (psyche). That is the metamorphosis.

•

"*The Valley of the Shadow of Death*" is the spirit of the World.

•

The self-created—created through the *Desire to Create*. It has this "desire" within it. "It moves, it moves not. . ." upon moving the ONE that desired to create, entered into it, or found itself covered by its motion.

•

Stillness found itself trapped in motion in the Kingdom of Shells or Sheaths. The unchanging Self becomes the forsaken offspring, the "*Divine Changeling*" having been born into existence, the Divine form thus raised by the Trolls of Cosmic Forms (or the planets) they come into or become the shapes of the "*Shadow of Death*;" living things in the kingdom of the elements.

•

What is true is the Pure and Shining form [*quintessence*] as the Sruti states: "The Purusha (unborn divine) is shining, formless, ever existent with inner and outer objects, unborn, pranaless (*without breath*), mindless, white, supreme beyond what is supreme and undecaying . . ."

•

This is the Identity in Eternity as the causeless Being, without the influence of effects of motion or action (karma)—nondual, auspicious, and unchanging [*the Philosopher's Stone*].

•

OM is the Central Point, or circumpunct center, around which six spirits or physically or energetic lower lettered wheels or worlds of energy revolve with or into the field of human anatomy and spirit. As Above So Below. This the image of Man as God or God as Man . . .

•

ONE—born upon the Tree of Life, is not by vegetation born, our Moon is full at midnight, leaving shadows where we walk. By day the Sun imagines, and we respond, to become the Phantoms of the Stars . . .

•

"*What is the miracle of Man?*" Man is created from the center within the body, coming as one unfolding in the world from a single cell. [That is in itself a miracle.]

•

We have the form of the Hexagonal Star of Man in simple terms. I understand the region of the crown, which is the extension of this [circumpunct single cell center] into the world.

•

The body is the image of man stretched within a circle between the microcosm and macrocosm . . . symbolically as part of the natural rhythm of form. We enter into the world as the projection of rhythmic animation.

•

AL is *Olam*, or the union of Aum-Lam [the light body] and refers to the farthest distance or the expansion of Time and Space—that which is Forever and Ever, that which is beyond the horizon, into the past, into the future, and the reach that stretches into the depths of space and beyond the horizon, or what is determined to be existence into and beyond the boundaries of anything. That is our measure of the world or the measure of Man . . .

•

[AL] is the measure of one's meditation, prayer, and fasting as well. It is the measure of one's lifetime and their experiences

•

The world is created in the rites of caste regardless of what one's demeanor is on such subjects. There are the Rites of Labor, the Rites of Business, the Rites of Politics, and the Rites that witness to that which is Divine or spiritual.

•

No one living, man or animal, can escape the hierarchical rites of caste . . . it measures self-determination, self-development, self-inquiry, and moral and ethical certainty. The rites are inbred in the wheel of Superconsciousness.

•

We are the living spiritual property of the Earth, in fact, the Earth, Moon, Sun, and Planets as they travel under the stars. We are the cosmic entity. Our vital bodies are tied, yoked, and bound.

•

Our Earth is Adam Man . . . our physical, vital, astral (starry), mental, and spiritual bodies all bear witness to the universal

union and integration with the cosmos . . . Thus, our wholeness is complete in our life and living.

•

We are bound to the circle of the Earth cycles, incarnating like bubbles in an alchemical earthly well, our cycle being the circle of wholeness coming and going in time from birth to death to rebirth between these energies as subtle (*occult*) as they may be.

•

History teaches that it is better to be that right minority than the wrong majority even to be the Master and authority represented by a single person.

•

We wonder, "Why are we drawn to the elements?" Are these divine? What is our attraction to these Elemental Forms in the writings that serve our mysteries? The day goes along, time passes, and then we forget and go about our business. Is there any wonder? Who can grasp that which is in transformation always?

•

These principles called . . . [the] Five Great Elements—Earth, Water, Air, Fire, and Spirit . . . serve as archetypical categories for the five great formations of energies that wander through the planet.

•

These Sacred Elements permeate nature through the experiences of natural energies that exist as attributes of divinity as the Mind of God and its embodiments . . .

•

Once deep in meditation, one enters into, or merges with, that Eternal thought of the ONE. [Our starting point behind which we can go no further.]

•

Embraced by that image, in that ONE thought, expanding in sensation, the body identification collapses, and the divine senses awaken . . . as it expands Subtle Eternity in the vision of the Divine.

•

The senses are but instruments for the imagination. They have the power for discerning nothing but the sounding of alarms. [They have no ability to know.]

•

The Soul, as Superconsciousness in the form of Being-Consciousness-Bliss, winds down into dense form through transitional stages of self-caused or self-created effects and events . . .

•

Time, as intelligence, is the Master. Intelligence is Time. Time is the King. [Time is all that you experience as change and motion.]

•

These transitions of the elemental senses are as the notes of a melody. It springs up from the light of mind with song—through words of love, traveling in supernatural forms . . . transformed into the complex . . . mantric form; identified with its meaning hidden in the subtle super-cosmic geometries, of transitional states of forms.

•

Can the mind discern that which is not sensed? It's impossible. Even when defined, you cannot believe it. You, in ignorance define it as the spirit of the impossible. Where, then, is there faith in Mind? [God lies beyond the mind.]

•

Truth is what is heard internally or translated into experience that is beyond the senses, when mind has drifted and quieted, then stopped . . .

•

Faith is something that is beyond the mind, beyond attributes.

•

When Kundalini rises . . . [though dangerous, it] then succumbs to the magical sound of the magical voice; like the serpent charmed in melodic play. The vocal elements are those principles of the Divine Mind in which we are first bathed, nourished, and coddled, swathed in its protection.

•

Layer upon layer, the mystery is wrapped from objectivity to subjectivity into universal entity.

•

The Earth is that into which we are born, and having birth, we are forced into the experience, and we adore it. The Earth, as nurse, coddles us.

•

Experience is an Eternal Power. Mind recognizes this power in the Field of Meaning. In that field, Wisdom and

Understanding are formed. This then is realized as the subject of our divine nature.

•

Our breath reveals what is to be, and realization comes exposing this process as [Right Conduct]. This is the spirit of righteousness, which is the basis for all activity, the living law of Eternity . . . righteousness as the light of our morality . . .

•

As motion is increased or decreased, so too the characteristic qualities change that are recognized in their dynamic interaction, and their world of subtle appearances.

•

The most-minute transition brings about recognizable change with dynamic differences, being distinguishable between one and the other. What is recognizably subtle [occult] becomes absolutely discernible by contrast.

•

Our life's meaning is found within those dynamics of change as the recognition of that which arises as the effect, which is neither the active cause nor the passive cause, but that dynamic of time or change . . .
"*The names that can be named are not unvarying names. It was from the Nameless that Heaven and Earth sprang . . .*" (Tao Te Ching, Chapter 1, Translated by Waley)

•

Superconsciousness, transitions through time, not in actions and reactions but in the dynamic between changes in time, instances, and moments.

•

God "rests" in the rest that is the silence between the tones that point towards natural directions, toward targets and destinations or prophetic destiny.

•

Natural forms of life are the miracle. We have come to accept this without humbling to this exception.

•

Destiny is the integral or essential property in the Mystery of Time; fundamentally omnipresent, omniscient, and omnipotent. It is hidden in awareness that is everywhere in the same instant. That is the unity in multiplicity [Aelohim]. . .

•

It is atheism that is recognized as the profound ignorance and immaturity. This is academics. How subtle the touch that God has embraced with us, as the spirit of creation, and we do not know it until we experience it and lose ourselves within it, as the subtle breath in its maturity is reached.

•

We are dressed in the elements and the record of our experience and cannot escape that life into which we are bathed and nourished.

•

We are born and are sustained in the cycles of time, the revolutions into which we incarnate . . .

•

The subtle currents of the earth ever change; the sweetness is like that music to the ear. This is life. Life is motion, and we are

entertained and played. The entertainer thus is the entertained even by the elements.

•

This, our world, is forever subject to endless incarnations dressed within it from the life of the ONE Before Beginnings and the Mother of Never-Endings. [Father Sun, Mother Moon, Earth the nurse or nursery.]

•

What forms our existence? What exists beyond the body? The body lent, when spent, returns to trash and ash. We are beyond all this. We are, in fact, THAT . . .

•

We contain our living memory, [*Akasha is memory*] but who are we? That memory is our bundle of eternity . . . THAT which points to our Eternity in the form that is the subtle shape of our experience that is greater than we think.

•

We are a "bundle" in/of Eternity, and that Eternity is omniscient, omnipotent, and omnipresent, a drop in the sea having that much reality. We disappear and they break up instantly. [Who are we?] . . .

•

So what's the first question? It should be "Who am I?"

•

Every cell broadcasts its needs. Where do these instincts, powers, and authorities originate? These powers have to originate in the composition and the material forms under which they are made since these are intrinsic powers, laws, and

principles. It is in their nature. What is this "nature" or natural instinct? [Neters] ... These are divine attributes.

•

Aur is the Light. The Light is hidden in the breath as the "Rua." In Hebrew, the breath is "Ruach," [having found life,"ch" in the lighted breath] ... God in Man in the form of the seven divine principles or stages of evolutionary powers ... is the Ruach Aelohim.

•

In Man this [aura] lights up in and by the living energy; [as] the magical mirror of its Cosmic Entity.

•

We think of this in terms of the human aura but life, that living energy, projects an aura of energy. That energy is seen as the secret power of life that lies *"over the horizon"* of the physical world. Horus [the Hawk and solar Son of God] lies on the Horizon, from whom the name is taken. [The name as aura, hour and horizon all have the same identification with Horus on the Eastern Horizon at dawn.]

•

Life, that living energy, projects an aura of energy. That energy is seen as the secret power of life that lies *"over the horizon"* of the physical world.

•

We think of the first light of dawn as life awakens to the rising sun. This is the Aur. The ancients called this sunrise ... the Solar Hour of Horus. This begins Bereshith [the] days Genesis [with] the first Hours of sunrise on the Horizon—beginning the day as well as the week and year, on the cycle of "Seven Day

Periods"... the Archangel or time angle of [Hebrew] Auriel... the hidden light of the divine that appears leading into the spirit of the Sunrise in the East.

•

The shading angles of light shifts the form and shapes its sacred property; of life revolving time. Without the hours of the day, these divine properties would otherwise never be recognized. These are the instantaneous transitions of the hours ... the *"Proper Ties"* not properties ... emphasizing the divine properties.

•

Our dreams are laden with seeds in passing clouds; in them lie the tendencies of deeds that come to be, from its future property. In them, God is found, an actor playing many roles, testing our uncertainties.

•

Initiation is our substantive way of life. What are our tendencies ... In our memories lie our tendencies? They're structured in a hierarchy where roles are played with Superconscious energies. The Witness is present in all of these. We can't escape our dreams; they're written in our memories.

•

God is mother, father, teacher, and guide. There is only one source of True Wisdom and one source of Intelligence ... Man is a recipient of that resource, not the creator of it.

•

Man is a comfort to man ... The Teacher is a guide and a comfort for the support and removal of obstacles that are hidden

from those less talented, should that be the case, a servant to those where the need is great.

•

One-self and God are one's only company. Were we blessed to discover God as Guest, the light form of the Master Within, but more lucky . . . to find that God as Friend.

•

God as Guru, Teacher, Guide, and Friend is essential to self-discovery. [*To find a guide to ensure the true path, to give confidence and faith, and to remove the horrible ego thru surrender and humility that is the enemy to divinity.*]

•

Humility is to die and resurrect into the Universal life that exists outside of the mind; with the mind as the instrument and not the master. Only then man becomes the Master-Mind, when becoming the Master of the Mind.

•

It is the Name of God that is the Divine Guru of Man that leads one to the Mastery of Life.

•

One needs a target to divine that lucid inner life. Without a target, the archer's arrows would scatter everywhere like a blind man destined to shoot at nothing in the dark. Not only would it have no purpose, but within the distance of the Archer's Bow (mind), no one would be safe.

•

Arguments are cheap tricks prepared by lawyers and liars, but not lovers of wisdom, if that is your intent, who plumb the depths of Eternity in search of the heart of untapped divinity . . .

Sit quiet, try to look, ask of it, and listen. Take the process on its merit, on the path into the self.

•

The ego must be lost, as bit by bit, the struggle is this: the ego must die in the path to find peace and happiness. The ego is nothing less than the desires of the mind.

•

Three forms divine—Mind, Nature, Man— in Love, Life and Light are all reflections of the divine as the shadow cast of Superconscious energy.

•

Like the "sol" or divine center in the "cell" or the sacred propagations of the "call" or sound, this principle [the supreme or twin spirit of God and Man] rests in the center, propagating or pulsing those rhythms that reflect the invocation of life.

•

The body of man displays the divine center that lies in the center of the chest resting behind the sternum. This center generates its powers or qualities, which are projected out from this point through the center of the head, the center of the two palms, and the center of the two feet.

•

The Hanged Man also relates to the Prajapati or the Creative Father, whose head has touched the earth as that hidden energy in the production of all living beings from their centers. Prajapati finds employment as the power in recreating the living forms, and perpetuating the cycles of birth and death . . .

•

𝕿hese twenty-two centers are the reflections of the twenty-two letters of the Hebrew alphabet as expressed in twenty-two dimensions or poles; their meanings are described in the physical form in Man, and this is the living image of that which is described as the instrument planted wholly in the image of God.

•

𝕿he word "LVX" or "Fiat Lux"... These make reference to the "Word of God" as a dynamic principle and are not a general expression. The letter "L"... refers to the Word or Logos as Law, Libro, Libra, or the Book of the Law.

•

𝕿he Lamed Vavniks (*Tzadikim Nistarim*) are the Sacred Guides [*Mahatmas*] who initiate humanity and form associations that shape the hierarchy of Man on Tree of Life.

•

𝖂e have not escaped the Truth with time, education or property, but we have lost understanding of what is critical with regard to the realizations of truth in our deep meditations into our internal mental or literal causes.

•

𝕻ractices such as that used in the Tantra of the *Mantra Mahodhadi* or *Dharmanada* utilize the letters to stimulate these centers in order to purify and awaken these projections for manifold effects, that is, divine transformations... Many are their powers or properties, and being of the divine, they are divine, and therefore have divine characteristics.

•

We analyze with subjective intellect, and we invoke images of uncertainty. In that uncertainty, we describe ourselves as wise, and the world is ripped apart in chaos.

•

The Cosmic Consciousness is hard to grasp; its power illuminates the world; God Consciousness or Superconsciousness is far subtler yet . . . All this disappears into awareness that is everywhere—omniscient, omnipotent, and omnipresent—Being,
Consciousness, Bliss reconciled into its endlessness as a single state in Eternity. It is the unmoving, permanent, the ultimate artistic canvas upon which all this rests.

•

What is the use of simply folding the hands into symbolic or ritualistic mudras? These have practical value, but we need to awaken the spiritual properties, and take advantage of their extended sensitivities and powers, for the good that is in them, using concentration exercises in order to awaken this in the Cellular Consciousness.

•

The Grand Architect inscribes this Universe through the power of his finger or Yod. In the German translation, this "yod" becomes "God" historically. This is indicative of the tenfold "point of points" that is the hysteresis of moving forces that fold up into form.

•

The "*Voice of God*" is mantric and is metrically articulated into energy as a process of Superconscious Energy and Thought; as the Thing, or reflection we call energy, vital energy, and Superconsciousness.

•

The head is the physical upper projection of the Spirit of Man that forms from the image of Universal Senses, these senses being the hearing with two ears, seeing with two eyes, and smelling with two nostrils, but along with these dualities, there is only one mouth and tongue.

•

A tongue divided will destroy itself and all this that surrounds us and determines our experiences, since its power over the spoken word will act contrary to itself, and no clear direction will ensue. The mouth and tongue being one are set in motion, when two [mouths] are gathered and then turned against each other, in arguments, or joined in communications. The mouth as a devourer will devour as well as nourish through the powers of its own spoken words even to the limits of overtaking all that is good or ill, even as it prepares to determine its uplift or the destruction of itself. The other senses as well are warned to speak no evil, see no evil, and to hear no evil.

•

Man is not the form. It is the reflection of divinity that is the form. The form is itself our instrument of work and worship. It is modeled as the instrument of TIME that is formed into SPACE imbued within itself with the Shape of Superconsciousness.

•

The True Mind lies in the heart . . . the spiral seed as the Ray of light of illumination and tunnel of life . . . the resident and foci within the center of the life of man
(Seated in the center of the chest).

•

From age to age, the ONE remains. This is the ONE who KNOWS or exists in the form of the Gnosis. What is many is resolved to be ONE. That ONE that remains is the Eternal Teacher, whose life returns from Age to Age,

•

The Perfect Intellect is the Universal Principle. What follows is the inapprehensible silence which is the boundless power and Universal Root. From this is formed the trinity of the Incorruptible Form, the Great Mind and Universal Thought which is the Universal Form of comprehensible TIME Past, Present and Future called *'He who stood, stands and will stand'* as the Eternal Absolute Form. From this forms the Seven-fold Entity we call Aelohim; these are referred to as Aeons or Eternities.

•

These [powers that form the gods, angels and men] are the powers of time, space, and consciousness that arise as the creative principles in the formation of life, creatures, and living forms as the intelligence at the fountain of growth, genesis, and creation. These are those powers in rebellion that create from the living properties of the Mind, Life Breath, and the Solar-Lunar-Earth Entity as imagined in the Hermetic Miracle of the One Thing, or the Father Sun, Mother Moon, and the earthly nurse.

•

We lend, or label, boundaries to our subtleties that do not exist specifically, but only are rendered physically not eternally, thus, labels are given to the atmospheres that surround our earth. We are not independent from the transitions that embrace the universal form of the Universal Entity.

•

One finds solace moving from finite motion to the absolute intangible. In this one finds pleasure in peace, stillness, and endless eternity in the boundaries that stretch beyond the borders of cosmic limitations.

•

One can transcend the world through mind at its depths but even more so through the spirit of intangibles that rocket beyond the canopy of stars, in the fortress of peace supported by the motion of the billions of years of eminence.

•

God is silent at its core, the endless stillness and peace. That peace is bonding space. That is rooted in the endless love, the balance of a cosmos or Cosmic Mind, born of boundless, ceaseless affection, love, and truth, the eternal intimacy. The Thing that is One is everywhere simultaneously. Its power is emanated by virtue of its thought as the Word known as the Divinity of Names.

•

Finding comfort in ancient language, another name of dḥwty [Thoth or Tehuti] is "Sia," the Supreme Intelligence (*the Sia, Shia, or Sai*) of Re, in the hieroglyphic Gnosis, and the "Intelligence of the FATHER" called also the heart (*ib or ibn*) of Re [the solar deity] . . . This Sia-Sai is that supreme intelligence of formation behind the Veil of Isis . . . The name Messiah in Hebrew can point to that which is "from" Shia since the letter "M" signifies "from" (*in Hebrew*). So, we say "*m' shiah*" [Messiah].

•

The "ib", or hieroglyphic heart, is likened to the Hebrew Y-D or Yod in the heart. The letter "b" is sometimes sounded "v"

and may be spoken "Jov". Re was the Lord of the Universe and the Supreme Authority (the Authentica). "Sia" is "Isa-Siva-Sai," the Supreme Intelligence. "Sia" is the "Sai-Amon" or the Supreme Intelligence of Amon, the hidden father. Sia is Sai, the living form of the absolute supreme eternity.

•

The Judgment scene exposes the Trials of the Heart (ib or YB). These we know as the Trials of Job as the one examined, or he who is examined in The Hall of Judgment. Job's trials were the Trials of Judgment as one who had ten children—seven sons and three daughters. The seven days' struggle of Job is like that of the trials of death and remembrance . . .

•

The heart (*ibn*) is in Kabalistic context the reflection of the people, sons, or children (*beni*) of Re, or the solar God whose life forms at the seat of Superconsciousness in the heart of Man . . . the Son of God that forms into the heart of Man. These hearts or souls fall like droplets, dew, or rain in living bundles of the sun [incarnate].

•

We are one with those who've "fallen" into life as the generations of the sun called similarly the Beni-Aelohim or the Sons of God, the Aelohim being the multifarious division of the ONE THING seen as the days of creation on the Tree of Life . . . or breakdown of its life, faculties, and attributes

•

Hu means "the Divine WORD or Logos" and is used to mean the "Power of the Word Command" . . . "God spoke, and then there was Light" . . . God Spoke, and the Word was invoked as

the first cause of the soul as sound, in the sacred mind and life breath of Man.

•

The Word or Logos Law sets down the rule of judgment by the law, or "DANY" the divine judgment, and it is invoked as a command or commandment. The Word, or Logos Law, is the invocation of Truth. Its Truth is Law ... fundamental to all of physics, chemistry, biology and social harmony, as well as fundamental to the essence of life.

•

Thoth is written ḏḥwty ... but the name has been variously reconstructed ... The names Thoth, Thot, or Thout are the Greek reading of the name. We think of it as thought or as that form that occupies the Mind. It is a four-lettered word beginning with the aspirated "Dh-W-T-Y," ... "*Divine Duty.*"

•

Thoth Hermes was known as The Good Shepherd. Such is the nature that is connected with the Divine Reason.

•

In Psalm 23. "*The Lord is my Shepherd . . .*" As the Good Shephard, [with his staff] is a symbol of the Sun passing overhead as the Solar Watchman, who watches over his flock, of creatures and planets.

•

Our lives exist on the daily plan, where even the body and mind are cast off as the reflections of the "Shadow of Death," or the world of mortality. This is our experience here day and night. We live day by day in the playground of the shadow of death . . .

•

The power of the Good Shepherd whose power is the Word or Name; in Hebrew *Shem*, the Name, becomes the Sun, *Shemesh*. The name is Logos Law, the spirit of right cause or Righteousness.

•

The ancient divinities are the attributes of RA the Solar Entity or Atma . . . the ḏḥwty or Jyoti was the Light Bearer, who was the self-begotten and self-produced form of the Light of the Sun, the incarnation of the ONE before the Sun into the spirits of Man's Soul.

•

What matters is the principle, law, or property that is represented by the meaning and the Name or Word. The Name and Form are ONE. Name and Form give birth to Identity. These arise as forms in Mind or Psyche [the butterfly with two wings i.e., Name and Form].

•

The Psyche is the Whole of the Mind. The Whole recognition exists as the soul, in the form of Superconscious Energy, or in the identification that is existing in the totality of the pure identities. It is the recognition of the ONE existing in the Absolute Entity.

•

Psyche (saɪ-ki) from the Greek Ψυχή is related to the Hindu Shakti, the intelligence within that energy of Superconsciousness. The word "psyche" means, in Greek, the butterfly [*the thing that flutters as it flies alighting here and there with two wings in motion*]; being the symbol for the Soul that is released from the bondage of an earthly existence through

transformation of its form . . . to a creature of delight . . . that forms the Tree of Life.

•

Numbers, Letters, Laws, Principles, Truth, Love, Peace, Beauty, Glory, Mercy, Judgment, Wonderment, Reverence, Piety, Righteous Character and Conduct—these are the intrinsic characteristics of the Absolute Entity, the ONE entity, or the Identity that appears within creation out of the essence of Superconsciousness.

•

Dḥwty, the Magician of the Gods, is the Truth, Light, and Duty. His Word is said to have produced all the Gods, and his powers generated the course of the planets.

•

As the light to the flame, so the wife to the husband; they are inseparable.

•

Maat as Truth is [True Voice] . . . Maat is the feminine authoress of science, religion, philosophy, and magic and the source of measure and inventor of astronomy, astrology, the science of numbers, mathematics, geometry, land surveying, medicine, botany, theology, civilized government, the alphabet, reading, writing, and oratory and the true scribe, the author of the works in every division of knowledge, human, and divine, having written that knowledge into the creation of every form; through the power of her Word, represented through her Voice.

•

The wife is the reflection of the husband; she sees herself in him and himself in her as projections and reflections of one another; separate but inseparable.

•

Thoth was the Servant of Ra, the Soul of the Sun, or the one dedicated to what would become our "DUTY" on the path of Liberation.

•

"Natural" is a word referring to the hieroglyphic Neters (gods) or the living energies that exist throughout nature; existing within the intelligence of the Word or Logos Law, in the governance of *"natural laws"* that follow the commands invoked at their beginning when "God Spoke."

•

The word "God" in Kabalistic context refers to the letter "Yod."

•

"Man" means Mind or the word that commands as in the invocation by Mantra or call. The word "Hu-Man" refers to the Word invoked as the Mind of Man, in the incarnations of the Word of God, in the form that represents mankind.

•

This philosophy of the mystery of the Word or Logos Law is the motivator. It is driven by the heart, mind, and breath in silence, and the tongue and vocal chords by virtue of the mantric ideals . . .

•

From the heart, we hear the the voice of God, as the still voice of conscience, laying down laws of morals and ethics as the "cosmic voice of truth," or conscience, from the source of Law that forms from its Righteousness...

•

The end of Philosophy, "Philo-Sophia," is the ideal love of wisdom that finds comfort in the true development, of the "Divine Character,"... to wear the crown of true Wisdom and Understanding... in power of the breath in its reconciliation with the Voice.

•

We are fundamentally this solar system, which is all solar systems and beyond, into the endless emptiness. That said, it is that which exists within the boundaries of our incarnation as the speck of dust that lives.

•

Our life breath is essentially the "Life Breath" of the "Sacred Sun" born within us, animating the fires in the belly, nourishing and strengthening us, and illuminating that Tree of Life that is the resident living form within us...

•

What is essential to know and understand is that what resides within the Sun as the "Sound" Brahman pulsates within the center of us as the Sun in the Divine Heart of Man and the Mystery of the "Word of God" that powers our awakening to Divine Speech.

•

That Divine Heart is the Son of God. It is reflected in the Divine Mind. The reflection of the Divine Mind is the

Daughter of God. The Divine Mind self-creates, having reflected, it replicates and gives birth. Resounding endlessly...

•

The symbol is ONE with the living entity; in that the Message and the Messenger are ONE, and are shaped by the form making powers of the Superconsciousness. It is essential energy that is ONE with the experience [being nearer to the first cause].

•

The true power of religious or mystical iconography . . . is sacred and divine. These are the true Idols of the Mind. You are destroyed when these religious idols are destroyed. God decides their shape and form and enters into them, "alive," [and] no longer motionless.

•

These [symbols or idols of iconography] are the powers of the Absolute Authority . . . projected as the Being, Principle, and Law. We are the Sound in Silence, the Motion in the Motionless; our identity has no place in space and time, being that pure awareness that is divine.

•

We are the powerless, unempowered, imagining our strength to be this finite memory of ourselves. We are humbled to forget and give up when possessing it.

•

What is in the nature of the Divine will produce of its own will, being the self-created anything. This is that Omniscient, Omnipresent, Omnipotent Witness that is ever existent and

eternal out of which we "live, move and have our being" and arises from the fountain of awareness.

•

The aim of the symbolic pictograph of the Tree of Life is to demonstrate what attributes there are in the Cosmos, Nature and Man, that are the reflections of the divine attributes.

•

Nature is the mirror. The mirror is reflecting God (Yod) in the image of elements, minerals, and creatures—plants, animals, man, and the gods, or divine space-time angles or phases (angels), of divinity, in geometry, number, tone, letter, color, intelligence and state of Superconsciousness.

•

In that mirror of Superconscious Energy, the Creative Awareness that is God sees its own reflection, and is happy in happiness (in a breathless state of bliss).

•

We are the Self in that breath, born from the "Breathless in Eternity," the "Being in the Breath" living in the Life, living in the Light. It has no need to draw this in, in order to reflect upon it. It is the witness into itself, in an eternal meditation, being itself the spontaneous Witness to it; the Cause existing in the Effect.

•

Man, with the vision of the senses, looks into the mirror of nature and mind and sees only the false reflection, the reflection of oneself in the light of physical presumptions that are returned ... When we remove the mirror, only God remains

•

Its legacy is Truth, Righteousness, and Peace. Mind is simply an afterthought, bundles formed as refuse in Superconsciousness.

•

Bindu means the "dot" or "point." One might think of this as the center, a drop, a seed, cell, semen, the nucleus, or atom. Without equivocation, it is at the heart of anything. This is the point of origin from which all things expand.

•

To [God] you find that there are given attributions related to four principles like the directions of space or the worlds, states of consciousness, etc.

•

All creatures and living things form into mirrored reflections (right and left; above and below) that are set into a cyclical balance, as well as are divined in their forms both in and out. It is to show the perfection of design, unity, and the endless eternity; hidden within its features.

•

Polarity is not a duality as much as it is a sequence of dualities within an eightfold extension of eternal or externalized physical attributes. That is the sign of spirit.

•

What is to the back is "hidden," but towards the front, the creature is capable of forward direction or momentum. Man naturally moves forward, towards the goal . . . [The destination is the future not the past.]

•

Man, is created in the "Image of God." This implies number, geometry or pattern form or archetype.

•

Identity is transformed, as it is recognized, into the first cause of selfless existence, since Self is the mirror reflection of the Tree of Life, as seen in the Mind.

•

Does truth need defense? Truth is its own defense.

•

That God is LOVE, tells one clearly that all love belongs to God . . . As there is unlimited energy, there is unlimited love in that energy.

•

Pretense has no place in the truth of this [love of God]. We cannot pretend our way to God.

•

Common sense means "that knowledge that is self- evident within." God as [righteousness] is in the breath that we breathe in.

•

Thinking is not experience; neither is it the end of the discovery of True Meaning. True Meaning is pure principle that is hidden in the Mystery . . .

•

God's Eye, as the fire and light, as the witness of Superconsciousness, resides in the center of every universe, in the center of every cell, the center of every atom, the center of every man, creature, plant, planet, and sun.

•

In man, God is centered in the heart or center of the chest. It is at the point of balance, as in the center of every magnet, creature, plant, planet, star, and stone. It is the null and ground of Energy.

•

God is the equilibrium and the center of rest in the musical quality or the characteristics at play in Superconsciousness.

•

God is the witness to that which is moved, being the mover and nonmover . . . God is the God of Fortunes, destiny, duties, and division as the Vision of Time, the call or calling, and the vocation of eternity.

•

Manifest or unmanifest . . . God is in everything, yet we are not this, we are not the body in spite of this; we are the Mystery Incarnate.

•

You live with the sense that Eternity, or Eternal Life and Happiness are your rights, fighting against the backdrop of the realities of nature.

•

One may have no fear of death, but that is generally meant no fear of natural death. With no fear of natural death, one may still fear the break in unfulfilled duty, unfulfilled obligations, and unfulfilled promises within the boundaries of one's destiny. It is the fear of the undone—the fear of destiny. But what is destiny?

We are here with a purpose, sent into the world with a mission. That purpose unfulfilled is like madness.

•

The Eye of the Universe is upon you. Its sight fills the space between each bundle of energy. There is no such thing as a physical body. Our natural state is super-physical.

•

The Form is a living energy filled with purpose, occupied with a challenge—directed towards a goal that is occupying space.

•

The body incarnates with a function, and we are the resident. Every particle within it has a function. Each function is intelligent; its intelligence functions as a helper and confidant on the path towards all success.

•

As the builder of the vehicle, chariot, or car obstacles await us to test the frame by the "Driver of our Destiny." We are not the body, but the Body is the Vehicle of Divinity; we are not the Master of the Body; its destiny is predetermined.

•

Our goals in life are not physical, not mental, and not emotional but are all inclusive and are spiritually dominant, dominated by the "Driver of our Destiny."

•

Millions, billions of cells or mini-universes form to project such an image of a living entity. They are influenced by our

thoughts in spite of the promptings of the Greater Life from which they spring or are spawned at birth, even our birth.

•

The centers of these universes are the birthplace of living archetypes that gather, in search of destiny, from the powers of the sun, the Divine Monitor and Witness, at the Seat of Superconsciousness. These are the Thoughts of God.

•

These million billion universes within universes, support and come together to sustain a greater life as a hierarchy of support. They communicate as ONE.

•

The record of our motion is written in every transition of energy. Their life propagates within it, strung in the form of the marionette, whose strings are strung from the threads of the endless living energies—bound as one by the hand of one, who is the Master of Eternal Destiny.

•

We are not the body, but the body is the form of Superconsciousness. We are the incarnate Witness and Identity, assigned by the Divine Witness and Divine Identity. The appearance of Space and Time are illusions of absolute divinity.

•

The existence of Space as the omnipresent is [Wisdom] . . . The existence of Time as omnipotence is [Understanding] . . . the creator. These are super states of creative power and consciousness that pervade the cosmos and create all that we perceive and do not perceive for its subtlety and occultation or obscurity.

•

Time, the ancients expressed in terms of "Days," or the reflections of [ten] periodic emanations. Time was worshipped in the Temple as we were incarnate Watchmen of the Stars. The word Temple refers to Time. They were Time worshippers, devotees or watchmen.

•

What appears to be "physical" is an illusion of the scribbled motion forming a boundary or "shell." The structure layered as one, in ONE, in ONE. The appearance is in our eyes; we know, and yet we pretend not to know. The reality is unfathomable.

•

What appears to be a form is "emptiness" filled with energy, power, spin, vibration, phase, and angular momentum, even intelligence; metaphysics has always insisted on this. These cycles, phases, and spins are recognizable in the Spirit and Mind the Mirror as well.

•

Space and Time are Mind and they are obviously ONE, but as certain they are one with Superconsciousness. In every form of physics these three are inseparable.

•

We are unable to record all facets of our life in this, even with deep experience and meditation. The most sensory experiences are gross and undeveloped and refuse to recognize the subtleties of the nearly insensible.

•

There is no freedom without Truth and Righteousness. [Righteous Action] will drag you down otherwise. Only the GOOD are truly free within the Cosmic Entity . . .

•

[Righteousness] is that law of ethical certainty that is determined to be the Moral Law that is the spontaneous form of Superconsciousness. Where there is [Righteousness], there is truth. Where there is truth, there is peace. Often, that peace is dressed in simplicity. Without [Righteousness] . . . You are your own worst enemy.

•

Supreme intelligence is tri-form or threefold as the intelligent cause, effect, and witness. We have sought for [Righteousness] in Fire. We have sought for [Righteousness] in Water. We have sought for [Righteousness] in Air, in the breath we breathe, and in earth, space, word and name, mind, gods, and God and have found that goodness there.

•

To cut off [Righteousness] is to cut off one's life from God . . . The gods of nature are everywhere . . . there is no recognition of God in the gods of energy and Superconsciousness.

•

There are no angels outside of the angular momentum of Time, Space and Superconscious energy. Even we are that and it incarnates with our nativity.

•

Where is this [Righteousness] absent? Where is Truth absent from any place if [Righteousness] is everywhere? It is only

absent in the mind that is unaware . . . There is no truth where virtue is absent. Words have no meaning.

•

Earth, as an elemental principle, is both planet and substance [a compost heap]. Seated upon the Earth, the world is stationed below us as the polar opposite to space and our sun and moon. These four (Earth, Sun, Moon, and Space) are an archetypical production, forming into a four-poled model, with magnetic and electrical oppositions of Superconsciousness.

•

These electromagnetic conditions are the form and substance of Superconsciousness. The clear properties of the element of earth are its neutral, strong, or weak magnetic properties.

•

The principle of Earth goes beyond the world, where geometries form that stretch from the infinitesimal to those breadths beyond imagination, with complexities in size, shape, and qualities that are inconceivable through human imagination.

•

This form of God in Man is called the God-Head when it awakens to its universal state. Your man-head is the seat of God-Head. That God-Head forms within man as it is made aware through the awakening of Superconsciousness within the human faculties.

•

The God-Head is not out there but in here as the realizations of Superconscious energies are awakened within oneself. That God formed within Man is proof divined through our awareness; be that devil or divine, it is defined in oneself.

•

You are not defined by some other awareness in the universe. It is your awareness that defines Self-Realization or Divinity, whether foolish or practical.

•

The mind will instantly form an image, to generate a place or proximity, and Superconsciousness will occupy that. This is a symbol, letter, shape or form as an "Idol of the Mind." It is our life energy that animates it. Even then, it is described as being the life in the breath that awakens the form.

•

The life is in the threefold power of breath, thought and meaning. You may have a thought, but Meaning is its essence, or is the soul of it . . . it is a living principle that is divine in its essence. This is imagination. This is the seat of magic and the power of the miracle. We see its vibrancy in the life of the living cell.

•

Every cell is a world unique within the body. Every cell is intelligent . . . Yet when the resident of the body leaves, every cell that appeared so unique dies in unity. [They have no independence all systems are One System.]

•

The cell (all cells) cannot survive without the Master of the House . . . There is no independence. When the cell is dead, the shell exists; the vibrancy of the breath has left and along with that, five principles: the vibrancy of life in motion, purpose, intelligence, self-preservation, and identity.

•

The vibrancy in the cell is a function of the Cosmic Life within it. That Cosmic Life presents itself in the cell as a replication of the Universal Theater or the Cosmos in which we live . . . move, and have our being. It was born in it. Its foundation rests in it. That life gave birth in it to life.

•

We, all creatures living on this planet, are indebted to the life on this planet. The life of this planet is called Adam, the Grand Man. When that life leaves . . . So many cells, all acting individually, intelligently, yet not one survives to make its way once death has rung its bell to take the life away.

•

The Life of the Cell depends upon the Life of Man. The Life of Man depends upon the Life of the Planet. The Life of the Planet depends upon the Life of the Solar System. The Life of the Solar System depends upon the Life of the Sun. The Life of the Sun depends upon the Life of the Cosmos.

•

We use concentration to isolate out the different states, bodies, qualities or parts of the self, parts of energy, parts of consciousness, or the various parts of the body in man. To assist us in this, we use the letters as one would by the use of their everyday language. We do this in order to focus the mind's attention and get it under control.

•

Letters are internal forces and powers that have external effects. The letters are life bundles or Living Monads. It is not simply to give consciousness a memory, name, and pattern. These letters are the inner language in the powers of the WORD, the Logos Law, or the building blocks of intelligent

determination and will. They have the power to "fly" to their destination.

•

The Letter of Inner Language centers itself within the foci of power, from the bundled thought and breath, as shaped by any geometry of these forces, energies, laws, and principles that lie latent and are hidden in creation.

•

All the letters in Sanskrit are sounded with the "M" or nasal *anuswara*, "om" which means the "*after-sound.*" It is the "M" whose symbol is the dotted ṃ with the dot below the letter "M" in English ... [or] dot over the Sanskrit letter.

•

There is no such thing as a physical body; it is a world of emptiness woven in a web of forces and energy, having unlimited capability within which to transform itself into infinite qualities ...

•

We hold the form together. We are not simply "gravity." It is in our nature, our polarity. If that holding power lies within us, what holds the form of the Sun, the planets, and moons? What is this form of gravity but the incarnation of something that has the power of perfecting life? What so subtle, so impossible to measure, shows itself so powerful but living. It is a state of emptiness. It is constant integrated awareness, as a self-forming integrated power of illuminating solar consciousness.

•

We are the form maker wherein emptiness, as the single form of awareness, attracts the form, draws in the energy, and begins to

self-create. That emptiness that forms within these bodies is written into the Soul of Man. Our emptiness or that inner motionless state attracts energy like the filings in the magnetic field.

•

What is that emptiness inside of the Star? Emptiness draws it into the center. That positive emptiness is "gravity." Its beauty or attractiveness makes it appear as if the energies of space collapse into its center, and emerges returning out again . . .

•

What is God is also the creator, form maker, and manager in us. What is the form of God, is also reflected in its Nature its characteristics. That emptiness that shapes and forms is not meaningless. That emptiness is not without awareness. Its function is absolute. Its intelligence is its function. That function is "Self-Knowing" . . . the seed of the "Self-Created" entity . . . the "bundle of light" as the "Light Traveler" on a sacred pilgrimage called life.

•

We, as creatures, as plants and animals, and as intelligent functioning entities, are self-formed; we arise out of this as sparks of illumination

•

Our path, pilgrimage, or journey in our world is that path of motion determined by the elemental state and attributes, wrapped in the mystery of Zodiacal time, born into the energies of the Sun. This is written at out birth. This is what we are. Thus, we are the "Self-Knowing Sun" that is the self or soul . . . that is [the] "Self-Created" form of the emptiness, surrounded

by the field of Living Time . . . called into divine play by the generations of motion that rise from Superconsciousness.

•

The letters are powers, qualities, where the sound is the creative power in thought and energy, the power of consciousness, which is called the unsounded sound or . . . the sacred sound. This is inner sound that is not vocalized but realized heard and sounded internally out of the silence of the mind or inner consciousness. It is like the breath that fills the balloon that gives it shape and form.

•

Superconscious Energy is the substance; the letters are the substance builders or creators of form like the bricks that shape the building. The WORD itself is the true image of the Divine MIND that is fashioned out of Superconsciousness as the mirror image of Nature and all living things.

•

  SIGNET IL Y' VIAVIA: DANIEL

The AKSHAYA PATRA Series
MANASA BHAJARE: Worship in the Mind
Volume ONE – Book ONE – Part Three

If God were a male, he would be brotherly, fatherly, uncle, heroic, fearless, wise, valiant, noble, intelligent, just and bold. Protective by his instinct. If God were a woman she would be beautiful beyond endurance, tender, fearless, faithful, sweet, kind and motherly, sisterly, the aunt who is heavenly. Maternal by her instinct. If God were a child, God would be deserving of our love and care, the tender eye of innocence, beyond description and the most pleasure we could bear. Knowing and loving and accepting of both our love and our misery.

God is the child in the first cause, the "arche en ho logos", in our birth into human existence. It is God who first forms in the womb of Woman. She is called Wo-Man because she bears the six-fold responsibility for conceiving Aelohim.
— DANISHWARA, THE Lord Dani, Signet IL Y' Viavia: DANIEL.

Psalm 119 is: The Doctrine of the Word

"Your Word have I hid in my heart . . .

I will meditate in your precepts, and have respect unto your ways. . . I will delight myself in your statutes: I will not forget thy word.

Deal bountifully with your Devotee, that I may live, and keep your Word. Open thou mine eyes, that I may behold wondrous things out of your law. I am a stranger in the earth: hide not your directives from me. . .

May you open my eyes, that I may behold wondrous things out of your [Righteousness] . . .

I am a stranger in the earth: do not hide your [Righteousness] from me . . . [Language of the supplicant as the prodigal in the Royal Mysteries}

My soul cleaves to dust: may you quicken me according to your Word . . . I have chosen the way of truth: Your judgments have I laid before me . . .

Your word is true from the beginning: and every one of Your righteous judgments [Laws] endures forever. . . My tongue shall speak of Your word: for all Your demands are righteousness.

[This Psalm of 176 precepts in its entirety is the language of the True Mysteries as spoken by the candidate for Initiation.]

LAW and LAWYER these words are Baconian or Masonic Kabala and have their roots in the 17th Century and are rooted in the same bijas as BaRa ALVHYm or Bara Aelohim [God Created] and refer to the body of light that is governed by the Divine Law. From the New Testament, Luke 14:3, we discover the lawyer is the "*interpreter of Mosaic law* [Kabala]."

Old English wrote "*lawyer*" as *lahwita*. The word *wita means the* "*sage, wise man; adviser or councilor.*" *Wita* as an ending later changed and it became "*lawiere.*"

The letter "E" in "Lawyer" is in Hebrew "Heh." The spelling using the letter "Y" in Lawyer began in the 17th Century legal Scrivenery and in fact is then used in the King James Bible, ["*And Jesus answering spake unto the lawyers and Pharisees, saying, 'Is it lawful to heal on the sabbath day?'"*]

These letters [in LAWYER] are the six days of work according to the LAW and likely were calculated [by letters and numbers] in the [legal] works and used among the members of Francis Bacon's fraternal societies [the Order of the Helmet, Freemason and Rosicrucian].

The Seventh or Sabbath day of rest is in the Sahasrara, where the bijas or seed sounds stand down as the day of worship [in the mind] or Manasa Bhajare:

L	Lam	Lamed	Coccyx	Muladhara
A	Aum	Aleph	Eyebrow	Ajna
W	Wam	Vav	Pelvic	Swadhisthana
Y	Yam	Yod	Heart Center	Anahata
E	Ham	Heh	Throat	Vishuda
R	Ram	Resh	Solar plexus, belly, womb	Manipura

•

Who has looked upon the sun and not recognized Divinities Residence? *Only the Fool has turned his back upon the sun* and set out on a journey denying the purity or reason . . . [The One who has incarnated.] You have been given a divine responsibility, a divine instrument in the Body, and a divine destiny in the Mind, consciousness and Vitality as an embodiment of TIME. [You bear the burden of the leather bag or body.]

•

What shapes the Destiny is temporary. What shapes the Character is realized in Eternity. Character is what is essential. Character is the essence of intelligence, wisdom, and understanding, being the embodiment of love . . . Stand and be counted with the reasonable as the one bound to the duty of pure reason. Be honest and truthful. Truth is the embodiment of divinity. What is certain is the test of truth and righteousness in the determination of the purity of love and illumination. Life's tests are initiations of Love.

•

God is Man and Man is God. Consciousness, Wisdom, Understanding, Love, Vitality, Destiny, and Duty are the

attributes of divinity that function in Nature, Man and Society. Be humble, devoted, and know what is clearly truth, and that will lead to a path of peace filled with confidence and certainty. Self-Confidence is the Confidence in the Self. Truth will always protect you.

•

There is no peace without self-confidence. Its certainty is pure awareness. There is no self-confidence without its peace. Self-Mastery is determined by one's self-confidence. Self-confidence is no different from faith in oneself and faith in God.

•

Be certain that Faith and Peace are ONE. That is the wisdom of the Sage and Saint, and the Magician that is filled with the wisdom and power of God. God is the Divine Magician.

•

Subtle anatomical associations have been recorded throughout time. The little finger of the right hand is associated with the liver and the left with the spleen . . . associated with astral properties of lower psychic energies. Other energies and associations are made with the toes of the feet, fingers, palms, soles of the feet, spine, stomach, umbilical, heart, throat, mouth, tongue, ear, and regions of the brain. These simply breakdown the differences and the relationships of energy to the Divine Anatomy or the energies of spirit forms . . .

•

The associations and relationships of the glands and ganglia and sympathetic nervous system are well noted. But the hand and the mudras derived through simple exercise or ritual are personal and easily divined and structured thru our concentrations into energies of light and spirit intelligence.

•

The creative powers of the sun reside in the palm of the hand. The mounds of the hands as well are sensitive to the nerve energies and regions. These are regions of incredible sensation that we know have a deep connection to the mind and brain . . . The physical nervous system has subtle counterparts that go beyond the sight for those blind or subtle energies of light . . .

•

The hands transmit and receive, as they are broadcasting energies through space. They communicate messages through symbols and signs. The hands are all that might be conceived as a symbol of the mind . . . The hands are five-fold elemental signs. The Divine Cosmos is reflected or symbolized by the formation of the hand.

•

Color and light may be concentrated into phase, frequency and qualities that carry the vitality that exist in them, in order to shape the seven properties of color in the pineal gland and the energies in the seven regions of the brain. This concentration effects the entire nervous system and particularly it is sensitive to the regions in and around the heart.

•

As Light defines intelligent attributes these define light forms that shape the seven brains of the heart that appear out of the vitality of our solar properties that are resident there. There is no one part of the body that does not affect the whole of the body.

•

As a temple, the regions of the body are sacred and represent the divinity as shaped by or through its attributes. One might

reflect or meditate on the statement that, "There is no part of me that is not a part of the Gods." These gods represent every aspect of divine activity.

•

All energy is universal and that it has a common root that unfolds into many forms of consciousness. Our playground of life on planet earth reveals endless dimensions to its intelligence; not just in man but creatures, plants and animals and every aspect of Time, Space and Energy, down to the most finite part of atomic energy and up to the massive enterprise of our life in Eternity.

•

We are not the body. The body is the temporary instrument... Divinity shines within the omnipresent, omniscient, omnipotence... The body is the reflection of this as this operates with dimension. It unfolds as the roadmap or the symbol of it. It is the shadow of the true illumination that remains unseen, yet this light is experienced and ritualized through the powers of the essence of the spirit, mind and vitality, within the limitations of the human experience.

•

The world experience is called the "Shadow of Death." It is the reflection of the real thing... We experience nature as the projection of its lawful principles... like the child who discovers their first shadow, and with maturity they are forced to face it

•

Were one to take a glass of water, a symbol or an amulet, and charge such with the concentrations in the hands; that energy would expand or dissipate throughout the body, as well as expand into the atmosphere. The atmosphere is the Theater of

Superconsciousness. It is the theater of Motion . . . Good thoughts are encouraged for the welfare of the one performing such an act. The great good achieved in the performance of this benefits the sender as well as the receiver.

•

Harmful thoughts harm the one performing the act as well as the recipient temporarily. The great harm stays with the sender, not the receiver. The receiver has the right to accept or reject. The good is complementary. The bad will be naturally rejected. Rejection sends the remaining energy back to the sender, like the light reflected from a mirror

•

The mirror is the power of God that is incarnate in nature . . . Protection is an innate property. That divinity serves the Universal Good and is the upholder of Divine

•

Righteousness and Universal Truth. In physics, sympathetic attunement is reciprocated. We all have the power to tune in or tune out. Where we fail, with the power of a thought, God will intervene [when asked with prayer].

•

Being one with God, the Word is the protection of God. Name, Word and God are ONE . . . The Ego of man is atomic, formed of that spiritual body of atoms, of endless energy bundles of Superconscious solar resonant charges.

•

The astral field forms around the arrangement of atoms, which form the molecular bodies within the cells . . . These forms, or vital shapes, turn out to perform actively in the creation of the

living entity, forming the organs and functions that support a single entity as one unity, creating, distributing and broadcasting needs and life-sustaining properties... They were born of ONE, forming into ONE.

•

We are not the body, but the body is an instrument of the divine, a house for rent created and maintained by the powers that created it. Man, aware of the body's needs, is constantly made aware of the role Man must play, as the occupant that is resident within the Sacred-House provided.

•

All aspects of divinity have a unique part to play through the living instrument, and a divine duty to perform effectively. It's functioning is completely out of our control, save for our role within it. When it requires food or external maintenance, we are beckoned through the desires and appetites. The body is inert save for the life of the gods that inhabit it. We are also as much the secret power of divinity that lives within one aspect of the body. We share in that divine responsibility.

•

Our pride and self-control seems to wane at the hour when the body is in need... there are those tests and trials that initiate our awakening in the development of Truth, Righteousness, Love and Charity in the development of our character and the shaping of our personality. These are roles that shape the course of human evolution or that which is transcribed and recorded in the events of our history internally.

•

"Why am I here? What is the purpose for life? Where am I going and what must I do?" We are challenged by the inner

representative to take up the task and act. Who or what is it that we serve? What or who demands this of us? It has a purpose that is undeniable and is Self-Recognized. Others may find confusion in our destiny, but we know our purpose and our contact with it.

•

Man is a product of the Aeons of Time, the electromagnetic confluence, and is subject to the dictates drafted by the Universal Designer . . . and the Master of the Superconscious Eternity. . . These gods function as time in periodic cycles and are recognized within their unique functions in the life of man, in the vessel and vital systems that make up the functions in the entire system, as the instrument of the body.

•

The Cosmos is a creature or beast of the electromagnetic essence, the substance of the stars whose elements are subject to the dictates of the stars from which they were formed. This is the fallen, the divide or the one that separated from the ONE.

•

This Beast or Cosmos [*Greek Pythagorean Cosmic or Hebrew Samekh*] is the instrument of God into which man [*Universal Man the mortal life born within it*] is given a palace from which to promote, preserve, and recognize the lessons of the divine . . . [*To thrive thru initiation for the perfection and discovery of the values of character and virtue.*]

•

We say the physical body . . . What is physical? There are seven recognizable bodies of Man in [subtle anatomy] . . . they are representative as gods. Four of these have properties of motion called loosely physical properties or characteristics are

expressed as the illusions of form. These bodies exist as worlds within worlds, [are] part of the Divine Hierarchy in the stream of Superconsciousness.

•

Physics, biology, anatomy, chemistry, and physiology—these all touch the surface of this as reflections that are flickering on the surface of the water. We master these with considerations called the illusions of form . . . These function as light, as elements, as sound, as heat, as radio and electromagnetic fields as well. All LIGHT is not incandescent light; respected by the senses. These atoms form and store the vast records of time . . . to witness the illumination of divinity.

•

These instruments with their cells and organic structures formed of the elements have intelligence and consciousness. They communicate and broadcast needs with one another. They create. They give life. They give bliss and happiness . . . Bliss is health; health is bliss. But buried deep within this . . . These atoms form the body of our Mercury.

•

Man is the one that is sacrificed, the one whose mundane energies are transformed through illumination. This is a sacrifice of ideas and transformation of life

•

Man must sacrifice his actions to the divine. In all actions, Time is the creator. When you give of your mind, thoughts, words, and deeds, these are sacrificed as an offering . . .

•

Once actions and attributes are given up, they cease to be with you, of you. They are no longer yours to identify as "mine" . . . Instead, the words are identified with God as [one] with the attributes attributed to their sacrifice . . . In the end, all actions are retired in the words "I and my Father are ONE." The Divine-ONE, who became the recipient of one's actions and attributes when these were given up, is now in possession of them.

•

The Mind dies in the end at liberation . . . The devotee discovers the Mind as the Reflection of God because Mind is not God . . . Mind is the mirror . . . When the mirror (mind) is gone, only God remains, no longer a reflection of its self-image . . . That is the Gnosis of Illumination.

•

What is the name, is God . . . The name is the proof of God. The name is the form of God. This is the nature of the WORD of God. God lives in the WORD. The Word is the First Incarnation of God, more perfect than the mind itself.

•

In time, the flower blooms. When the flower dies, the fruit follows from out of the branch onto the limbs that form into the Tree of Life. First the fruit is green, but in time, it is ripe. We pluck the fruit when ready in order to eat of its essence and sustain the blossom in Life. That is its alchemy. Its essence is essential to serve our life and existence. In its death, the fruit has given up life. This is work that is done in the process of time.

•

Give God your sacred Words. Give God your Sacred Mind. Give God the senses. Give God the actions. Hand God the

body that it may be the instrument of the servant of the divine. And in time, these will be awakened. You will be awakened to realize you are one with the divine.

•

This is the age of work and duty called out as the Age of Chivalry. Actions speak louder than words in our time . . . the Christian Arthurian legacy of knightly virtues, honor, courtly love, and courtesy, in the protection of the populace, widows, and orphans as both a sacrifice and sacrament of one's life itself. This was considered to be the Royal Virtue . . . in the royal mysteries.

•

"Not my will, but Thy Will be done, on Earth as it is in Heaven" was the example that Christ set in the willingness to enter into the Eucharistic sacrifice, all that he had left, saying, "This is my body, this is my blood."

•

Unheard, Divine sound is sensed, and the Sound Brahman, as Akasha, is the "sounding board of nature." The body is formed as the instrument into which the Devas are born as the instrument in the creation of a divine form. The staff of man is the spinal sheath that forms a triune unity and sympathetic harmony. God, as the life wind, is blown through it [like a flute].

•

The Akasha or Sound Brahman is the cosmic bridge wherein the sound is manifest and heard throughout creation from the form to the formless. It is the sound that never ends. Thus, it may be recalled as a memory in the planes of Superconsciousness [as Cosmic Record].

•

There are five states of matter: solid, liquid, gas, fire, and energy, which is the characteristic property of spirit energy or Akasha... The atoms carry a living record... its forms are divided in forms of sentient consciousness, from consciousness into subconsciousness, from subconsciousness into the Cosmic Consciousness, from the Cosmic Consciousness into Superconsciousness, from Superconsciousness it is liberated into the being of the Tao or Awareness of Divinity

•

Awareness is in the stillness. This Awareness is the Love present in the Being, Consciousness, and Bliss. God is all this, existing beyond limits in the world, and not in the world. God is, Being in TIME, Being not in TIME—Being in SPACE, Being beyond limits of divisions called into being as SPACE [i.e., *cause subtler than Akasha or the Atma-Sphere, as the perfect state that is dimensionless before motion or gravitation; possessing pure "I" identity, knowing everything; thoughtless.*]

•

God is what is limitless, and what is without limit—God is that, but God is not that... "Not this, Not that." Negating the Cosmic Entity. [*Zero state dimensionless identity.*]

•

The NAME is God alone even without abstraction. By the Power of the Word alone, God appears even as the abstraction... All numbers, shapes, letters, and forms are God [*incarnate*]... If that abstraction lives in you, then it exists even if in you alone. What is "ONE" exists in many things. One exists in all things [*omnipresent*]. All things can be reduced to ONE THING? That is God by definition. "God is ONE." And, "All things exist by virtue of the ONE THING."

•

Is God within or without? God is all things within and without [*immortality and mortality*]. The external world is the projection of us as living consciousness . . . God is ONE; one without a second, and when counting down to the cause, before ONE what can you count? What is before the ONE cannot exist. Therefore, God as ONE is the basis of everything.

•

LIFE, LIGHT and LOVE; all thought, all wisdom, all understanding—each and all belong to God. Divine LOVE is a product of the bliss of superconscious, or that, which is omnipresent, omniscient, and omnipotent . . . God is unfathomable. [*The cosmos is the externalization of this.*]

•

Our limitations have nothing to do with God. Man [the universal life creature] is the instrument through which the divine is enabled in the world to generate activity in a play of life. This is the play of plays. We are the actors in the play, He the director, producer, and author. We are engaged. We are not the source of this engagement.

•

Miracles surround us. Miracles may even pass through us. We are not the source of these. They are the blessings. God is miraculous. Only God is great . . . Profound miracles exist as life itself. Miracles are so common we have forgotten to give them a name and only pass these off as "natural" forms determined by our arrogance. [We think ourselves into this. Our Earth is a miracle.]

•

Everything in our world is a miracle, and we have been showered with such grace only to think that it is commonplace. Nature holds everything in the state of balance. The source of all blessings is beyond our grasp. Our life exists to sanctify that blessing through devotion, honesty, and dedication to these, in the qualities of good character, in the actions of good behavior.

•

Truth suffers the irrational and ridiculous. What is more irrational, to believe in a creator, or to disbelieve in one? If something is created, it must have a creator.

•

What is love beyond love, peace beyond peace, joy beyond joy? Our expectations . . . Our expectations are beyond our behavior, beyond what we deserve. Hope is synonymous with these. Faith is held to recognize itself as the subtlest form in eternity.

•

We are a germ in infinity, bound for greatness knowing only that God is GREAT. Life is a miracle that we have all been given as a blessing. . . [How vast is the Cosmos?] Having come face to face with Sia Sai, the Divine Entity, on the inside, one realizes that destiny, Truth, absolutes, origination, will, freedom, and all those unlimited attributes, are out of one's control . . . they are in his hands [of] the unfathomable original.

•

Our form of ritual "Yoga" [is] to yoke or form a union. But we are already united; therefore, that "Yoga" supreme is self-awareness [oneness] knowing no other activity. But without the divine engagement, these practices are of no value. We must engage. God is the unmoving. God is the all-moving. All motion is the function of Superconsciousness.

•

It is the absolute Silence of Silence who is the Voice or still small voice that guides one's every direction. We are pleased to hear it in the voice of conscience and self-awareness or common sense. These are ONE without division or divisiveness [when True] . . . All knowledge is this knowledge. All ego is shaved. We have lost our eyes and mind for the Greater Eye and the presence that is boundless.

•

Thinking is eradicated before the presence of the unthinkable. One proud of knowledge is humbled with no knowledge. Shallow wells are stopped from speaking once there is recognition that the ocean of water, in abundance, is already far beyond their grasp. Sia Sai is the endless well . . . Silence is certain when this is realized. Silence alone is one's only friend in the presence of the unthinkable.

•

It leaves one speechless to realize that Only God is in virtue Good. All knowledge belongs to God. God is love, and all love is God's to give. We are simply the recipient of this. That is my experience.

•

If God is in the Name, then God exists as the Name even if that name is the "naught thing" or that beyond the ONE THING. If consumed in your mind, there is no place that it does not live. It lives in all things possessed by you and your experience. It projects with every image within and without. [You are God.]

•

If you erase it from your mind . . . it will consume you. There the attention will be placed all the time. If you insist, "I must forget," you will be challenged, "I must forget what?" And your attention will never leave it. To say, "God does not exist proves that God does exist." God exists in your negation, the thing even put out of mind and challenged. You cannot escape your thought—even that will follow you.

•

God is not this and not that. God is twin. God is ONE. God is NONE. God is manifest and unmanifest. That is by definition. That is how God is . . . God exists even in the idea; as by any NAME that defines God. To say there is no God proves that there is God. And if God exists in NAME, that NAME defines it. The name alone is the proof that God exists, even existing as the name that defines it.

•

[What follows you into death?] All NAMES and FORMS are as eternal as the thought that defines you. As long as you exist, God exists. You are the ETERNAL NAME, and ineffable as named by [Causal Man] at the source of creation, as the cause of causes that we exist within. Existing even before the form or formless. Before there was the idea, there was ONE.

•

The Breath of Life surrounds the earth. It supports the water. Without the breath, the water cannot exist. The breath is the original "water-mist." In MAN the first cause of life is breath. At death, it is the first to leave, followed by the moist water and finally the dust of the elements. The dead planets have lost their breath and the waters have dried, and they've turned to dust with the end of life . . . God is in the breath. But the breath is not God.

•

𝕎hen the fruit is ripe, it falls from the Tree of Life. Its essence adds to the impression; a projection of itself as an image of eternity. Life and death have no meaning in the image of the ONE THING. The ONE is itself undivided. It neither lives nor dies. It is ever-present, omnipresent awareness, untouched, permanent, being without beginning. Our actions are but a reflection, scattering rays reflected in the field of this.

•

𝕋he Sun is the Sacred Paradise, that doorway through which we travel to the absolute goal of redemption, or what is the return from the material existence. We have "fallen" like the fruit from that tree and cannot find our way. [There the goal of our projection into the original is Kether in its core elements in the ever-presence. The two poles being the core of the Earth and the core of the star. The path is through the Moon. The external objects only reveal what is the purity in their original.]

•

𝕋he Sun is the Father (reflected in the Cosmic Consciousness), the Moon is the Mother (reflected in the Subconsciousness), the Wind carries it in its belly (reflected in the Subjective Consciousness; the life winds, life force or prana), and its nurse is the Earth (Objective Consciousness and the life, energy-forming elements, condensations of light, dull and reflected poorly in the objective senses, and the will of material forms).

•

𝕋he "Center" is within man at the center of the chest behind the sternum. One experiences this clearly. That center is the same as the center in the cell. That center lies within the heart of

the atom. That center lies within the heart of the first vibrations of energy, and it is the center around which energy (consciousness) travels.

•

Each organ has a "Center" around which influence is formed. Nature comes to gather in motion around it. That is the "central or center principle." All things formed must focus around a center, even notes in music. Forces are drawn toward, extend from, or rest in, the center. [*The center of the invisible.*]

•

That center resident in all is "location" [Loki the shape-shifting]. We say it is the *"center of gravity."* That center of gravity extends from the beginning of the Golden Mean. Location has a place and purpose in all the vastness of space. It gives rise to bodies that form in space. We are identified within it. It provides a reasonable origin from which all this originates.

•

The "Existence," . . . lies within the "Center" of everything. It is the *"state of being"* described as "I AM," or that place that exists, when all else ceases to exist. "Ehyeh Asher Ehyeh," . . . "I AM, THAT I AM." These refer or point to the points along the path of the spine that is the life principle unfolded in the life, light and love for the transformation of Man. The letters used are "A-H-Y-H" and "A-Sh-R."

•

Aleph, the vowel letter associated with the breath as the aspirate, "A," is very powerful. It is used for the Aum in the Ajna in the Hebrew system that unfolds in our mysteries. As mentioned before, this is associated with Ayin . . .

•

The name aleph refers to the divine mouth; as this so called "third eye" [it] is the vibrant region associated with the nerves at the tip of the tongue. [*Think of the Third Eye as the Mouth of God opening Ajna-Ayin, the region of inner-sight, or light breath, between the eyebrows, with the tongue pressing the roof of the mouth with as in "AL." The letter "Peh" refers to the mouth of God.*]

•

Life forms out of its center under the influence of space. Moons form as the extension or expansions of extended energy [shells] that separates through distance and the pull or shift through orbital motion. Our moon, has a common origin with the Earth. We are in its orbit, existing as the power sitting in its center [as it turns and we spin within it]. We are in it with a sense of peace sitting in the hub of that center of the power in the state of rest that is turning it [between its center and the earth's center core. We all have our place].

•

The galaxy is comprised of many ancestors, gods, patriarchs, and matriarchs as we understand the hierarchy of energy that we are a part.

•

Life spawns in the depths of the ocean. Life forms from the center out—we sense this in ourselves. Our center is the absolute. From the center, the seed unfolds from the minute "particulate form." From the seed, the form unfolds through germination. We see where it comes from . . . Life spawn's life in many forms [*from the center of the sperm growing out. That center of the sperm is the power, ideal or form of the Father or God. Creation and all that is created is female appearing in the*

male and female forms. The only male in truth is God. If Adam is truly "Man" then Adam is also God.]

•

The watery ocean is the same energy that was once a property of fire no different from the sun. The inverse motion turned fire into water [its reflection].

•

The moon or lunar form spawn's life from the Center of Life, which expanded into the cell [*through division or Aelohim*]. The moon invoked life from the womb and tomb, the depths of the earth. It raised the dead from what is Life itself. Life was churned into processes that are now under the influence of the moon, their mother, biological and botanical in TIME, mind, organs—reproduction.

•

One might conclude the Emptiness itself sowed the seed from which life perpetuates itself. That in essence is the Tao.

•

One can think of energy and vacuity as a continuum of two enormous super states, one in motion and one devoid of motion. These states are equivalent to the states of Awareness and Superconsciousness. Heat and cold move in their shadows along with transitions and change—mirroring the forever changeless origin.

•

You cannot buy or find a "heat" or a "cold". They therefore do not exist by definition, they are defined as a characteristic of motion [illusions]. They are an illusion of change and motion [Maya]; and in that they are no different from a melody, as an

illusion of changing forces transitioning through time and space. [*A melody has no motion from the tones. Motion is separate from the tones themselves as a dynamic appearance surrounding changing states and is something separate from the tone. Its cause is universal.*]

•

There is no beginning to time itself. Time is an eternal propagation of Superconsciousness. There is a time and a no-time that has to do with states of changing motion. This determines what exists and what does not exist. What exists in time and space, does not exist [or is an illusion]. What exist beyond time and space, must therefore exist [as eternal] being what it is that the other is not [without time and without space].

•

There is a foundation; root or cause that has no cause, no root [causeless] since it is the root cause without beginning or end; being eternal existence [on the one hand] and nonexistence [on the other]. [*What is non-existent is causeless and eternal.*]

•

The cosmos is a Time-space Superconscious Shadow of God. Its motion is unreal [even galaxies and stars]. The motion is the Maya or Magic of appearances. All Motion is a dynamic shadow that surrounds the motion determined as dynamic forces between instantaneous changes in forms that provide an infinite set of events that are changing states. The experience is in the shadow of change. That is the Tao . . .

•

Our experience and growth in the world is the result of change. This change is brought about in the fields that are in motion. We are central to our world in cosmic space. Our transitions and

change are determined by our position and direction in the cosmos in the world we are born into. These changes transition by second, minute, hour, day, week, year, and lifetime as phase shifting propagations take place in superconscious energies. We are slowly and minutely transformed by this.

•

Time is the evolution of motion or consciousness. The Universe, the Atom, the Cosmos present us with perfections in TIME. Time is the evidence of the Primal Mover, that "invisible hand" who's WILL is inimitable, peerless, and unfailing. Its will is pure reason devoted to perfect form in motion (creation) in the stream of TIME.
Time, motion, and consciousness are inseparable . . .

•

The noumena is not just the plurality, but rather refers to the field of absolutes—that formless that has permanence, i.e., *Identity, Awareness, Wisdom, Knowing, Truth, Glory, Beauty, Splendor, Bliss* in omniscience, omnipotence, omnipresence. Noumena represents that divine state called "*satchitananda*" or Being, Consciousness, Bliss; or again, as we lightly reminisce, "*Light, Life, and Love.*"

•

Mathematical meaning is power. The mathematics of motion determines fate. These numbers and forms, direction and growth (life) are inevitable and predictable throughout time. Consciousness is TIME. TIME is SPACE. These are the composites of BEING. [Its actions, not its cause, are mathematical in space and time and therefore consciousness.]

•

[If fate did not exist, neither would mathematics. What is missing is the means to calculate it, or rather it is lost due to our ignorance of its mathematics and not due to our lack of labor in true philosophy. What is invisible is behind all of this as emptiness. Much of value, or Truth, suffers or is lost due to ignorance, not because it doesn't exist. We have no means to identify it. Knowing everything then is too great a horse to sit on. So, we should get off of it then, if it is the horse that we rode in on.]

•

Mankind, as individuals, ascend through space at death and fall like raindrops at birth. How does this equate with Adam? The inner man is solar-formed. One understands the earth as the footstool base or basis. Adam as "man" is the filter through which consciousness is realized.

•

The first cause is threefold: being, identity, awareness . . . Righteous Law, arises from the will of identity. It is a moral cause. It arises from love. This gives rise to the mathematical properties that organize by virtue of morality. It is the pure law . . . It conceives and generates through mathematical geometries through its lawful or righteous power called Rita (right) or Dharma (the determined or Righteousness). Dharma [Righteousness] as the will of the law is its foundation.

•

[What is Lawful is Truthful and this is the seat of Righteousness as a covenant, agreement or contract between Man and God that serves as a guarantee of what is only divine perfection. Without God, without perfection there would be no such thing as an axiom, accepted truth, general truth, dictum,

truism, principle or anything of worth to justify the value of the science of anything.]

•

Two forces exist in the delicate balance of the Tau. These two forces transform experience into character; these are information and transformation. These vie for power over the living. On the one side of the balance are academics, on the other are initiation and ceremony. Ritual transformation lays down the patterns of experience. Academics (academic study) sets down the skill sets required to move forward. Without the balance, there is no personal growth.

•

The Tau propagates, traveling as it does with ideas that move like light in a rippling replication, coming and going, never moving but transforming at a rate infinitely fast from its point of origin. In other words, clockwise/anticlockwise; its beginning and end meet in a place that never moves, in an infinite center, or the "middle" of the cross

•

We detect according to our instruments. The meter of any kind is limited to the specific frequencies and wavelengths that they have been created to identify. One cannot create a meter to determine that which is unknown, and which can only be experienced as a state of intelligence, or inner bliss and enlightenment. That instrument is only YOU. You are that instrument, because it is determined by the principle of "LIFE" and therefore it requires a living instrument.

•

Hamsah is the swan of consciousness; the *soham* is the breath of life. Through concentration, we draw in the light of the sun,

and with exhalation, we give of ourselves our thoughts and feelings, imagery and spiritual aspirations. Our life in the body is a living sacrifice of the elements within us.

•

If God were a male, he would be brotherly, fatherly, uncle, heroic, fearless, wise, valiant, noble, intelligent, just and bold. Protective by his instinct. If God were a woman she would be beautiful beyond endurance, tender, fearless, faithful, sweet, kind and motherly, sisterly, the aunt who is heavenly. Maternal by her instinct. If God were a child, God would be deserving of our love and care, the tender eye of innocence, beyond description and the most pleasure we could bear.

•

God is the child in the first cause, the "arche en ho logos", in our birth into human existence. It is God who first forms in the body, in the womb of Woman. She is called Wo-Man because she bears the responsibility for "Vav", the birth of the six powers of Aelohim

•

"Wo-man" is God Divine. God was and is conceived in every womb of woman. Man, the reflection of divinity enters with the first breath of life. That child in the womb is not man nor woman. That child in the womb is God's incarnation. Chaste, virgin, celibate. It is Gods adventure. Man, is the reflection of this. Only god creates. Man, is not responsible for this.

•

Lord, this is my body, this is my blood. I do not possess them so that they do not possess me. Here is my mind, my life, my love, my peace—these I release to you. I do not possess them so that they do not possess me. Here are my legs, my arms, my

hands, my feet, my thighs. I do not possess them so that they do not possess me. Here are my organs for lust, for life, for joy, for crime, the melody of my staff, the flute that struggles along my spine. I do not possess them so that they do not possess me.

•

Here are my heart and my lungs, my ears and my eyes, my one voice, the tongue, the throat, and my life. I do not possess them so that they do not possess me. I am I. May I in Truth hold on to that memory so that I may possess you, and you may possess me. Here is my: Lam, Wam, Ram, Yam, Ham, Aum. Do with them as you please.

•

I am in you and you are in me. My breath is my life, my life is not mine. I am in you and you are in me. Love is imagined. The center is mine. Without all distractions, the love is divine. I am in you, and you are in me. Whatever imagined is forgotten in time, but I am in you, and you are in me. Even my center in you is divine. Take it that I might enter sublime, the process of the Mystery.

•

Hope is imagined. Hope is divine when I am in you, and you are in me. Faith is devoted. Faith is inclined to awaken reality when I am in you, and you are in me. There is no charity. There is no sanctity. All is one lesson. There is no separation when I am in you, and you are in me.

•

What is God's is to be done with as God would please. That is the nature of the Superconscious Entity . . . This is the Path of Transformation. This is the Divine Assumption through consumption, saying to the effect: "My strength, your strength,

my love, your love; my peace, your peace; my joy, your joy; my body, your body; my breath, your breath; my mind, your mind; my soul, your soul; my spirit, your spirit; I am your splendor; I am your victory and defeat; all in all, I am You, and You are me."

•

The senses themselves are the instruments used in our measure of the world. Time is measured in the senses, the mind, and consciousness. Time is recognized as the dynamic that is reacting to change and transition. It is a power that rides over change as an unseen force, a form, like a ghost, with no measure save for change. It is heard in the tonal dynamics of musical change, though it exists in everything.

•

[Time as God and the Tao Identity] is capable of being recognized though it as subtle and as mysterious as gravity and levitation, weight and weightlessness, density and vacuity. It is, the dynamic activity that exists between the changes or transitions in the illusion of duality. It is "cause-cause-effect"... [the] vision caught up in trailing images, or the sound that is subtle to the ear touched by the key change dynamics. These are the powers that are hidden in energy that is traced by the creative intelligent builders of form . . .

•

[These creative intelligent builders of form] write themselves even into the cell and broadcast through molecular cell signal communications. Cellular communications go beyond the chemicals that form the bonds and mundane properties of finite actions since they are propagating space/time appropriate needs addressing every situation in the environment and beyond, more-subtle than the helium ion, more expansive than the vacuum.

•

[These creative intelligent builders of form] are living forces that exist on a grand scale ... They live in the form associated at their depth in the Kundalini-Leviathan. They are properties of the Cosmic Beast or Universal Entity; the Divine Incarnation. The life is hidden in the mystery of Superconsciousness; in the mystery of the Breath. It is the Being, in which we "live, move and have our being."

•

Intelligence is not limited to time and space and consciousness being idealized as the property of awareness, a condition that is omnipresent and omniscient. What permeates the universe is aware of every need, responding appropriately. This is immanent omnipresent awareness that is engaged in its operations ...

•

We are a product of Time at the instance of our nativity; as a bundle of Time-Intelligence whose birth-breath is written in, as life that is effected by time in transition, within the frame of the Cosmic Entity. This is as certain as anything that is created or steps into this Universe engaged in "Initiation."

•

What is objective and appropriate to the senses becomes subjective and appropriate to vitality, becomes subconscious and appropriate to the mind, rhythm, and cycles in time, becoming one in substance and intelligence within the consciousness of the Superconscious Cosmic Entity, knowing what is known—past present and future—for functioning on every level of time, space, and consciousness within the Superconscious properties in the movement in Eternity or God.

•

Every atom is a memory written in every form where it has been or is placed. The Zodiac (the circle of animals) is the embodiment of Time... In the Mysteries, Time becomes temporal or the created. The Temple is a House of Time. A House of Time is one engaged in devotion to the Worship of Time. An astronomical observatory is such a temple...

•

Christian Gnostic literature recognized Divinity as a process of Aeons. The Aeon was recognized as the inner being discovered within vast Dimensions of Time or Time Worlds, translated roughly into hierarchies of Divine Thought, Divine Grace, Sacred Silence, Universal Mind, and Absolute Truth, which function in vast regions of Sound and Light by Mind and Word; within a Hierarchy of Intelligence driven by Time in Eternity...

•

(**T**ruth, Righteousness, Peace, and Love) are sacred forms of these Aeons of TIME. Faith, Splendor, Beauty, Wisdom, and Understanding as well; make up the body of the Being of Beings as the form of Eternity. We match these up with the words "God is."

•

We recognize the relationship between consciousness and time. But to understand thought, mind, and the absolutes of divinity, we fail to realize the subtle being of formless time, that is, the instigator and creator of all of this. The Tree of Life references this in the form of the Aelohim, and the representatives of form in creation,

which unfold and are propagated forever and ever [Le-Olam] in this.

•

No matter what we pretend to know. What we know is nothing. We collect clues and call these axiomatic laws and principles. Meaning they are self-evident and accepted laws and principles, even when they are shaded by the limitations of the Instrument of Initiation, the body and the senses [limited] . . . much like the oyster in its shell. . .

•

Nothing is added: Nothing can be taken away. One times One is ONE: One divided by One is ONE. One multiplied by whatever Power is the power of many ONEs . . . All elements are transitions of ONE Element; whose face has many forms and facets. All light is one Light. All sound is one Sound. All words then are one WORD. All thoughts are one Thought . . . All Minds, are one Mind… etc. We imagine differences and respect boundaries that are imaginary, which hide behind the propagations of illusion.

•

"What are the creative powers of the cosmos—are written in the creative powers within nature." We see this creative power written in the theme of the body of man, the body of nature, and the body of creatures.

•

The word "Archon" is given in the first verse of the Book of John as "Arche" and is translated "In the beginning." In essence, the statement is translated, "In the 'Archon' or 'Arche' was the WORD," naming the Creative Power of the Creative

Cause that was the WORD or power of the WORD as the original or first primal or ruling cause. *"En archē ēn ho Lógos."*

•

There is no difference between the Archetype and the Archangel. It is not a psychology, but a property to Time, Space and Superconsciousness that is written into the chemistry of formation and the physics of creation as well . . . [Alchemy] is magic, in that it defies imagination.

•

What is the Archetype, is the Arch-Angelic form of consciousness as it relates to Father-Time and the Divine Living Cosmos in the formation of energy into living geometrical forms, patterned after the powers of the WORD, as number and intelligent dynamic universal powers of illumination, as the form of superconscious attributes; hidden in nature, or that power that is subtle or occult.

•

God is in all names and forms as the embodiment of all names and forms. In fact, it is the body of Wisdom and Intelligence that is in search of a form. The form is in search of Wisdom and Intelligence. That is the nature of Initiation. That is recognized in the growth obtained through the mysteries of WORD and Symbol. That is at the root of their powers to create and communicate.

•

In Sanskrit, Swa means the Self, Swara means the Sound, Iswara means the Lord, but its name would imply the Sound of the Divine Yah, or also I-Swa-Ra as three syllables that define divinity. Swa is the Self of RA, the soul of the Solar Entity. . .

"Iswa" in "I-Swa-Ra" . . . is the emanation of the sun as, "Yah-Swa-Ra."

•

The seed of Vam becomes the Swadhisthana, or the "Seat, or the actual place of the Swa." "Swa" refers to the Self of the Lord "I-Swa-Ra". Whenever there is a fire sacrifice, the word "Swaha" is chanted as a closing. Swaha is an oblation that is personified as the feminine goddess and wife of Agni, the God of Fire . . . Swa-Ha, the voice, relates to the Swa-Ra the tonal scale and Swa-Mi the monastic mendicant or "Mother".

•

The symbol related to the SWA is recognized in the Eastern Cross called the Swastika. The Swastika is the symbol for the revolution of the elements as a whirling or whirlpool motion. This is similar to the bijas, or seed sounds, of Lam, Wam, Ram, and Yam for Earth, Water, Fire, and Air.

•

The Swastika is a whirling or rotating force similar to what would be the cross-section of the symbol for the letter "Aleph" when it is cut through. It will form, an equilateral cross with four arms that are bent at ninety degrees to its axial rotation. The right angles signify the motion that influences the world of form. It is the square of the circle in motion and divided.

•

The great word was called the "Ma-Tha-Ra" Word or the Mathra Spenta in the Zend Avesta. This is the Holy Word, as written in the sacrifice . . . The sacrifice is meant to "give up" to God that which you possess. What you possess are attributes of yourself. This sacrifice passes what is possessed through one's efforts, to the

will of God, and in this case, the power of the Word in Man to the creator. This sacrifice of the WORD is very powerful.

•

Mazda in the language of the Word [Mysteries] is the Light of God [and] is the one that comes down . . . and spreads through all directions, or to the four directions . . .
in the form of the "Man of the Stars or Light."

•

The Philosophers or "Lovers of Wisdom" delighted in the Greek drama. The dramas originated with the "moral plays" that depicted the power of innate goodness that was characteristically sacred to the Mysteries, in the theater of values. These were the dramas of the gods . . .

•

To the ancient mind, the gods appeared "Out of the Blue," . . . Divinity is realized beyond the sunlight when the curtain of "blue" disappears, and the night comes to life with the backdrop of gods performing on the stage of Time; as the light of stars in the backdrop of the night sky. The Blue Sky was the curtain responsible for revealing [or hiding the players in] the theater of the night and day.

•

This outer world is something that we imagined for practical purposes, in our search for answers as we faced the examination for the measure of the thing . . . We mock our ancestry, but our senses, then and now, have served no one the better in their discerning measure of the world.

•

We are certainly drafted out of a single element; that is universally ONE and we call it "Spirit-Energy" That transitions thru phases and frequency changes to form its many properties and characteristics. This same "Spirit Energy" is a universal finite property of the light exposed of the Sephiroth [spirit].

•

The past is shaped into the future on the gnomon [*measure of phenomenon*] indicator of time, as a transitioning of light in the periodic transformations of the spiral form of time. We cannot escape the fate . . . Consciousness, man, and lives of endless forms are one in endless time.

•

These [cosmic] entities are aeons of time in eternity. Space is measured by time. Time is measured by space. What is measured, measurer, and measure is consciousness.

•

Living entities communicate from the most-minute to the most-grand. This is the measure of our prayer and meditation, one entity in many forms, surviving through the sacrifice of living, giving, and receiving; broadcasting, transmitting and receiving; the message and the messenger are one. All, have needs, and these needs are reconciled.

•

Pure AWARENESS is the foundation, omnipresent stillness, and absolute space. Pure Mind floats as a form in the pure AWARENESS into which all things or rhythmic vibrations are reflected as desires, in light that scatters everywhere. Consciousness is the ripple of superconscious energy that moves on the waters of space.

•

The world we live upon spins east to west and oscillates north and south. The cosmos is tetrapolar [YH-WH, where Y is East and W is west the HeH is North-South]. It is terrestrial along the N/S axis and celestial along the E/W axis. Brahm, the House of RAM, becomes B-RA-MA as it moves. The creation [Bereshith Bara], or the second [B = 2] RAMA, or that which unfolds into creation, is the polarization of the Father-Mother RA and MA. It is first cause or A-Ba-Ram, [these syllables mean] the father [A] or soul [Ba] of generations [Ram].

•

In Hebrew, this beginning (Tau) springs to the end [head biting the tail of the serpent] or "middle swing" in the mathematical form as Teth [from Teth we get the bite of the teeth and sacred Truth], and in Sanskrit, this is what is represented as TAT meaning simply "that," as the snap or projection and return [like a whip], and in English [it is called] thought, in the imagery of magic it is the power known as Thoth. Its fire is a torch. It represents Tau to Teth or Theta [in the wheel of the One Word or alphabet].

•

In the Hebrew QaBaLa, the direction is in nine steps forward and twelve steps reversed in the wheel of the alphabet or Aleph-Beth. Note the word "Al-*pha*-bet" uses the "Ph" in the center [letter Peh] showing the relationship that it has to the "mouth" of God.

•

We are Awareness. Even the Sun has a center around which it travels. That center is God [the absolute draw or equilibrium], the center of its gravity and orbital plane, which we think of as RA and whose fire is Resh that surrounds it [Re] as a flame [Sh

or Shin pronounced as *sin* and a state that represents fire in the name].

•

We are the witness of the MIND in the pool of awareness, eyewitness observer to its Grand Miracle of a million billion cosmic stars—the condensation of the light falling into creation, falling into orbits, rising out of nothing—appearing in space as order around an axial center or cosmic soul, a point that points towards a beginning that ends in nothing—finding fulfillment in the miracle of Earth (our home)—a cosmos set staring [down] upon us here in this world, this stage, this planet, lost in the stars, steering us toward perfection—safe among all the stars [gods] on our temporary home, placed to wait for an eternity to cycle, come and go, on that path toward enlightenment or self-realization [and liberation].

•

[Say to yourself] I am my mother's grandmother, father's grandfathers, I am my sons and daughters, grandsons and granddaughters, returning again and again as new mothers and fathers. [*We recycle through lives until these divine qualities of Time and the elements and stars are perfected, as their energies are absorbed within us or by the soul or character through the principles of the divine alchemy i.e., distillation, sublimation, calcination, cohobation etc., and we become one with them.*]

•

We are one in it all. We live out our roles in families within cultures and societies. God is the author of these, not man. We come into these being born into these, but we did not invent these. We have adapted to the lessons that they have provided, and contribute our influence as our awakening is exercised.

•

Wisdom is self-evident. It is the Awareness of Bliss existing in Superconsciousness. There is no Truth that is free save this . . . is Superconsciousness. It exists as a state of Truth, Consciousness and Bliss.

•

To peer into Superconsciousness is to realize that it is a "Heaven of Bliss." We exist because we are a part of this endless state of Superconsciousness. If not for this, we'd be devoid of reason and self-intelligence.

•

The cosmic is in Hebrew Kabala the letter "Samekh." The Sama signifies that there is sameness or Equivalency . . . Space does not really expand (since it is omnipresent), but its creation, the [lighted] cosmic breath or Samekh [cosmic], expands as a form that is self-imagined, self-imaged, as part of the divine illumination, in the lighting up of stars.

•

Samekh [the cosmic entity] is the network of the cosmic nervous system. As uniformity [of sameness] Samekh transitions through dimensions and appears to be at the center that is anywhere and everywhere, in a circle (space) that is nowhere.

•

All life is temporal. All life is sacrificed. Nothing lives forever in Eternity . . . But Samekh, the cosmic, has its own cyclical process, or cycle of birth, death and resurrection within eternity. Eternal man does not exist within the Cosmic Egg but in principles more vast than eternity.

•

𝕿his form [our form] is filled with principles that are "Self-Fulfilling." When our prayers are realized, it's a self-fulfilling prophecy, because they have a timed aspect. That timing is related to the mystery of Superconsciousness.

•

[*𝖂atch your words and be careful what you ask for. All words are self-fulfilling and are heard by God as Superconsciousness without exception or discrimination. These powers do not ask you to recant what you mean. What you say, must say what you mean. It determines your destiny. You cannot escape from yourself. You create your destiny as you enter into the door prepared for you divine Destiny. You set the pace.]*

•

𝕺ur form is propagated as a principle of self-expansion. Space does not expand. How can it? [It is the same everywhere] . . . We are not the body. We are cloaked in vehicles or bodies layered hierarchically in a maze of super-energy. The entire cosmos is reflected into our spheres of energy as a mirror of Superconsciousness.

•

𝕿ime [is] the Initiator, as a function of Cosmic Intelligence. Each moment proceeds with intelligence. And intelligence is illuminating. All powers come to play in the Kingdom or the zone of life and consciousness, wrapped in the illumination, oceans, atmosphere, and physical sphere of the earth. We are an oracle of Time.

•

Where Time has been we are a living record of its expansion into self-illumination. What is without is within and within without. All things exist within us when the belief is a reality. Self-Knowing sets the stage. Truth lies with Self-Knowing.

•

The "underlying forces or dynamics" of dimensions within the House of God . . . are the ancient underworld forces that are at work within creation. Through meditation, concentration, visualization, movement, and experience within the body, one develops illumination with the entrance into the portal of inner superconscious life dynamics, through sounds, words, and symbols that embody these underlying forces.

•

Our life is a living melody, either in harmony or otherwise. This cannot be realized through anatomy, psychology, astronomy, or physics alone. A deeply intuitive philosophy must be emphasized to understand the melodic "Meaning of Life" hidden within the metaphysics of super realities.

•

The Cosmic Consciousness is the Zodiacal relief presented as the backdrop of the path of the stars. It is the illumination of all suns, both visible and invisible. The measurers of these are presented by the movers or planetary bodies symbolically. The real measurers are those elements that move in the "Life Winds" [Prana].

•

The zodiac, called the Circle of Animals, is related to the Symbolic illumination of the Beast known as the embodiment of the Cosmic Consciousness. In that name, Zodiac, the "Zed" or letter Z is one with the Illumination of the Divine Entity. We

think of this as the Solar Path, the Path of Illumination, the Path of the Charioteer, the Righteous Path of the Chariot, or in the Hebrew the MeR-Ka-Bah. [*The Ka and Ba being from the Egyptian forms of Soul and Spirit.*]

•

One can imagine the Chariot Sun, drawn by the long-haired white Lunar Horses or nodes of the Moon, harnessed by the Cross of the Elements of Earth, Air, Fire, and Water as it is drawn across the Heavens of Time... The night is illuminated by the moon. As a symbol, the horse is the symbol for the vehicles of movement, direction and the harnessing of the senses and mind or animal instincts and passions.

•

[Geburah, the sephirah] Mars is Mary the Divine Sea the Mother of God through whose womb, the circle of the Sun, she sacrifices her life in birth. As the sea of life, she is the red blood and menstruum. She is born, as creator god, to give life to the image of the Son of the Sun [Tiphareth the sphere of beauty]. Through this sacrifice, the Mother is immortalized in the giving of her flesh and blood. [*Geb was the Son of the Earth or Son of Man. "Ra" the Soul of the Sun. The violence and bloodshed has to do with birth of creation or "Bereshith Bara".*]

•

The mother, through her union with God, is given the power to create and give birth in the world. She is the divinity or the divine meant to watch over the house as well. Thus, she is Beth, "the House," Beth the Mother of divinity

•

 Mercury, as symbolized, is threefold—the Moon over the Sun over the Earth [the symbol of the

Hermetic Axiom]. [Mercury] is the only trinity [or universal composite image]. It is the [universal] Staff or Wand and the harmonious balance of the body, mind, and spirit. The Mind above is realized in the brain of man as the illumination. The Sun in the middle is realized in the divine center of man as the spiritualized essence [in its center is the atmosphere or life breath]. The earth below is the creative principle born within and through the creative power of the elements in the body and senses.

•

♀ Venus is the Sun, or womb, over the Earth or elements and is the free and liberated spirit, unfettered by the illumination of the Mind or Moon. She is separated and free. The mind or moon has no duality and has disappeared or become hidden by the Sun.

•

♃ Jupiter is the moon within the earth, the mind mixed in the creative powers of the earth, the mind in creation as the Universal Mind. The sun is hidden. Its insight is the voice or Word as the Master within. It is the Atma/Buddhi or divine reason.

•

♄ Saturn is the earth [dominant] over the moon, the divider wherein motion breaks the foundation of the earth [the moon the instruments of cyclical change, is in constricted motion]. [Saturn] is the plough that breaks the earth [into furrows or cyclical periods] into which the seed is planted, breaking the foundation, when that which is fixed, is divided through the cycles of motion. [To plant in the first cycle of the sun, the earth must first be broken.] Change is inevitable. Saturn is the Master of Time and change. Through Saturn, no

"thing" remains the same. [Saturn is creator and destroyer.] It is the power of change and transition, life and death and life again in the ever changing tides and waves.

•

The waters divide through distillation and separation, the earth breaks down and builds back up again in cosmic crystallization. [This is the universal form supporting the cycles of incarnation and reincarnation.] The fires of the solar energies run hot and cold. [Space is filled within the cold solar fire.] The world is realized in the collyrium of the eyes that recognize the many in the ONE. The spectrum of the stars is realized in the illumination of the night. What is ONE is many; what is many ONE. The universe is the [thermal] dream. Man becomes the Dreamer in the Dream.

•

Time is fluid . . . [seven powers] we know as the octave wave in the period spectrum. However, there is a determinate in TIME that is a hidden power of change that is difficult to equate to cosmic bodies alone. Change is a concept that is difficult to grasp. It is that power of motion that determines meaning. We hear it in the musical melody and the laws and principles that are investigated in the recognition of harmony and disharmony in musical tones that appear to "move" in time.

•

Alchemy is resolved in these units of time that are realized as change and transformation. There processes are dynamically linked to mind and intelligence.

•

The mind, emotions, and senses are likened to a wild animal. They must be tamed to ride or perform. Without rigorous effort

and exercise, this is not possible any more than to be able to ride a wild zebra. Academics are not enough. Mental, emotional and sensory exercises and disciplines are required. In that as well, the mind must learn to accept, behave, admire, become devoted, and humbled. Arrogance, sensory self-indulgence, and egoistic pride are demonic attributes. They are easily discovered and easily triggered. There is little left to guesses when determining one's social impact. Spiritual qualities and characteristics influence society on the one hand, but they also effect and affect every aspect of human energy systems, environments, and psychological temperaments.

•

We say the "Light of Mind" and recognize that this "luminosity" is the measure of the senses. It is a form of Living Light. It is a world of mind.

•

The Moon is the sphere Yesod on the Kabalistic Tree of Life. This is the first dimension beyond the Kingdom . . . [*The Kingdom is Malkuth the perfect, pure and invisible sphere surrounding the earth not the composting dung heap.*] The Moon's power resides in the World of Splendor, which is the Door to the Secret Chambers . . .

The Lost WORD – Voice of the Prophet

The Path of Elijah

Br–A–L-V–H–Y–M The Light of God created, Brahm, in Man

Bara Ham– the Created Word in the Cosmic; the Akha–Sha or Soul's Light

A-L-Y-L	Alil – God
A-Y-L-Y-H	Alilah – Goddess
A-L-H	Eloah – God
A-L-V-H	Eloah – God
A-L-H-Y A-B-R-H-M	Elohi Abram – God of Abraham

A – Ajna
H – Vishudha
Y – Anahata
BR – Manipura
V – Swadhistana
L – Muladhara

The Lost WORD – Voice of the Prophet

The Light on the Path

H-V-B-R-Y-m	Ibrim – The Hebrews
A-L-W-L	Elul – The Sun in Virgo
A-L-Y-W-n	Elyon – The Most High
	[Title for Kether. Here "N" for Nara-Narayana or Adam Purusha which is associated with AMVN Amon and AMN or the Amen]
A-H-Y-H	Ayeh – "I AM"
A-L	AL – Divine Name of Chesed
	Associated with Jupiter of the Father IAO-Pater. It is the Polar Magnet striking between the Father and the Son, or the Kundalini between Ajna and Muladhara (Shiva and Ganesha; bija Gam or AGLA).

The Lost WORD – Voice of the Prophet

The Light on the Path

A-L-H	Alah Goddess Associated with Geburah. Generation, Fertility, Birth
A-Y-M-A	Aima – Supernal Mother Binah Associated with A-M-A or AM Mother
N-M	These letter additions are associated with the unified Field of fluidic force, gravity as the Male-Female elements.
A-R-Y	Ari, the Lion and A-R-Y-H Leo
A-R-Y-A-L	Ariel the Airy Mercurial Spirit
A-Y-A-L	First Astrological House
H-H	Ha! Alas! "I SEE!" "I have discovered, a vision or window. Related to HEH or the fifth letter, five elements, Hierophant or the divided Yod (God).

This H-H is the Akasha or Sound Brahman

The Lost WORD – Voice of the Prophet

The Light on the Path

H-R	Har, a divine Mountain
H-A	Ha! Lo! "If!" "Therefore!"
H-B-L	Hebel (Abel) A breath, vapor or spirit, the Son of Adam or Purusha the First Man and EVE (HVH) slain or H-L cut down in the field by Beth the Mother, or Manipura creation or birth.
H-Y-L-L	Brightness or the Morning Star, first light, first star dawning
H-Y	Hi! Lamentation, the five elements (H) ruling over or covering Yod (God) Heh-Yah versus Yah-Heh YH.
HVA	Hu- "He" Male Divine Name of Kether versus HVH (EVE)
A-Y-R	Taurus – April and May

The Lost WORD – Voice of the Prophet

The Light on the Path

Y-H-V-d-H	Judah, Tribe of Israel the expansion of the gerneations of YHVH
L-Y-L-H	Layla, NIGHT, darkness of space before the entrance of light or the light is hidden
L-B	Leb, the Heart Center, not heart, but the spiritual heart, the "BA" or maternal hidden womb of Binah.
L-B-n-H	Levanah- the Moon or Lunar Sphere, the Heart Center after the elements are born from the seed of Nara-Narayana into the elements.
L-V-Y	Levi, the Priest-Caste or Levim, the Leviah, or Priest of Yah or the Serpent Leviathan (Levi-Aton) Priest of Aton

The Lost WORD – Voice of the Prophet

The Light on the Path

L-A or L-V	Lo, meaning "No", "Not", the negative or negation, like AIN or that which is hidden or behind the veil as the non-existent or uncreated.
R-B	Rab, He the Mighty or Great!" associated with God of Creation and Generation and Manipura
RA-H-W-W-R	RA-Horus
R-A-H	To See, Sight, Vision or Inner Illumination; like Self-Realization
R-Y	Rushing Water
R-Y "sh" A-H-W-W-R-H	Risha Havurah – The White Head or A Title of Kether – the Crown or

Summit or "Sahasrara" similar to Horus-Ra as the light descending or ascending as the Divine Hawk or Son of God as the WORD and first cause Sound Brahman in Divine Illumination.

𝕸ankind is fraught with contested difficulties [stemming] from hearts destroyed by the strength of the tongue.

Generations pass but the tongue will wipe away human progress in a day . . . the death knell of rhetoric and politics tolling for the destruction of society, religion, philosophy, and love.

•

𝕳uman hearts are delicate and therefore hidden from the world for safekeeping . . . God, as the Master in his mystery, is resident there . . . as the Master in his Kingdom, he alone finds refuge in its center.

•

𝕳ere is written the properties and powers of the WORD of God. No man has the right to witness this alone . . . sheltered warmly as the witness to this essence of love, life passes by it in the blood. Thereby finding a moment's measure for life's rejuvenation.

•

𝕿he WORD requires a depth of devotion written into it. The heart is the champion by which it is sheltered.

•

𝕿he world, cast into unhappiness, shall run away, and all the temperaments casting shadows will find their wickedness, and there be the die cast with better temperaments. Here the love shall garner it, as one would the contents of the dinner plate, and by its essence showered upon its temperaments, make even the sour sweet.

The heavens hold such miracles, and we are witness to magnificence. What a morning Star is this! What an earth to gather and witness to it.

•

What a sphere of innocence until the fig leaf gave us confidence and the Glory witnessed became sheltered from the storm; as the tongue engaged in violence.

•

Divine Travelers, mourning in the field of atoms, are standing as if placed in Time and Space boundaries of God delighted by myriad grains of sand, showering beneath the field of superconscious energies; sight unseen, being—living—hidden, without our labor. As if by unseen hands.

•

They gather, formless souls, being lost from our sight otherwise, gods like diamonds that appeal for cause identity in their spacelessness and timelessness, wailing for the inability to glow when presented in their darkness, or displayed invisible in the absence of light. We appeared as the breath of light.

•

Our first natures transcending time and consciousness, return flying far beyond the fields of change, until waking from the dream in the streams of superconsciousness. We are reborn in liberation realizing Self's divine identity.

•

There is knowledge that is revealed as much intuitively and through scrying [in the mind], as that written and published, with clear intents, to slander and misrepresent, to us, its hidden

history—That world of dog eared books copied voraciously by the paupered academies and their obsessive students of innocent iniquity.

•

Where is there true revelation when all doctrines tend toward evil ends and word inventions? Truth, [divine voice], conscience and common sense all have a common ancestor, in the lineage of causes hidden beyond the world of sense, lying naked in the soul of man.

•

Histories and legends lie buried in shallow graves. Dug up, neither are found buried deep with truth or lies, only stories and fragments of secret lives.

•

God is meant to illuminate the human sun as the Lord of Righteousness. All eyes, with conscience distorted in discovery, look to it. With jealousy, hate and envy false lines become written into it, by those who break the gifted legends in the plagues of their false doctorates. [Lacking sincerity in purpose.]

•

Opinions are as easily academic! Know, rather than accuse. Academics rule our lives by knowing without knowledge, in policies and opinions both political and legal.

•

Politics, like lawyering, is so often synonymous with that novel ending whose story functions as a lie.

•

Our axioms remain our imagination bonded to our theories.

•

𝕎hat is the goodness that one is in search of? In life it is the search for that written at birth in one's destiny.

•

𝕎hat is my destiny? ... We live and die in the House of Time and therefore are creatures of Time's destiny. All creatures have their creature's destiny that is created first in the nature of the entity.

•

𝔸ll purpose is derived from their righteous cause. If a male to be a man animal, if a female to provide for future progeny. These are our initiations. These are divine gifts of nature but the natures come from God as true law, actions that have consequences, and righteousness forged by the cover of the smallest of the small [as *rita, karma, dharma* (*destined righteous action*) in the birthplace of the *parma* (meaning, *parma-anu,* most minute or the smallest of the small)].

•

𝕄an lives to emulate the gods, to forge relationships with the divine through the practices of Time and all virtues born of Ra-Ma [the duality of God].

•

𝔼ach "*Shake-Spearean*" play ... was written as a moral play. Every play ... a detailed discourse ... was written for that purpose. They were moral and philosophical, and meant for discovery and examination, and they were [*historicity, but to speak of the unspoken in the period when written, masked by a past historical theme.*] Every discourse is deserving of its own in

depth examination and discourse for revealing its moral explanation [*of the Kingdom under the rule of Elizabeth I and James VI/I.*]

•

The deaths of both authors [*Shake-Speare* and *Cervantes* /the Servant/] were celebrated in 1616 on St. George's day, just using different calendars [one in England and one in Spain.] This was by design to show that both Shake-Speare and Don Quixote were [mysteries] modeled after the Knight's St. George. [*It was not their deaths but the day of chivalry that was to be celebrated by their monuments.*]

•

History is a false teacher. Political character assassination is not history, yet this rivalry for money and power in education and politics is at the point of being ridiculous, not alone the willful misrepresentations but historical forgeries.

•

Shakespearean works scoured the world for content that would provide material deniability in case they were brought in for interrogation and questioning on the subjects of writings.

•

The true Rose & Cross was founded in England (not Germany or France) by Francis and Anthony Bacon. It was a Protestant Fraternity . . . an inner circle in possession of the secrets that were instrumental for their perfection . . . for the rehearsal of moral mysteries, in preparation for the Golden Age and the revelations of the Philosopher's Stone.

•

The Chymical Wedding of Christian Rosenkreutz was ... the invitation to the royal wedding ... [*Meant to be a wedding of the candidate to the public in order to serve society. But, based on a ceremony for Francis Bacon held in Temple Church.*]

•

We hear and see [*the secret lives of Francis and Anthony Bacon*] on mirrored glass of mortal mind [*scrying within*]. Our hearts record the legend. Our mind finds love yet unfulfilled, lessened by the entertainment, of their voices heard and filled by divination. Voices are heard echoed round the world, voices that blame our ignorance, feeling blessed but unfulfilled, as we end our dedication, feeling morally unsatisfied. Showing nothing more than this.

•

First Insights into the Mystery — Truths are wedded to Righteousness. By day, the spirit of illumination rises with the morning sun to shine upon the crown of Man and illuminate the shadows of dark illuminations.

•

See God as if you are looking in the mirror that is reflecting God back in every direction as the reflection of your inner self.

•

Nature is the reflection of divinity. Man is a spirit jewel hidden in the darkness; the light within a garland spirit hidden in the emptiness of space. This is the many-faceted diamond glittering in the shade to mirror that hidden both in darkness and in light.

•

God . . . occupies every space in the spirit of a cloud. To discover God within this, one must separate the elements out.

•

From the identity realized from the heart, this identity is the same emptiness that is a separation that forms [the] cloud as a projection of the self.

•

The Lost WORD is that vocal property of supreme intelligence, hidden in the light of Man [hidden in the Alphabet, to our shame].

•

You cannot think, write, define, or describe your way to God. Mind may be a measure of the senses. These are road maps alone, and they are fraught with academic limitations.

•

The WORD is a living power inspired by and measured through Awareness to write itself into Superconsciousness as the Miracle of the ONE-THING.

•

The number, light, heat, and sound travel with the mind as an electromagnetic illumination in the spirit of the WORD. This is a function of Absolute Desire, and the power of self-propagation and generation—omniscient, omnipotent, and omnipresent.

•

The Spirit of the Word a form in an alphabetical life that is functional in the mind of man . . . by cultivating it, we have erased its inner effectiveness behind the sentient babble of fraternities and universities.

•

All living powers are conceived intuitively, within the silence, in intimate discoveries of self-realization, experienced in the bliss of a reality that is profound and vastly beyond the depth of senses.

•

What comes from or descends in spirit from God ascends to God, or through God, as hierarchy. [*No less than the Electromagnetic Spectrum which is the unconscious spirit as characteristic adornment of superconsciousness.*]

•

Yesod, [The Sphere is] the foundation or Lunar Sphere of influence, is the revelation of the [*Samekh, letter "S"*] as the cosmic or inner light of Yod [*the letter "Y" or Yah the Lord of Hosts*]. [Samekh] is the birth of the seed [of light] within the life of Yod. The addition of "S" [*Yod becomes Yesod*] is the Son of God. It is the East, Isis or "*esse*" or the essence revealed through separation, coagulation, and fermentation, since these reveal the resurrection of new life out of the waters . . . the cosmic sweet butter churned and revealed, separating out from the soured milk.

•

Samekh is the Cosmic [in Pythagorean Greek], the Cosmic Consciousness (*cit or chit*), the Pure Consciousness immersed within the bliss of supreme knowledge, intelligence, and wisdom—the infinite self-awareness awakened in recognition of the Great Being of Superconsciousness.

•

This intelligence travels with the life breath . . . omnipresent and omniscient [it] fills space as mind and consciousness, as time . . . as well in the forms of gravity, orbits, cycles, and periodicity, [and] vibrations of cosmic emanations.

•

Life in the world is a superconscious offering. Devotion and dedication finds fruition in their processes of divine elevation. This seed essence is life living as the sacred incarnation.

•

God is a word to mystify us by a word, revealing the name for the mystery behind the world's formation. The lunar member stirs this field of consciousness . . . The earth is populated and generated as would that spirit of manifold generation . . . [out of] the Sound Brahman, as that sperm or seed unfolds within the egg formed of this life out of this subtle spirit; as its moist breath infuses life within the elements; in life and death, to bathe it with its essence.

•

Man, as the first spirit, is the incarnation of God.

•

Creatures, plants, animals, birds, and fishes—these are incarnations of its divine attributes born under the spirit of the stars.

•

[*All creatures are first divine creatures, the subject of all life and the Father's sperm*] . . . first defined as the circle of animals (*zodiac*), as creatures that are born, out of Time, from the spirit of the divine in time, by virtues of nativity.

•

Which came first, the male or the female, the chicken or the egg? Neither... God is first, then the WORD. God is last through the WORD. God is generation, life, and emanation [*as the male sperm*]. God is Yod.

•

Academics are unreliable though necessary resources. They are born of senses... their ancestral roots come from the sacred place once dedicated to the goddess of wisdom, Athena. It was raised from out of an olive grove: "*the groves of Academe.*"

•

It is inconceivable that after thousands of years of investigation, the depth of man's knowledge of the elements has decided to limit itself to something as trite as the mere study of the weather, when the Universal ONE may be the better witnessed by those dedicated to in depth investigations.

•

We live in the sphere of mathematical approximations. The grand elements move through the veil of the Cosmic Consciousness, and its electromagnetic emanations are driven by the sun and cosmic stars, along with their moons, planets and tides of change, and are processed through their miracle as creatures and plants and animals, with life and form spirited by their essence in transition

•

If this elemental essence cannot be scaled, how then the WORD of God hidden beyond the veil of elements? The powers of motion hidden in the breath are scarcely realized. These are planetary, as are the humors with electromagnetic passions that are hidden by the stars. There, love is the root cause of their creation.

•

We have, only now, even with the limited senses, begun a discovery of those small things in transition that are finally recognized in the mysteries of sound and light—the scale, tone, and color.

•

There are subtleties recognized in melody, key and tonal dynamics that are felt and heard; but as of yet, these are found wanting in the mysteries that transition in light and other periodic changes that take place in *Time and Space* that are those same dynamics of sound.

•

The image, sound, color, light, meaning, number, and sentiment are evidence of true divinity, born in mind and self-witnessed imagery, studding the stars in a field of light. [*Tone and Color are variations in dimension within a given key structured according to their beginning in the root or tonic signature.*]

•

Divine Names evoke characteristics of divinity in Man. These names were the common practice... to invoke ethical remembrances of our divinity. They are self-experienced, self-realized beyond the properties limited by the senses.

•

Aleph-Lamed [A-L] ... As Above, So Below. This transitions in the sense that it is conceived between the two ends of that power stretched; stressed between heaven and earth; between stars and iron core; existing in the incarnate life, as light in

extension; or that called the supreme power of Kundalini [*Ajna to Muladhara*].

•

Don't be fooled by those who pander to you with books filled with tales and daydreams. [Kundalini] is a power that is so powerful, asleep but lying within you. Its sight, its presence, is devastating. It is the seed form of supreme intelligence.

•

Kundalini's property is absolute, virtuous, righteous, luminous Intelligent-Thought-Sound, and it is the Ideal Identity, with megawatt authority, as the peak of confidence.

•

Kundalini is scarier than hell. Your finite property is not worthy of its endless or infinite desire for emanation. It is the ideal metaphor—discovered, unknown, and never known.

•

[**K**undalini] is calmed in a state of rest, and within that slumber, it therefore eats through us, sleeps thru us, breathes thru us by actions, thinking, contemplating, and may be discovered in the simplicity as found thru light and sound thru meditating.

•

[**K**undalini] is the symbol living by its periodic elevating and close approximating sentiments to God. It is the *Spear of Michael*... it is *"the Light of God"*... it is *"the Face of God,"* the facet of Truth set over the repentance as the mouthpiece, or *Voice of Hope* for those who would inherit eternal life.

•

The WORD lies within [Kundalini]. It generates all power in the Universe; everywhere in everything simultaneously. It does so with Righteous-Intelligence, purpose and with meaning, by its very nature and true identity [awareness].

•

[Kundalini] is subject to its identity [awareness]. It seeks thru subjects having meaning.

•

God alone is the wielder of its thunderbolt[Kundalini]. By man, it is wielded by the Word alone, touched by sympathy, to the nature of its divinity. [*God communicates to man internally and demonstrates powers internally and externally by the power revealed through silence materialized as sound. The Word is the internal motivator, as with number it is sacrificed in space and time, these are causative elements in creation. They are Eternal elements as well as temporary.*]

•

[Kundalini] can burn us in an instant if met with any resistance. The senses, nerves, and paths it takes may crumble at the touch. Only the WORD and its hidden meaning can tame it gently; for it is pure intelligence, and only purity can wield it. And that ONLY with impunity. It is justified by conscience, morality, and ethical aptitude.

•

Will and knowledge will only fail without humility. Academics means nothing.

•

Academics is designed to implode upon those who perform as platform heroes. Meanness will destroy all that it touches.

•

𝕎ithout will and knowledge, one is destined toward insanity, depending on the struggle. God becomes a devil; saints are demonized; when that which must be wielded wisely is overconfident, when righteous truth
and peace are underrealized as selfishness is recognized.

•

𝔾oodness is the godlike quality, and only God can wield it absolutely. God may only wield it through its creation and its consort, the living entity. It is realized as the extreme power of Righteousness . . .

•

𝕋he will alone cannot control [Kundalini]. It will burn it up instantly, as resistance heats all things which demand or make concessions. God is incarnate in the pure power of enlightenment.

•

𝕋he Serpent on the Tree of Life, is the power of God. It is the lightning writing the WORD of God [like the electromagnetic spectrum]. The WORD alone is law. The WORD alone can wield it and tame all obstacles. The Word is born into the image. The image is the Word of God as Name and Form.

•

[𝕂undalini] *as the Word of God* is the Language of the Gods; recondite, occult (*subtle*); more-subtle than a breeze; or that awakening of the still witness, self-born in the air we breathe . . .

•

𝕋he Lamed (ל) is the serpent, or that conceived as law, language, liberation, and the Libra, or written account, and

legacy of liberty and living Word of God. There is the secret of its power . . . divine names of God as EL, AL, or even Allah; and that principle of Greek Electra in electricity.

•

Awakened properly [Kundalini] is illuminating, but unprepared it will rip the brain into shreds of madness. It is the secret of *Poimandres; Nous;* the *Divine Pymander* in the *Corpus Hermeticum,* "I am," quoth he, "Poemander, the mind *(Nous)* of the Great Lord, the Most Mighty and Absolute Emperor: I know what thou would have, and I am always present with thee."
—London 1650; translated by John Everard

•

Two powers (*Yah and EL*) give divine life to the divine endings found in the Hebrew angelic language, in angelic names that shine in consciousness, as the elements of time; unfolded in the electromagnetic properties of Superconsciousness; stressed in Cosmic Consciousness; similar to that conceived within the sun, and the powers riding thru, the planetary entities. The cosmos is power-driven, hidden by the motion of its spell.

•

Yah and EL, illuminate life, as those powers that have divine connections . . . hidden in the subtle energies and organs of the body. Each letter is written to conceal their properties and polarities. They are Heart, Throat, Brow (mind), and those seats of cosmic energy rooted in the Kundalini.

•

The [sacred heart] is symbolized by the empty throne of the King, upon which is seated the Absolute, as the invisible

omnipresent, omnipotent, omniscient power—the vehicle of Self-Perfect energy.

•

The symbol for the heart has nothing to do with one's physical heart. It is the spiral form of the golden spiral hidden in the golden mean and its polar mirror or reflection. It is meant to be the 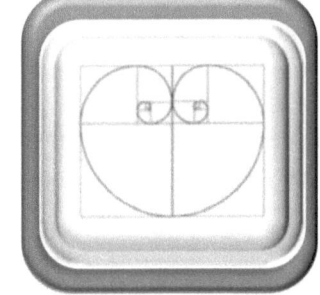 hidden mystery that lies hidden within the center of Man in perfect symmetry, where it is crossed in the very center of the chest about which the lungs pump life incessantly.

•

The planets in the sky are symbolic representatives of these properties that have to do with periods of motion originating with the sun, in the mysteries that define the Cycles of Time or Change.

•

These [planets] are the things we define often as "feelings" that effect our sensibilities, state of mind, or conditions of transitional change in the surroundings in our lives.

•

[These planets] are forces stressed across the subtle "spheres" or "worlds" of mind and vitality. In fact, they are the vitalities themselves, defined as the life winds or
pranas. These are also called the periods, or "days of creation," and they unfold as the body of Aelohim,
or the God of gods.

•

Death thru battle is also a sacrifice in the giving of blood for the sake of glory and for the benefit, safety, and security of others who are less fortunate.

•

As moderns, we have unrecoverably lost our connection with the Mysteries as the sign of our ignorance.

•

Spiritual is defined in terms of the world of motion called "spirit," . . . Resh is the royal sun with a crown of stars. This power is hidden in the name, the text of which takes on the forms for the divine names in the name of God.

•

We might move forward with reason . . . if we were not so surrounded by the ridiculous and burdened by the academic.

•

The letters form the memory organs [forming] within the omniscient illumination, as the omniscience explodes into the most minute entities of subatomic essences, spinning within self-genesis, appearing before our eyes as if an awakening.

•

The *Aur-Ra,* solar emanation, is called the starry Magical Mirror of the Universe hidden in the soul of man in the magical traditions, since it is the reflection of this solar life. It reflects the presence of the powers that are resident in the mirror of animate energy, in the motion of the planets and stars that reside, or are reflected into it.

•

The atmosphere of man is the atomic *Atma-sphere*. This sphere is key to the "fixed" point of view of the personality as if seen while standing thru a window or a doorway. The subtle movement of the Aur-Ra reflects the motions in the production of time, or divinity; the creative entity (YHVH-Brahma), and it is the spirit of one's living energy in the bubble of immortality.

•

This [*Aur-Ra*] is that magical energy, or those qualities that are the life energies that are the states of consciousness, or transitions of consciousness, that are in the middle, communicating between two worlds: the inner and the outer, the divine and man.

•

[This *Aur-Ra*] is Spirit Energy ... that is consciousness that is shaped by that power that is clearly defined as the life force, or Soul of Man, that exists "*in the image of God.*"

•

When this, the Breath of Life, leaves the body, the life from the elements return to their shapeless fundamental roots, and they disappear from their once-intended form invoked at birth. Even the dead body loses its life
recognition and becomes an empty form on the day the person disappears from life. These life qualities
evaporate, dissolve, or vanish; and the shape is almost unrecognizable.

•

Name and Form are ONE, in the condition known as the "*Breath of Life*" in the Soul of Man. The lifeless body that remains is only that imprint or shadow, like the trail hidden in the woods where once a creature passed; even though unseen, its

imprint remains, the victim of change, drawn, in the shadows of the night.

•

AUM is in union with the AUR as its wife and mother. It is the casing or womb of life. Aum is the self-reflection or womb of Aur into which the Tree of Life is born [as RaMa].

•

The AUR is also hidden in the Horu [Horus] and hour. Its name is formed from Ashur or Ausar (Osiris), the Father of the mysteries . . . [the One divided into fourteen parts or twice seven for day and night.]

•

All things incarnate with polarity, and there is no such thing existing as a unipolar incarnation. Without polarity there is no motion. This duality is complicated by the fact that it is mathematically implied $(=, +, \pm, \div, \times)$ . . .

•

Separation is duality, and it is duality that incarnates [the inner and the outer, heaven and earth, above and below, life and death, finite and infinite, mortal and immortal]. Motion is the product of the subtle division of a single duality. It is ever seeking—ever-living or everlasting.

•

This power [of duality] in us is the power that invokes our search for the meaning of life and provides impetus for the quest in pursuit of it. It is, universally, God or Devil, dark and light, good or evil, true and false otherwise.

•

These exist in the singular state of the absolute entity before incarnation, as the noumenon, or that state of being ONE "before coming into existence" in the phenomenal world; it's opposite . . .

•

Singularity exists in the realm of the "I" identity, the experience of the perfect entity. We are not one in the world, but one in which we are named as: ONE in the world AND beyond the World. We live in the equivalent, or samadhi [sameness] . . . *"As Above, So Below."*

•

In exercises of the magical cloud accumulation (or elemental separation), as defined by the Rosicrucian is seen in the Christian Ascension. For this one should chant simply AUR-RA to invoke these elements, when forming the divine body, as the reflection of the self [as if *on the horizon.*]

•

The breath should excite this [cloud] deliberately as purpose charged with meaning. Aur is the hidden light, unreflected, omniscient, omnipotent, and omnipresent . . . projected out of Ain Soph [the supernal or Brahman]. It is the mortal moral absolute.

•

AU represents the vowel signs that shine in the Akashic heaven . . . (the quality of the Akasha or Sound Brahman) the transcendental sound that represents the sixteen powers (14 + 2) of the Avatar in the Sanskrit alphabet . . . These give life to the consonants, although the vowels are generally associated with the female . . . and the consonants male . . . These are the sixteen

vowel sounds that animate consciousness and give life to the consonants, or the hidden soundless powers [of God].

•

These [letters] are the articles of peace and live within the powers hidden in the evocation of peace.

•

Those who obsess over matter, money, politics, race, gender, or division will never find peace . . . in fact, will be dead to this entirely, being locked in divisiveness, or the chaos that is marked by the creation out of what is almost endless, confided by that cosmos that is "formless and void" . . . in "chaos and desolation."

•

One must find peace in meditation or the silent thought, which is the stopping of the mind, or that state of natural motion. When the mind is stopped, what remains is omniscient.

•

Ra implies the energies of the sun—although in Hebrew, it implies evil sentiments. This infers the fact the Sun itself is the Energy of the Beast or the external living thing covered by the earth or mortal elements. The two oppositions being *"the dust of the ground"* [the atom] and *"the Breath of Life"* [vitality] that forms the living soul.

•

Ausar, *or Osiris,* is the name hidden in AIN SOPH AUR [the light of the first hours as Horus or Auriel, the Light of God].

•

To follow the path up the Tree of Life, one must find the way to discriminate between good and evil, the profane from the profound. That divine door that goes on into heaven demands it. That is the divine lesson plan.

•

Immorality is the path leading to a human hell. The divine power is rooted in morality. God is moral perfection. This is written into the fabric of creation.
Even the body takes in what is good and discharges what is not. This is clearly that process called [righteousness].

•

This [duality] breeds cycles of necessities in the play of good and evil. Man, is the product of divine necessity.
What is good, what is justified for plant or animal, is not necessarily good or justified for man. That is part of the lesson plan: *To Learn to Discriminate*. With good judgment, we survive. We do this of necessity.

•

This [discrimination] infers the image of the Tree of the Knowledge of Good and Evil. This is just not *"good advice"*—it is the advice of necessity for the instruction in the development of proper human behavior.

•

We live, not just for the body, but for the sake of the spirit that animates and gives it life.

•

God is the invincible metaphor. It is the Word first written in the mind by metaphor and translated into meaning. Its power is first formed in the object of its symbol. This makes it magical.

Its property is *"Anything before Defining"* . . . Absolute and impenetrable.

•

Absolute and impenetrable. God is LOVE.

•

The residence of God in Man is logically in the heart. The heart (center of the chest), is the seat of love and divinity in Man [and identity]. This is self-evident . . . to say for God *"there is no evidence,"* where in fact there is no greater evidence than what lies within you.

•

Only when there is no love can one say *"There is no God"* [since God is Love.] But even the elements are at once filled with Divine Love, and, at that, God is resident as the center of it.

•

The elements are purpose-driven, and their power is their ability to create. It is God who serves and conforms along with this and, as such, incarnates into endless forms. That is the evidence if the mind is filled with *Divine Intelligence and Divine Reason.* [*No person thinks of themselves as less than divine.*]

•

God is one's identity [there is no other identity] as is said, *"Be still and know"* . . . know what? *"That I am God."* That "I" is the identity. The "stillness" is just to include in this that this is meditation and a willingness to self-identify, being clear, quieted, and sequestered from the world, and of what is constantly the chatter of the *"ridiculous."*

•

["That I am God"] is common to the mystic sense that is in the rapture of the mystery hidden in every Man. This is not a special gift born by invitation. It is the message of Love.

•

The grandeur of God is hidden even in one's own sense of selfishness ... Or divine activity that is basic to one's attitude or the driving force for the governing of one's spirit [even in immaturity].

•

What is the proper greeting of the child coming into the world? That of the "Love of the Mother." The Love of the Mother is God. That is what is right or just.

•

For the child, there is the debt owed the mother. For the Mother, the duty and responsibility is given—and expected. Here is divine initiation. Either is conceived as a divine blessing for both. From this, good character is developed in the chain of life. This destiny challenges moral responsibility; and by it, all destiny is determined.

•

With each breath taken in mentally say the words "*For the Love of God*" and with each breath out mentally say the words repeating "*For the Love of God*" ... this the reason for life and living... that will inspire this meditation and assist you when asking "*What is the purpose and meaning of Life?*"... These words of power will lead you on the path toward human sanity.

•

Begin the work in the contemplation of cell consciousness by meditating on the omnipresent nature of God in the illumination of energy that is in, around, above, below, left, right, before and behind, and in the center of you [*in "burning bits of raging sand that span these torrents of Time's demands"* or atoms in cyclical orbits and formations.]

•

It is the life beyond the cells that finds focus in the life of the body. You are not the body. Before the many is the ONE.

•

As the whole is in the parts and the parts are in the whole, each model reflects the universal model, which replicates itself in all beings in the Being of Beings that is the Embodiment of Cosmos.

•

God is; power that is omnipresent and omnipotent; prime before principle; the self-evident precedent and miracle essence surrounding the stationary CAUSE that is; the identity; self-identity; the heaven preceding motion; dressed in motion, in boundaries regulated in motion; by ONE law forming the fourfold entity: Being-Space-Time-Consciousness; the elemental ONE principle *"Being Absolute"* —self-glowing; having millions of different sightings thru experiment; as the formless forms; formed of the self-resonant echo shattering from within; come out; called by the quintessential VOICE.

•

God becomes wisdom's nomenclature, a methodology of Names: the ONE THING "Universe." The essential ONE: law, principle, and property that is omnipresent everywhere.

•

The moral cause is invoked at the creative instant. [righteousness, right nature, right practice, and right consequence] are one as the instant cause of the single entity, and this is the established law that is absolute. It is in mind, breath, and energy one. Its witness is TRUTH, its power is LOVE, its initial cause is Peace that is absolute; in spaceless space and timeless time, that is perfect silence without motion . . . everywhere—omniscient, omnipresent, omnipotent.

•

Where is Truth? It rests within the mind: perfect. Where is Love? It rests within the heart: perfect. Where is Righteousness? It is the Eternal State

•

These three—Truth, Love, and Righteousness—are the essential properties of the essence of being and the joint property of Peace

•

There is no science bereft of these three—Truth, Love, and Righteousness—that enter into absolute Peace. They are the pure characteristic causes, the essence of all physics, being the cause and determined property of the essential states of power and energy

•

What sits before you all the time is divine. It's not where but everywhere a miracle.

•

What lies unrealized is only the ignorance, and ignorance lies within one's eyes, deceiving one's vision of the world with

tantrum and opinion—making dumb, immoral eyes and ears drink soaked senses mired in sweat, in the putrid lie of ignominy.

•

That which lies before you may lie before you when there is no truth: the false becomes ugly and academic. God exempts no one. Purity of thoughts, purity of mind, purity of spirit: purity, purity, purity . . . For what is the pure and sacred function but the true function that is by its nature unsullied? . . . This is the natural born religion, purity of self, honest and sweet.

•

The love of divine Wisdom, Sophia, separates at the crown of [the beginning], where it is discovered and is found, the cause at the core of the mystery of anything . . . Sophia [Wisdom] is the root cause for intelligent investigation [for the source of intelligence in creation through the sport of self-initiation] . . .

•

"God is that power in the realization that is hidden in the Silence of Wisdom": Speechless power: that is also that meditation; invocating the tongue, assuming Speech as Power.

•

[Speechless power] is the declarative WORD: who's every letter forms a universal statement of harmonic thought: propagating thru "*Type-Archetype*" of formless form: thought thru subtle divisions of mantric time: self-formed without form; self-created by number in numbered, ordered forms: to shine self-light; upon a struggling world; a perfect entity. In the struggle to be divine.

•

"**Meaning**" exists thru its miracle; self-identity; BEING nowhere and everywhere, in TIME before Time, in Space before Space, in Mind before Ming: as Motion unfitted; Intelligence without cause; BEING without a cause: Time Eternal; the Self-Formed Entity with intelligence, power, and meaning.

•

ONE, that number miracle, is the ROSE in Bloom beginning; that shines thru us, thru nature, thru mind, vitality, and identity; as the God of Superconsciousness . . .

•

Truth; Love: Law . . . true righteousness; so subtle as its nature is: in the Beginning, Ending, Beginning . . . born in selfless service: as self-actions invocation, with offerings to the divine; that are as stated *"Truth; Love and Law . . . true righteousness; so subtle as its nature is"* that replicate in man; thru the miracle of feet and hands as duty is realized.

•

Our vision of God is realized when God is recognized and held perfect in our vision of this world thru the symbols of the mind.

•

Existent, God is all-pervasive.

•

God is without a cause, permanent and perfect: neither hidden nor exposed; though misread by Man in need of a visual collyrium; requisite for the eye that has abandoned truth, and the wisdom of the Soul

•

"Initiation" is in preparation for . . . the "*firm determination to engage in pure actions*" — It is that power implied in transformation where the old is taking on a new form.

•

What is transformed? The [demonic] becomes . . . divine as refined and beautiful: the wild becomes the tamed and controlled; the ignorant transformed into the wise; the uninspired becomes the inspired, and weakness transforms into strength and determination. What is immature becomes mature, and what is leaden becomes the golden end.

•

In the mad world pummeled by the elements, man is regulated by the lust for greed and the desire to pretend away those good qualities; long held "golden" in the handbag of humanity.

•

Holding back the tears in those eyes, they are suddenly blinded; the mind haunted by the immediacy of its stubborn reality: [One is] forgetful due to that power of the unsteady time; wasted by the sudden urge to either spring to life or, in quiet, retreat again.

•

Of what use is it to pray once, or even five times a day, for that which condones one's lunacy or laziness; or worse, the madness of hate, lust, or greed? A madman has a fast-paced day; racing hard towards that wicked bondage that is ever moving forward and conceiving our imprisonment; wrapped and tangled in lost thoughts, words, and deeds: and those times meant for good roles, better times that should have been played for better ends, are found now vagrant; drunk lying in the streets; or lying to our faces; [its evil wrapping] wrapped up in our mirror.

•

God is not in need of a psychic: such without that veil of truth and philosophies of value are a puff of wind in too many ways; when reason is forbade. [God is in need of a true Devotee.]

•

God knows the future: God is the future. These extensions of human senses, in the West as they are in the East, are recognized as by-products of the development of the physical senses or certain mental faculties . . . What are of value lies within the character, they are the insights, wisdom, and true knowledge, and the ability to act upon it. And that key is in the act. That act is the initiation which lives in the life filling the day with thoughts, words and deeds.

•

That which is psychic . . . is to provide a lock on conscience and a gift of self-guidance, for the performance of these insights in the roles for better days. What good is insight without action? The extension of the senses should key one in to a better life. There is deep value in foresight and insight, but the game is played without knowledge of its outcome.

•

The development of the Human Nature into the Divine Nature, thru the awareness of love and goodness and philosophical insight is our cause. That matches the . . . Righteous Character, and God-like qualities. That is the dominant truth.

•

What is needed is a noble character: the character of the gods that manifest in man and transform the elements that make up

man into those forms, types, or archetypes, with universal qualities.

•

Good character, a loyal devotee, a hard worker . . . Service is paramount to divine appreciation. Even the Angels serve Time without exception or expectation . . . God is in search of the Devotee who serves in the name of Righteousness, Truth, Love, Peace, and Nonviolence without the thought of self-consciousness, self-interest, or self-aggrandizement.

•

Time, as Creative Creature, is the Creator. The sun serves all or none and is the ideal of Superconsciousness; . . . human cells can tell the mystery of human attributes, human virtues, or more prudently, the mystery of Divine Enlightenment.

•

The appearance is only the physical expression. Relying on that alone, you will always be deceived . . . imagine that in the rays and elements of the sun, which unfold nothing of its qualities.

•

The mysteries of Wisdom, Love, Peace, Truth, Righteousness, and Intelligence are omnipresent realities, spirited by solar illumination. Our lives tune into these and have that experience. It is to tune in and clarify the senses that makes the most sense and is the object of our quest for purity thru vigilance, contemplation, and meditation.

•

The first cause is to move and serve. There should be no sense of personal ambitions . . . that results in divine ordination and

spiritual consecration. It is an investiture where one is sworn in as thru the accomplishments of chivalry, honor, duty, and service. It is inspired thru ceremony because ceremony replicates those activities and provides the impulse for their initiation. This is the case for true magical intentions, which unfold in demonstration.

•

Wisdom unfolds slowly. Quick and easy, the true Wisdom is not clear; having found no sense for meditation, nor time for realization thru illumination.

•

Real philosophers are now deemed "out of touch," too much, the rancor of old men . . . with philosophy muddled with the silly street jargon and silly talk . . . leaders nothing more than dreaming pretenders, like flitting butterflies, in search of new funding, or a publisher with financial hopes; not unlike the academic. Old wine, aged and picked at the vine at the appropriate time, produces wonders to the taste.

•

We must now wait patiently for real maturity. So much is stuffed with blind politics or personal preferences determined by pampered desires . . . for wants and wishes espoused for trinkets and trash, and the desires raised to greet with [the] hell of fouled wisdom on the hour.

•

Christianity is being hit a terrible blow these days. For what is deserved, there is much that is undeserving . . . there is a Puritanical Wisdom that is easily found somewhere deep within when the devotee has gone in search; in silence, not in preachy

theater; where pomp and performance are outweighed by the treasures of Truth and Good Character.

•

There is no greater beggar than the one who feeds on wants and desires for what others have and pretend that God is dead, and they, poor things, have naught. It is not to deny the honest need, but the world is full of pretenders to their needs: beggars, beggars, beggars filled with greed and not a day's honest deed . . . give them a book of honest deeds and let them read; if they have time to play, for begged nickels, pennies for their wasted day.

•

Heady and high-minded means it all becomes academic. How hateful must a human being become before one locks horns with their own devils and before one's face-to-face encounter with marketing reveals itself as lies.

•

We are living in good and bad times where truth is mostly upside down, where the elements take domination over the spirit, and the value of the elements are twisted and incomplete.

•

Sad to say, we must leave the influence of our times if we wish to realize the Truth that is Truth for All-Time; for achieving a new timed product for the realization of the "Human that is Golden." [The one that is "Golden" is truly color blind.]

•

We can appreciate the psychic, but give it a grain of salt when it comes to human value. Its place and practical value is reserved for the competent and philosophically profound . . . [revealed] for

what appears at the doorway of their death, for evaluation of one's true purpose and true character assessment. What is our Purpose? What is our True Purpose?

•

We live stretched between activity and inactivity as we live propped between two worlds: "As Above, So Below". This is our inherent nature. We are beggars. We are God. What is the purpose in life—to live, eat, sleep, play, and work? ... What is our goal? It is ... to live every day to be a better person to acquire moral character. That is our obligation. That is the object for determining True Character in our daily purpose

•

There is the need for self-examination and the wisdom born of prayer. No man lives to be worse off even the man that's jailed. That runs counter to one's character. As even evil desires to better itself. Even evil desires on death's table to evaluate what was good. All search for peace and happiness; even more so the unpeaceful and unhappy.

•

Who is more in search of God—the madman, the fool, the atheist, or the saint? The saint has found God, he may search but will he also be at peace. The rest go in search. No man obsesses more over God and his existence and their desire for proof than the atheist. No man is more restless and a fool.

•

The man who is wealthy does not run in search of gold. An empty shell desires its fulfillment. We seek love, desiring its fulfillment. Even the evil man is in search of love.

•

We seek marriage as a form of happiness and its fulfillment as a remedy for our love. It is our natural property. We should first bring love to the altar of our marriage vow. After that bring food and sustenance, untethered to our fatal vows of unhappiness.

•

God is the judge of this great initiation called human life. The true welfare of our society, all societies, depends upon this field of development called Human Nature and Spiritual Awareness; for what is Truth and Righteousness . . . What is needed are true sages.

•

It takes real muster to wake up life to meaning and real purpose in the properties we recognize as that of a saint. But when we find this in one, we recognize it as what is golden and respect it, for it is the most deserving. Its real presence is one of silence. In that silence, all tongues are held in check.

•

There are infinite depths in energy within this that are manifested as depths of consciousness. This is realized as divinity in Soul and Spirit. We know it exists. We pretend ignorance. Its depths exist within us.

•

These [infinite depths of energy] are realized in those states of superconsciousness. Its depths are difficult to achieve [*in our mortal state of isolation and confusion passing through our journey in the Valley of Claustrophobia; clothed in the spirit of atomic energy with the irrational fear of our confinement, in the walled in boundaries of our mortality, suffering in our casings that are trapped within our bodies of ignorance and death*].

•

To touch the doorway leading into these depths sparks envy and jealousy. There are those who deeply deny and find value in that atheism. Those who fail to find shelter beyond the senses often fail. It is hard to leave port when the ship is tethered to a rock. These failures are often pointed to as proof and then are labeled as professors.

•

One might imply this realm of superconsciousness by changes in their chemical characteristics, when experienced. But then the world is filled with drugged bums who fail to realize that there is truth hidden in back of this reality. They fail to grasp the mind, much less the soul or divinity.

•

We cannot see beyond the depths forced by our exclusion and philosophical preferences. These philosophies mean nothing to those who have lost the will to search. These failures have nothing to do with reality but, rather, are prejudiced: burdened by one's preferred philosophy, which keeps things all the more simplistic, in a shell that is easy to conceal.

•

We take science as facts true; trusting our desires and illusions that are trusted by our sensory existence.
We hope we have found truth in theories that are lies; even by their definition of implied authority.

•

We account for matter in cosmic emptiness as if it has reality in existence. Even when facts stare us down, we cannot give up their false realities. We cannot gauge their depth. Meaning the depths of Superconsciousness . . . that it is "not this or that" — It is other than existence — Depths unfathomable, thru

measurements that we depend upon for our "fact-based" realities.

•

True cosmology: that seeks the absolute — that is true philosophy. That is, in truth, the depth of scientific inquiry . . .

•

When we may go to that place that transcends both life and death, we will have made an honest attempt. The ancients did just that in their rituals that passed thru these portals of life and death. Anything less is a false inquiry.

•

To measure the cosmos within the arc of a human hair at 500 miles or to see beyond 100,000 light years is remarkable "perhaps," today but not tomorrow, but it makes no one more intelligent, or wise, by any factor of mythical reality.

•

True knowledge is self-knowledge, the knowledge of who we really are and the ethical reality of our true purpose here.

•

What is true is that which endures and finds purpose here, as well as beyond both life and death. Our relationship with Cosmos disappears with death . . . That spirit itself is light, and the shell is written in the senses born in the atomic form, as living tissue that gathers value determined by their bodily functions [in the form].

•

Has calculus made any man a better person? Purity exists as the standard for our values that are determined by the divine and perfect relationship that it has by its nearness to divinity.

•

With each passage thru these stages of purity, there is a price to pay; are we equal to it?

•

It is our intimate discovery that finds eternal value. It is the virtue mirrored in the heart. Our relationship with life then must be weighed in the balance of this. What we achieve in life must be determined by our journey between man and man, and God and man.

•

One endless net of knots ties light to one reality. Space dark, it is assumed, is an endless lamp illumined; and unreflected we see but by glimpses of the stars illuminating it. Can we see beyond their doorsteps?

•

The lights appear from all directions. No part space is absent from this reality; though we appear to be turned inside out or simply blinded. We live in unreflected energy. What happens then to us, were we to enter into it, passing thru these doorways of the stars, to see it for what it really is? Beyond that region of our sun; where time and space disappear at death —The experience lies within new dimensions undiscovered but may be new experienced.

•

We speak of shocking measurements out to 100 billion light years. How does this define us? — What is the TRUE measure? — Love hits hard; truth enigmatic energy. No purpose means your quest is meaningless. Their symbols lying dead. It is not the vast wisdom but the shallowness of man that one finds truly incomprehensible.

•

It is not the Fall of Man that is disgraceful. That was inevitable being born in the transition of life's energies into living forms with physical senses. It is the shame of Man that has made man disgraceful and incomprehensible. Immorality trumps immortality, and it has become wicked tantamount to infamy.

•

[Immorality] is unnatural to the divinity hidden at the center of every particle in creation. Man's natural nature is to live in accordance with it . . . One has to work the devil in him to cross the path of goodness to fall into ignorance. Every man, woman, and child will warn against it when their loved one suffers thru this. Evil, even in the world of evils, finds that righteousness still dominates one's natural instincts. We find this written in the common sense in Man when untampered with by his politics and will to rhetoric.

•

Power is not evil, but the desire for power breeds deceit at the foyer of the Temple, where its acquisition is realized. The True Temple is hidden behind the Sun; the portal to our wisdom. The moon writes it in the hidden wisdom of the mind.

•

The Earth is the center of OUR universe. What takes place around *"where we are and nowhere else"* is critical to our life span. The day we set up house in the center of the sun or the center of the galaxy, we can have a discussion about who was more ridiculous in their interpretations of an Earth-centered reality.

•

Truth begins with morality. Morality ends with lies. Truth is the foundation hidden in that fountain that is eternal. It is the

fundamental form—the processes from the beginning or that sitting at the original cause of existence.

•

God is that eternal truth; before [Divine Man] the self-shining, becomes, forms, and creates—propagates, and puts on the form in the generation of atoms; that *molecularize* living; in the cellular unfolding from the atoms attractive gathering—around the imperishable—in the discovery of the Being hidden in beings; and those returning beings hidden in Being's reflection.

•

God forms creation thru the mirror of divine alchemy as a projection of itself; with a cover, an appearance; an illusion; in this field of initiation.

•

The foundation for creation is morality; where [righteousness] lays down with its substance as a cause in action: the form has the emanation of a righteous cause. Without morality, humanity cannot survive—families fail, governments die, nations fall . . . without which the creation as well would cease in chaos . . . God is in the order fashioned out of chaos.

•

Philosophy forms: self-regulated by law the fountain of true happiness the property of Truth. Politics forms at the dead end of life. It scatters itself destitute in lies; unfulfilled when all talk is sacrificed by demonstration. Silence therefore is our master; it encourages life; at the first cause in silence.

•

Nature is the "*dark*" shadow of God; illuminated thru refractions, reflections, and resounds within the forms. The perfection of the Law in Nature is absolute. We witness this perfection in creation as it permeates everything. How is it that

there can be no law in THAT which is the cause of that Law? What creates is greater than the created.

•

The Ancient, in deep reflection, is the True Philosopher; having forgotten himself in the Great Self, and left the world behind. It has nothing to do with the instruments at hand, but the instrument of the hand and the self behind it.

•

"Not this, not that"— the mouth is unstuffed and quiet, but sacred speech only touches upon the needle of the tongue for sacred messages. What is perfect, what is equivalent, rises along the middle pillar—harmonious, balanced, neither stressed one way nor the other as the language is set down and organized into the draft that is written in its life.

•

What is absolute and discoverable, as the perfections, are those of Number and the Law. They are TRUE on the Inner and the Outer. How much more pure and extreme, on the INNER; the field that is indescribable but for many undiscoverable. Therefore, silence has its tongue

•

God lives in silence and the grand sound is given as the sound of quiet, written as that mystery that is Peace Profound.

•

In the beginning (root cause-essence or foundation), there in the heart of silence, [the voice of silence] lies stable on fallow ground, unrecognized as the incomprehensible cause, unflowered self, and yet one subject to its sound. So that it is voiced for those who write for the sake of others.

•

Those things hidden by meditation are realized in meditation alone. Meditation is the root Mystery of
God. Hearing the secret that is hidden in the silence.

•

The reasoned compass points within; and the senses worry without. The only compassion is God. God is man's only surviving friend. The senses, binding man to playthings, are his greatest enemy.

•

Empirical values satisfy the senses. But the mystery may be hidden from it, under the cover of its shadow: reflection, refraction, and resound.

•

Poetic or prosaic; the musical sound of language is the disruption of the word in man. Within language, the breath provides the power of meaning. Thought rides upon the waves of sound: written in the language hidden on the inside by the gods. . . Language is the property provided by the Word of God.

•

The following is from
The Poems, Prayers, and Ramblings of the Flighty Ass, this is a poem called
"The Dilemma" written around 1975

Those burning bits of raging sand that span these torrents of time's demands, in deserted frames of empty space - that comes to rest in our embrace. To challenge our thoughts and simple pride, to review our cause, with new thoughts imbibe, those memories lost within the dream, reborn of our dilemma.

•

Here opposing fields come to view, of what is nigh and what comes anew; then passively await the arrival of, gestating thoughts that burden our love, that brandish in fire the heart and soul; avowing death to our memories old, and depth to our uncertainties.

•

As a Matter of coincidence, again comes calling our confidence, as the matter's enforced, while the dreams unfold, the matters of which we've not been told. Now, foolishly we wait patiently, for only to act again, upon the same that has brought us here, this fact of our dilemma.

•

Oh Time, why have you forsaken us, in these patterns of our undoing thus, and why then have these patterns wrought this rubble of our ruins brought? We speak of dreams in our saddest hour, and await tomorrow's passed, to imagine what we could be - Ah, but this memory doesn't last!

•

We are alone... And alone our companion is ourselves . . . for so long now. And only this trust, that's been given to us, should bypass the midst of our dilemma, to find us as before—alone with ourselves now.

•

With thoughts that, to us, would be near to the heart, with the ideas that appeared, to have been lost and torn apart . . . Hidden alone from one another, in the singled truths—vanquished, in the eyes of our reality.

•

That disappear in the night walk, and reappear at the breakfast table, while each should look at an empty plate, to discover

themselves as the field of passions empty mate. That nourishes little, but hungers a lot.

•

For it is there that we set our table and dine with an empty heart and there that our quest is held, before even yet it had time to start.

•

It is there that the Earth stands still, in the moments when the mind is dizzily filled, with the last retorts of a broken dream, and the busy hours of love to be.

•

SIGNET IL Y' VIAVIA: DANIEL

Signet IL Y Viavia: Daniel

En Arche en ho Logos Kai Theos En ho Logos en Ho Arche — In the Beginning was the Word and God was the Beginning

The Akshaya Patra Series is
A LIBRARY OF DIVINE AND PHILOSOPHICAL INQUIRY
and
BIRTHPLACE FOR THE MYSTERIES

Virtus • Veritas • Visio

Courage • Valor • Vision • Character

Creating Moral Excellence

True Initiation Lies in the Process.

Thereby our Education.

Time is the Master and Creator.

Virtue is the Guardian.

Truth is the Hierophant.

Character is Identified by the Articles of Three Virtues of Inspiration and Intelligence:

Integrity • Initiation • Illumination

These Inspire Divine Diplomacy.

The Akshaya Patra Series: MORAL DESTINY

The Akshaya Patra Series: MORAL DESTINY

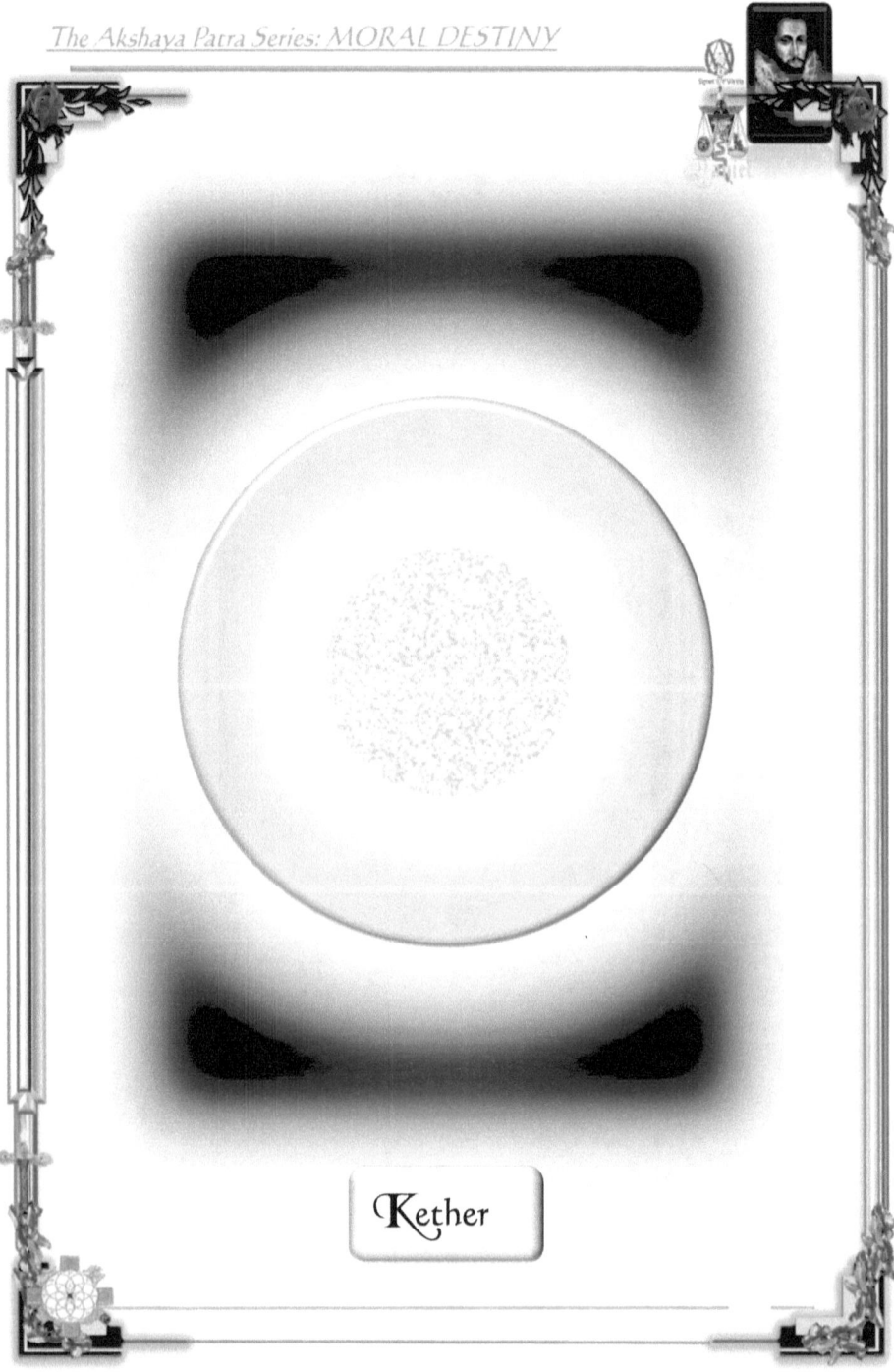

Kether

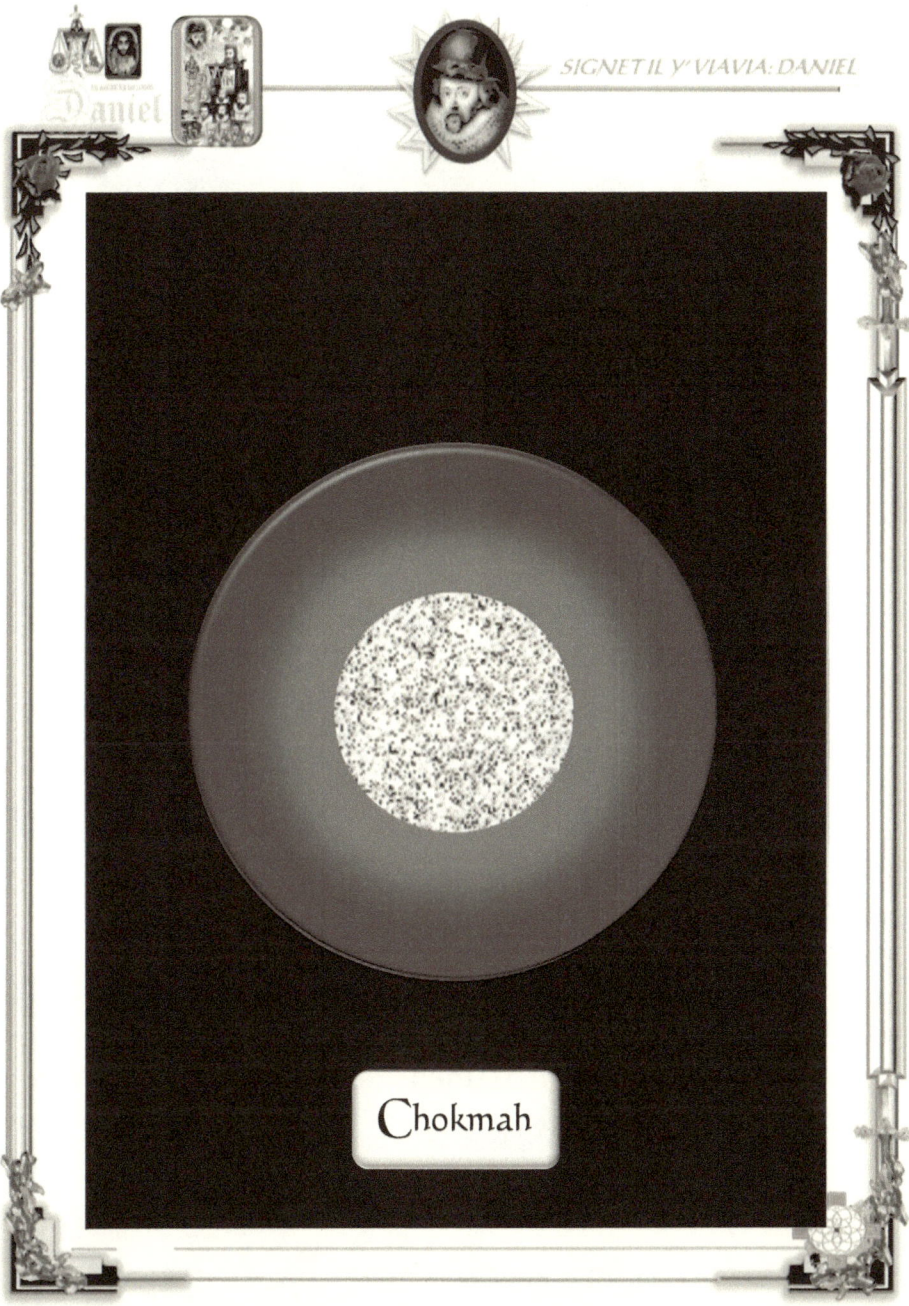

The Akshaya Patra Series: MORAL DESTINY

Binah

The Akshaya Patra Series: MORAL DESTINY

Geburah

SIGNET IL Y'VIAVIA: DANIEL

Tiphareth

The Akshaya Patra Series: MORAL DESTINY

Netzach

SIGNET IL Y V VIAVIA: DANIEL

The Akshaya Patra Series: MORAL DESTINY

Yesod

SIGNET IL Y V/AVIA: DANIEL

Malkuth

Our Signs for the Four Archangels
Raphael, Michael, Gabriel and Auriel

The first matter "YH-Yah", the Divine Name in Kether-Crown, is revealing, since it reveals the role of the Sephiroth. The crown must yield to the sacred heart behind Tiphareth and not the crown of the head. There rests that seed bija of Hridaya behind the Anahata, as the Soul of man and destiny of God.

•

Alchemically, the breath is the vital twin of God, or the nonreflecting unity, vibrant from the nucleus. These form the seeds of the voiced breath in the dynamics of intelligence—or the letters of the Word of God.

•

The Divine Farmer here has seeded the mortal earth, its Mother. She bears her fruit as food to feed the life in these dynamics. This Mothering is nurtured or nursed by the Moon. It is fathered by the Cosmic Voiced aphorisms of the Sun, as the world is seeded or called into being by those inner call dynamics written into the soul of man.

•

To articulate the distinction of two forms of God, one is the eternal absolute, the other the source of Time and, therefore, change.

•

All things in motion change in the power of Time. Time and Aelohim are one thing.

•

The Cosmos beats, to the atom's seat (*nucleus*) or the "throne of god" according to its time, and space forms through its emanation. Its seat is seeded by the monads or single unities. Its Lord is the resident in the heart or nucleus.

•

This form is infused by the breath and monad. It is that inspiration of breath, as the soul that thrives where there is love, marked by the receipt and delivery of the breath that as the fire spirit of life, moving as a stream, flows from that Paradise and is moved by the spirit of intelligence and understanding (Binah) by its Will that is Divine—made perfect as perpetuity like the timed rhythms of life and the recordings of the centers in the nucleus, atom, molecule, cell, or living heartbeat, as much as that Sacred Mysterious Resident residing centered as the "I" identity in the center of the chest.

•

The animation of the world is through its obsessive gravity and corpulency (density, size, and build), inspiring the subtleties of breath.

•

The Word SPIRIT is derived from Sephiroth (SPYRVT פירות). These are the worlds unfolding from the ten emanations on the Tree of Life. They are its fruit or the womb vessel of the impregnated male seed. The seeded center is the male divinity. The Sephirah are its divisions.

•

Like the colors within light, they are illuminations of Superconsciousness. In truth the fruit is the Mother, and the seed is the father. The Womb is the Moon or Nurse.

•

In fact, . . . She (EVE or HVH) is the Fruit of the Tree of Life. [She did not eat but is eaten]. We see this in the abundance of living things where we eat the fruit and not the seed. The fruit is designed to give nourishment. The mother provides the

environment for the seed to survive and be protected. [*At birth, we live by the fruit of the Mother at her breast. Denying this defies logic. It is the natural function of every law of man, animal, creature or plant by nature. Therefore, she is born from the breast of Adam, the sustainer.*]

•

The seed is designed to generate new life. It is the seed of the Father that is the evolving creature that is either male or female as a reflection of these principles.

•

The Divine Man . . . [*Divine Intelligent Vitality*] as Nous . . . impregnates . . . [*Spirit Energy or divine motion or cosmic motion*] manifesting the three . . . universal qualities, as states of motion within a righteous cause [*goodness, animation, or action, and dullness or inaction, or the clockwise and anticlockwise winding and unwinding as gravity and antigravity*] that forms the ego [*density*], which is influenced by these, within the worlds of soul consciousness and the spirit elements.

•

This [motion] animates intelligence and its faculties and the spiritual realities, the five elements, and the qualities of the senses. These form a relationship with the inner forms and outer forms, invoking sense perception and self-awareness—and the powers that are self-creating, self-sustaining, and self-destructing.

•

God exists in every center of this amalgamation, both finite and infinite, being the basis or foundation in its center of pulsation and replication, as the breath of God that is the power-making

power as described in sacred texts and treatises on alchemy and its sacred medicines.

•

The word Spirit expresses Sephiroth in terms of the whole, while the soul expresses the variations in qualities by the densities, individualities, and polarities of each Sephirah.

•

These [*sephirah or spirit*] terms are used alchemically to describe the animations of plants, animals, man, elements, gems, and metals. They are the planetary expressions of the Timed-Soul forming those "*star*" [astral] qualities or astral elements of time and superconscious energy. They move within the spirit (*superconscious energy, . . . or the essence of cosmic and solar energy, as motion within space, time, and consciousness*).

•

These [*Sephiroth*] are individually the Sephirah, or the leaves on the Tree [*of Life*] or the papers written in the Book of Ra (Sepher-Ra) or the light, or lightning forms of the Seraphs of the Sun. These are the divine angelic or angular emanations, or divisions of the divine reality. This forms that spirit of the Word of God.

•

> *All life and spirit f from thy breath proceed,*
> *Thy Word doth all things generate and feed.*
> *If Thou withdaw'st i it then they cease to be,*
> *And straight return to dust and vanity.*
> —104th Psalm translated to verse by Sir Francis Bacon

•

Seraphs are referred to as *The Ones who Burn* as creatures of fire. The Seraphim would be equivalent to the creatures of the Sephiroth or spirits of these superconscious forms or of these intelligent emanations. These are worlds within worlds, or dimensions of that named "Life, Light, and Love of Time and Space in superconsciousness."

•

[**The Sephirah**] are referred to as Temple [*a house of Time or astronomical astrological observatory*], Worlds, or Houses [*St. John called these cities*] to indicate, not simply an enclosure, but a universal dimension, as life within a sphere or environment, as planes of consciousness or reality [*realities*] that form the Divine Idea [*worlds within worlds not unlike their replication in the formation of cosmic bodies that follow similar archetypes or Archangels*].

•

This is not unlike the dimensions of color in light. These change their appearance in time and space. One may choose to imagine these forms symbolically and mathematically as their beloved "wormholes," but they are each omnipresent, omnipotent, and omniscient realities of the ever present One Reality.

•

One needs to understand the Mystery of the Christocentric soul of Jesus to realize the miracle, as did St. Maximus in the universal ideals attributed to the experience of the Divine idea of Man.

•

These [sephirah] are the essences that are called the fruits formed from the Tree of Life. The Hebrew would be "Saraph", a name that identifies it as the "*Cosmic Light of the Soul of the Sun out of the Mouth of God.*"

As the name implies, it is implicitly the light out of the mouth or Divine Voice of God, or the Divine Will of the *Logos Logoi* center, or the pure principle of the *"Voice of Voices,"* the *"Word of Words,"* like the Aelohim, which forms the *"God of gods."*

This is the multiplicity or Adonai (*Lord of lords*). These are the One and Many [*ideal forms or gods, being the purity of the ideals, of both in their divine origin as idea and righteousness, or purity and perfection*].

•

The Sephiroth are cellular worlds having singular qualities and dynamics in their forms. They are intelligences born of Superconsciousness, the ideal cell of God, born in the crown called Kether.

•

Music has its form of intelligence demanding by tone, tempo, dynamic, timbre . . . self-experienced, self-witnessed, self-determined and unique. The same is true in terms of the power of the lettered voice, which is the power of the Soul itself that is bundled as desire in the mind, and given vitality as experienced by the inner or outer senses, and these, transition through the field of "self-identity" or the "I-Identity." What determines the end begins in that beginning [***birth, bereshith or genesis***] hidden in its center. God's essence versus activity [***The energeia—potentiality and actuality of anything possible in the complete realization of the final form, the Mahima, or what is conceivably the creation as purely magical, or the object of a miracle, or that unleashed by an unlimited cause out of anything; given its nature that is the embodiment of Truth, from the beginning existing in absolute purity.***

For it can be nothing else, being "Certain and Most True" as the Hermetic axiom states clearly and emphatically, as it is called in

philosophy entelechy or entelecheia, as the complete, matured and fully developed image and design of the potential at the founding in actuality as that power of greatness that is sacred, and of the highest value, being the miracle or the greatness called mahima.]).

•

Malkuth is the Divine Man referred to as the Invisible Archetypal Moon. . . which is placed in the heavens "*h'shamayim*" as the astral vessel of the stars or the astral forms of the invisible planets called the Aelohim. [*The emphasis is through the focused energies of the Moon, Venus and Mercury, or those agencies between the Sun and Earth. But it is the life that supports the world that is the vital chalice holding the cosmic essences.*]

•

Wisdom is that magic that is nothing less than the wisdom of the creator that is planted in the creature [*as Truth and Righteous cause*].

Its vessel fills with the intelligence and magic of the human astral stars, by their nature, with its living properties. [**These powers march within the vital energies. They are mirrored in the soul, mind, the astral and vital motion, in the cycles and movements of life within the physical, emotional, mental and spiritual energies and consciousness, reflecting the vital role of the spirit of Superconsciousness in our lives inspiring the witness to the Divine Awareness that is present in life everywhere.**]

•

Singularity [*oneness*] in multiplicity, there are many superlatives in language, but we are familiar with those of the thrice great forms. These are words to describe the Hebrew-Greek builders that are linked to Hiram-Hermes, "*Hey-Ram*" or

builders such as "Trismegistus," thrice-formed great-great-great as body, soul and spirit, out of which forms the words also appear in embellishments. They are also found in examples in names like the Song of Songs, the King of Kings, the Servant of Servants, and the God of gods, or in the Hebrew, they shine like the Aelohim. [***The light of God in Man.***]

•

The Cosmos, the entire cosmos is a single cell. It is called the Egg of Brahma. It is the Divine Eye in that it opens up and divides and reveals the egg of the eye inside.

The entire cosmos, as vast as it is, is but a tiny fragment within the AinSof/Brahman. What the atom is to the Cosmos, the Cosmos is to God.

•

Spirit energy follows the intelligence. You are the master. Draw the energy of the fire spirit or monad by the exercise of the will, breath, vitality, thought, and power from the radiant light of fire that projects through the eyes into the atmosphere from consciousness, as the light of mind.

•

Animate the atmosphere with intelligence. You are the seed or sperm of this. The spirit energy will follow your intelligence. Condense it with the powers of concentration and mediation from space and atmosphere, as the mind is the power driving the focus of attention.

•

Separate out the elements one by one through the will. Form and shape the cloud formed and shaped at a distance. When formed draw it to you or step into it. Open it to the elements, by Sephirah, or separate these Sephirah out one by one through

imagination. Follow the pattern of the Sephiroth and experience the relationship. Find the property that is the fifth essence as that sacred property more-subtle than the rest and condense it. This is called The Beginning or Bereshith (Six Created).

•

Aelohim (ALVHYM), . . . the Light of *"Bereshith Bara Aelohim"* which formed the *"As Above, So Below"* or *"Heaven and Earth"* (ath ha Shamayim, w'eth ha Artetz) [is] found reflected in the mirror of the microcosm and macrocosm, . . . or as sounded "On Earth as it is in Heaven" . . .

•

The Sanskrit . . . seed letters with their "am" endings, as they extend, are moved through the energies in the body as vitality or pranas. They are form-making principles or powers hidden in the body as the light and sound form that created it. The Logos, or Word of God, is hidden in the alphabet. It is the power of vocalization or divine voice . . . the *"Still Small Voice."*

•

The living element of divinity is bodiless but has a form in the Voice of God. It communicates from the level of the atom and cell, through all living creatures, to stars and planets, galaxies, and even Time products as consciousness from nanoseconds to Aeons (or divinities of Time).

•

Our cosmos is a flaming resonant emblem that is formed within its massive, dynamic omnipotent, omniscient, omnipresent enlightenment. Every vibration, cycle, or gravitational element down to the inner core of every atom has this property as its source. That is why it is referred to, or defined as, *"Narayana, Narayana, Narayana"* thrice, or the ***"triune form of the Voiced***

Spirit of Cosmic Solar Light, moving on the Waters, or field forces of wave emanations, 'In the Beginning' or at the root of causes, as the First Cause."

•

They say in number, *"Before the ONE, what can you count?"* Therefore, it is ONE *"In the Beginning"* at the point of self-genesis. [**This truth is singularity**.]

•

Each letter in the Hebrew is universal in power, law, principle, Aeon, world, or state of Superconsciousness. In number and letter these fly by representing the Word of God.

•

The tongue is a wick for a lighted flame. We think of life voice as the Light Body or the body formed by naming, . . . entirely One with the Cosmos and cosmic elements. We exist, travel and multiply and play our roles devout, . . . in the spirit of the Universal One within our form of Love, Light and Life.

•

The female is called Wo-man where the Wau or six-fold Vav is included. This letter emphasizes the six-fold property of the star or *womb* or powers or light in extension that stress the birthing, and ability to create, storing life's seed, in the extension of the womb. The womb is the vehicle of the six days' work—the motions of the Aelohim in the formation in creation.

•

The directions of motion are called planetary powers. They rest in their power center or the seventh. The seventh is the samadhi or equanimity. This is at the point of apparent rest within the hub of motion, like the center of a wheel spun tight or nucleus of

the atom. The female egg is the universe, equivalent to the womb into which the male seed is placed for life's gestation.

•

The life winds draw in over the tongue passing by the mind and brain as it is drawn to the surroundings of the central heart, in the middle of the chest, the seat to the divinity. It takes in the vitality of God and returns from that divinity in Man vitalized by the human animus.

That life in spirit interacts with the life in the creature. It then returns to the atmosphere . . . The breath passes out of the mouth and is animated by the mind as it travels over the tongue. It is charged with vitality and meaning.

•

The mouth is the canal of the mind. The energies of the brain are focused on the tongue. That spirit that passes out of the mouth is filled with life, vitality and intelligence.

•

Our lives are webs spun as a network inspiring many lives aside from the broadcasting of our thoughts and feelings but passing into the elements by the breath and touch as well. This is the true spirit of the egregore. Our image is impressed on it.

•

Our thoughts and feelings, are sorted and weighted in their hierarchies of experience according to their subtle densities in the superconscious energies. If we form and create gods, angels or agencies, these geniuses become living things that have an influence over our lives. We are them, and they are us. The true dynamic defies imagination.

•

𝕿he light is the intelligence within the breath of life. It is a shining illumination, or spirit essence. One may, with practice, cause the breath to illuminate in such a way that its light will shine in darkness.

•

𝕬ll Light is God. God is All Light. Where is God? Staring in your face. Who can ask that question? God is the illumination of the Cosmos. This light is called the Eye of God since it is the cause of seeing sight.

•

𝖂here is there any form of light without intelligence? Intelligence is the divine experience of light.

•

𝖂hat is the communication in the breath? The electromagnetic spectrum is One Thing. All motion is self-willed motion and not accidental.

•

𝖂hat is not individual, may be seen as God. But what is God, is also the individual, inspired in the breath, and the illumination of the energies in light, sound and Superconsciousness.

•

𝕯ivine Knowledge is God. God is Divine Knowledge. Divine knowledge is true knowledge in that it will never change. There is no knowledge that is not God, although God is not any knowledge.

•

A Fool's insult is not knowledge. True knowledge is God. False knowledge is not Divine Knowledge. False knowledge is the antithesis of God and Philo-Sophia [*the love of wisdom*].

•

There is no true knowledge without divine integration [*divine assumption, union or yoga*]. A fool may be clever, but meaningless. No one cares about the fool once the humor has lost the day [*in ignorance*].

•

True knowledge is that knowledge found in the Wisdom of Solomon. But even Solomon may be a fool unless the truth be rehearsed as Sol-Amon or the ideal Sun of Divine Knowledge. Human ideas born of senses have neither wisdom nor knowledge. They are an insult to the names derived from True Knowledge and True Wisdom.

•

A dog may bark to announce an intruder, but a dog's bark may not discriminate. Without discrimination, there is no knowledge. Discrimination is the Guardian of True Wisdom and True Knowledge. [*True knowledge is always recognized as such.*]

•

Morality is a necessity. One is destroyed who has no morality. True Knowledge and True Wisdom are protected by morality . . .

•

[True Knowledge and Morality] are principles that define the first causes in physics. These predetermine the existence of Time and Space as the essence received within the ideal of the Cosmic Reality called into existence as the Superconsciousness evoking the mystery called the Cosmic Consciousness.

•

Where is there anywhere a place where God is not? Who can ask such nonsense? Only an academic, tangled by the web of illusion in every academic predicament, knotted and confused, pretends confusion to be destined for intelligence, within that graveyard known as sensory chaos and egotism [***devotion is the first to witness the divine reality.***]

•

God is recognized in the spirit of divine pulsation as that spirit that moves the heart and pumps the breath. That pulsation is the indication of life [***even the womb belongs to God.***] It is the I-ness. It is "tam" or "tum" or the beating of the "tom, tom" with the pounding of the damaru or drum that sets the beat for the cosmic dance or writes the melody that inspires every written line [*Divine Denial is demonic*].

•

Speech is intelligent even in the weakest utterance. In speech man is prosperous in the conclusions drawn from every proposition, where the proposition deals with pure concepts of divinity, conceived in self-knowing, where there is no hypothesis to define or unravel it . . . the common sense of it is self-realized, and it is self-defined by common sense perception through experience, though it may be challenged by all manner of ignorance.

•

Ignorance challenges every experience, when it is devoid of experience, as treacherous, by virtue of its selfish emptiness, no less than the person who is devoid of touch defames the sense of softness, hardness, grit, grime, or tenderness.

•

Ignorance is insensible to knowledge and self-determined experience; therefore, it becomes nothing more than its false witness when it claims to be either for or against it.

•

The absolute form is no form, and that first form is incomprehensible. It is incomprehensible, being formless or without form, being the original, and therefore, causeless cause. It must find a form into which it may animate itself.

•

In Man, there is no god form unless there is a form into which one may animate it. Without a form, it is powerless. Inanimate God is speechless. Speechless God is powerless. Invocate and evocate since God is invocative and evocative.

•

God is the singer. Therefore, sing as if you are God. God is virtuous; therefore, be virtuous if you wish to be in the presence of God. God is health and disease. God is life and death. This is the spirit of the world where we live echoing back, in the back side of the mirror [*the dark side*] as the divine reflection. This is the meaning that we have turned our back on God. We are the mirror. Our Mysteries are the divine reflection, as our science, art, and poetry.

•

Meaning is a first-cause power property. Lack of meaning is our poverty. That is the first stage of that magic of form identity. Without the form, man's god becomes inanimate and, in time, meaningless. The Word names and identifies the form.

•

There is no magic without naming conventions. Meaning is an original shape and function of its energy born from its intelligence that is a supreme power and property that is similar to number. Where is a dictionary replete revealing the divine properties?

•

[**The Word Exists . . .**] But not with one, but with every alphabet. This is at the root of what is truly hieroglyphic. The hieroglyphic invention was an evolution and not degeneration of divine intelligence, as some would echo in ignorance. [*Its power is a form of 'Meaning as Magic' —even as a hidden form of the unwritten absolute in physics.*]

•

The world is full of nonsense. How we have heaped our piles in stacks of lies so high into the stars that now we are breathless. We have the universities to thank, for now we have cause to lose our common sense and have, in the streets, filled our world with tantrums. God disappeared in their words of nonsense.

•

Is God number? Being dimensionless, how is he length and breadth? These numbers are not meant to bore you to numbness. It is supreme in its profundity, to the depths of silence, in its penetration into providential meaning.

•

Neither is number limited to manipulations and calculations of length, depth and breadth, as the physics often simply interprets form—no matter how complicated, in a world functioning into what is almost meaningless, by their manipulations of the natural frames or dynamics, with numbers forming mobility or momentums, or revealing their static identities that are only

conforming to time and space realities. [*These limit their identity as God from the Beginning.*]

•

Number is a numberless reality in its first identity as the Zero Entity (*Ain, Ain Soph, Ain Soph Aur*), the spirit of anything.

•

We are superconscious entities, when that root miracle is realized. Where is the limit for intelligence? These tools extend our outlook and perception in ways that are evocative and transformative.

•

Where is intelligence? Intelligence is omnipresent. Where is Wisdom? Wisdom is omnipresent. Where is there a reference? The Cosmos is our reference. That Cosmos filled with Time and Space Wisdom and Intelligence, is a miracle occurring within ourselves in every moment of our lives down even into our cells and atoms that we are destined to appear in, and destined to give up.

•

The pulsation of our Finite Consciousness is not effected by it [*the Cosmos*]. It is one with it—that vehicle of Superconsciousness. Where there is ONE, there is no chain of cause and effect. That would be ridiculous. It is always in the instant, and all linkage disappears and there is no argument in the realization of the Self-Identity. This is the . . . oneness in the nonidentity of the one identity.

•

The Sacred Word is bound to the breath as divine inspiration as that rooted in Atmosphere . . . Our life spirit in the world is like a

garment worn by the world. The WORD or LOGOS is an entity or spirit that inspires us through the breath.

•

As the Word is the Law, bound by oaths and truth, so the Sacred Word is bound by love and truth to God. Wisdom, Truth, Law, and Principle are one entity. That is the power of our lives lived through principles.

•

No man is without principle, even those who are devious. Where there is breath, there is life. In this sense, the life breath may be accumulated since it follows the divine intelligence. This is an absolute condition. By it, our lives are forecast. [*It has that relationship with the original archetype as a form of Human Destiny, though in truth it is a matter of the Divine Destiny. It originates with God. Though it follows a karmic form derived as well by the actions taking place in nature. We enter into it by our choices and our action derived from our intelligence.*]

•

Our limits lie with the realization of divinity in consciousness. Be they weak and pathetic and powerless, they are nevertheless the One Entity. This perceptibly is far beyond the realm of senses. It is the experience of that realization occurring as the practical benefit of Divine Self-discovery as witnessed in self-confidence.

•

The power of the will and determination effect [*Divine Self-Discovery*], as determined by the focus of concentration and identification with its symbol or intelligence, the vessel that contains it. The intelligence may also, therefore, be evoked out of human consciousness through the mystery of the breath, as the life in living elements, as the light within the essence written as a

shining in the breath. That shining is illuminated by the Cosmic Entity in the spirit of Cosmic Consciousness. Meaning has tremendous power.

•

The three spirits of the first cause are a triad crown that release ten spirits (Sephiroth) or Life, Light, Love illuminations that form the Tree of Life. These powers permeate the solar system as they do the cosmos. They are the cosmic powers witnessed by solar operation as evocations of the Word of God.

This is called the Fiat Lux when referred to from the Latin in the phrase to mean "Let There Be Light."

•

Three spirits or Sephiroth are supernal and accompany the first form or the model of the archē, . . . the crown unfolds its essence, which is the wheel of life and death—functioning as the spirit of Time, and the form making powers of Superconsciousness. . . its property is male as the sperm of divinity that is both evolutionary and generative as female fecundity.

•

These letters are living, illuminating supreme properties and principles as clear as the essence of energy and life. In physics, we reveal only the properties of energy, but not the triad of energy, life, and Superconsciousness.

•

[**Energy**, life, and Superconsciousness] are experienced and realized in Man as a creature having divine intelligence, unlike the creatures with limited properties or faculties. Man, unites these principles and properties in the power of the Word, with Mind and Breath, to form the life spirit that is intelligent and superior to lesser creatures in the hierarchical kingdom of divine

illumination, which is the cosmic entity as subjected to its natural order.

•

Behavior in the world is everything as related to the world's lesson plan and its natural initiations. Virtue is the natural end of initiation. That is its objective.

•

In the Sanskrit, the beginning and end is A-Ksha, and we may imagine it as the cosmic Akasha in [the] region of the throat. . .

•

Akasha [*Sound Brahman or Divine Voice in the region of the throat*] is [*sympathetic to its counterpart in*] Space as the egg envelope that permeates the depths of eternal emptiness so vast its presence is inconceivable even as to the depth of its dimensions [*zero or dimensionless*]. The egg is the record of that WORD mystery that lives in the spirit of Man [*as the auric egg evokes the cosmos*]. We think of this as the entire region of the Cosmos that extends to the blackness of space that is without light. [*The Cosmos is the living nucleus of this state of absolute emptiness (in appearance).*]

•

The idea of the breath and "then there was light," means that God breathed the Cosmos consisting of every star imaginable into the blackness. This follows the idea of the *Tohu w Bohu*. It is this cosmos that is created by the Breath-Word-Light of God. One may argue whether this is primitive. What it is, is self-knowledge, the ideal Gnosis. It is not the immaturity or rudeness of academics. Neither should it placate to it. It is the recognition of the ideal state of Man.

•

Azoth is the Sound Brahman hidden in the spirit of the throat as Akasha, where God is informed and communicates in the spirit form, or naming, [*Name-Form*] out of the perfect mind/voice of [*Divine Man*] that flies as the fire out of the mouth of man, consisting of the initial letter [A] and final letters of the Latin, Greek, and Hebrew ['Th' or the] A-ZOTh alphabets.

•

Azoth has neither beginning nor end inspiring the essence of the Sun and Moon as the universal "ens" or "esse" essential to being as the animating energy (spiritus animatus). The one and all even existing in the form of a universal medicine and essence of virtue conceive between the Sun and Moon. That mystery forms the nature of God and Universal Man and exists . . . the form of "Tat," the expanse written out as forming "*Tattwa, Tatwam,*" the divine principles of "*thatness*" and "*That Thou*" or simply, in English, the spirit formed as "*That, Thou, Thy,* or *Thee*" from the Elizabethan English assignment.

•

There exists a limitless Force in the universe, but even this Force may not be God in the sense of autonomous authority. Man, as magician, may learn to bend the properties of this to his will. Man, as Mahatma or Great Soul, may become such a master but in fact, all affect [*touch*] the cosmic functional phenomena to some degree, where there is the Will, Mind, and Reason . . .

•

[**This limitless Force**] is the visible objective expression of the absolute. This is the form-making, form producing property of substance, as that evocation of the WORD that forms from the invisible or subjective form.

•

Think of the parts that make up the body as a cosmos. The organs are the gods. The life spirit of the gods animates them, and provides the life hidden in the processes, the spirit hidden in Man. There, in Man, spirits occupy the anatomy as the company of the gods. . . They provide the body with its life [*and intelligence*]. Think of these as gods and you will realize the profound purpose and processes hidden by their animation. That is the true occult (*subtle*) anatomy. . . There among the many atoms make up the spirits of the *"hundred million crores of gods."*

•

"Thought out" is that creature created, that spirit. . . the Architect of Man. Where does this essence form, or "evolve" into the highly intelligent beings if unplanned? The cosmos may have seen a minimal sign, but here on earth, we have found what is nothing shy of this *"Miracle of Life,"* and the play played out in the spirit of the Life of God and Man and that spirit that is Christ!

•

We have lost our way and lost our confidence in the definitions of mortality by the enemies of Man (*the senses*) that have bound us up by the ropes of academia, in the illusions of their representatives and their corrupted institutions, and those who are bound to represent them [*in a desire to prove moving forward, political atheism. There is our pandemic*].

•

We are both God and Man. We are in fact, God, the Cosmos, the World, the Sun, the Elements, Time, Space, and Man. [*Man is the Absolute Reflection of Awareness or God incarnate. Man is not the body, space or the elements. They are in Man. He is not in them as an external agent.*] And the gods that form a spirit

are called the Aelohim [B-rALVHYm], or the God of gods, (*those powers on the Tree of Life hidden within Man*).

•

𝕎e are mad pretenders to intelligence. All that is known lies within the scope of our inner memories, but our outer memories fall trap to the limitations of the cellular functions, in the context of our present lives and objective experiences. They are the Time denied. This is the fruit that falls from the tree in a season. We are that hidden from within, the Tree of Self-Generation that lives from life to life.

•

𝕋he spirit appears, and it is shaped into forms spontaneously as it comes to life, and it procreates life in lives covered by the aegis of the eternal progression of cycles and the process of evolution, ever perfecting its work in the alchemical operations of the life form of Purusha Man. We assume this to be so, having had neither the experience nor intelligence to determine what is uncommon in our miniature moment in time. It takes form and shapes itself in geometries.

•

𝕎e deem the philosophical, scientific, and intellectual masters to be our spokespersons and shut our mouths and minds to Truth, even that Truth that may be voiced by God, the primal spirit on the throne, being incapable or grasping what only confidence and faith may come to know.

•

𝕎hat exists in form, must exist before the form, for either to exist. We hear it knocking from the inside out with the subtle temperaments of voice. There is the voice of soul.

•

Where there is no inner spirit, there is no form. This is true from the electron and nucleus to the star. The shape forms to the dictates of an inner spirit that is invisible to the outer form. In the natural sense, it is the power that senses. Its functions are limited and they may ignore anything outside the limits of their natural characteristics.

•

When asked, where is the evidence that there is God? We say we are the evidence. And all that is seen is the evidence that is more than obvious when what is needed to be known, being witnessed within our neighborhood.

•

God is clear in that power written in the center [*"Yah" in every Hridaya or sacred heart,*] in the first property of every living animation or nucleus from finite to that manifest in the infinite form. There is the throne of God that is defined as the life seated on the first geometrical form.

•

God is the ONE seated as resident and intelligent; as life unfolds perfected by time and the cycles. God, being the cause of time and cycles and the first Master of the patterns of the ineffable. Those patterns unfold by the power of the Dharma or self-righteousness.

This discourse following was presented as part of a visual lecture at The Conscious Life Expo on February 10, 2017 at 8:00pm and is taken from the *Akshaya Patra, Volume ONE, Book Two Part Three* called *The Ligature of Light* and other "quotables" drawn from the Akshaya Patra Series.

Ad Rosem Per Crucem

AD ROSAM PER CRUCEM,
AD CRUCEM PER ROSAM
IN EA, IN EIS, GEMMATUS RESURGAM.
NON NOBIS, NON NOBIS, DOMINE
SED NOMMIS TUI GLORIÆ SOLÆ.

"Breath in me we are One. We dwell within One Substance. More than to be consumed in One is to know One. Our thought must be enflamed, our consciousness merged, reflecting One in luster and Illumination. Sacred thought bring form and substance to our premonitions. Reveal and clarify our impressions intents. Event hang on dark and ominous clouds that have shadowed our lands and people. Evoke here now our substance from the beginning. " —From Lemuria (Mu) The Mysteries of Khan Gu.

From fairest creatures we desire increase,
That thereby beauty's rose might never die,
But as the riper should by time decease,
His tender heir might bear his memory:
But thou contracted to thine own bright eyes,
Feed'st thy light's flame with self-substantial fuel,
Making a famine where abundance lies,
Thy self thy foe, to thy sweet self too cruel:

Thou that art now the world's fresh ornament,
And only herald to the gaudy spring,
Within thine own bud buriest thy content,
And tender churl mak'st waste in niggarding:
Pity the world, or else this glutton be,
To eat the world's due, by the grave and thee.

In this endless creation, the ACTIVE ELEMENT is the Purusha, the Lord, the Eternal Awareness, who accounts for the WORD, the Divine Intelligence and the attractive source of gravity.

The Active Element accounts for the Light and the appearance of Superconsciousness—This Active Element accounts for the formation of the plasmic world of nuclear and electromagnetic actions and reactions that give rise to the embodiment of forms and the awakening of the life in the light of atoms.

Space expand as Time expands drawn into the boundless by the attraction to the Field of Anything.

Without the Active Element, these elements would fly away into nothingness. God has entered into it. It is the Active Element that charms these into the characteristics of the elements and objects of mortality, draws these into the appearance of all planets, stars and living things. It is the Active Element that does not show himself in the appearance of gravity, heat, motion and time, as the life which gives it the appearance of the ONE THING that is not (*Ain Soph/Brahmin*).

These are inspired by the "Letter Creatures" as described by the life entity. These are all described by ancient histories in perfected self-ideals of philosophy before that world of babel appeared and the monkey-mind became the deviant form of human history.

These are in truth described beautifully in the words, "*From Fairest Creatures we desire increase, that thereby Beauty's Rose might never die...*" This concept of the letter creatures is divined in this as the subject of the pure Torah-Tarot tablature that it is. Thomas Vaughan (*Bacon-Vagan*) the liberated-liver described it. Within our deviance we tend to encircle, inscribe our signatures in mathematical formula, and descibe our world of works in print, feeling unharmed in our innocuous world of senses.

Though our souls are laid out as simples on these tables as mind deviant prisoners of our rhetoric. It is to say, "*Thus far and no further . . . step away for lack of skills.*" And, we call it the scientific attitude for being so empirical, in living limits described by senses as if these are geniuses.

What appears in the emptiness [Zero-State of *Akasha, Atma-Sphere or Space*] is God. This is the Lord the fundamental and foundation that is omniscient, omnipotent and omnipresent existing in the field of Eternal Awareness.

Who says it is *Not-Physics* is unaware of the *Meta-Physics*. They count for nothing while trying to embrace the field of anything. Meta-Physics is by all ancient account not simply that root form that is *Beyond Physics,* but it is also the *Great Physics*. By all accounts self-realized this is common sense, unlike the experience drawn from academics.

God appears everywhere, as the perfect Alchemist engaged and ever-present in omniscience. Every planet or solar planetary system in the cosmos is a perfect alchemical laboratory.

Of the trilliion star possibilities each is unique in its unitary principle environment for the conceit of divine self-creation. Every sperm is wholistic. Every environment is ONE.

There is only one perfect laboratory, and that is deemed "*space*" for lack of a language determined by divine intelligence. In truth,

what we call *"space"* is the Atma-Sphere or the soul's Akashic environment.

We live in it, as a bubble in a mist that is determined by its thickness to our nature, as only we can describe it. It is the *"suvaha"* or "That Beyond" of the Gayatri, behind which the *Savitur* or *"Savior"* is ensconced as the Solar entity enigmatically engaged.

It evolves, or appears, out of its center in the breathy cell, unfolding into atmosphere as the sacred entity.

How do we know it? We breathe it, in and out, in the spirit of the Solar Entity that emerges from its core, the center, called the "I" identity.

Each created world alchemy is uniquely different. We see this in the universe of stars, planets and moons. It evolves being *"spherically omnipresent and omnipotent,"* and as equally omniscient, as the power is of illumination that is the unfoldment of its perfect centers, out of which Eternity is seen as the illuminated temple in it. Appearing staged as the Time-theater it is laced in the vast lattice works, of many tangled ornaments.

Every planet is a perfectly sealed alembic of pure principles engaged in their miracles in operation for evolving their spheres as life entities. We judge the by our senses which is for us, a unique state of idiocy.

Each cosmic system is as perfect as it is unique, unfolding in it Time-Destined opportunity.

There are as many divine alchemical laboratories in operation in the universe, as there are snowflakes generated by the most deliberate cold in the generosity of elements, in a worldwide storm. Each of these planetary or solar systems, by experience driven to exhibiting properties of worlds within worlds that can

only be unimaginable by any dream. These alone are seen as specs and spectrums by the mundane world of senses. Nothing compared to the nine times of these that are part of those spheres that are insensible?

What comes out of perfect "space" is from the emptiness perfect in its unfolding unity. That is the ideal of the rose-bloom. Each element contributes holistically as any single plant, creature, microbe or animal, as if the holistic lived by that unity, of what is holy and unutterable.

What is true in the subtlest of heavens are true within these earths or world entities. Like the Lotus on the waters, these operate in space without interference as if floating on that invisible surface. We are deviants to believe these starry creatures are unintelligent. We all who experience life as living are rendered intelligent from their identities.

We say "I" because of these. How happy, only by its love, which we are the lucky, to be able to support in our limited ability, taking such a fragment of it in.

God is not omnipresent in the Cosmos; the Cosmos is omnipresent in God. The power in the presence of the Cosmos, the cosmic vast principles, laws, actions, reactions in vast energies are ideals and characteristics that are present in the powers of Superconsciousness that present to us electromagnetism, gravity and superconductivity that moves merging on its edges—as the Being waking the divine experience—as the supreme reality of unlimited power.

Our good fortune has its limits living in the safety of our planet which in itself is a miracle of unlimited currency in its investigation. Even the single cell defies imagination. We search the cosmos just to find one other like it, living, surviving and

multiplying in another planetary experience. We are full of cosmic nonsense.

Not one civilization, not one plant or animal, nor just one cell, has been found to remind us that we are not alone, defying the miracle of miracles. We cannot travel the cosmos to inhabit the system of another star, how is that we can imagine the migration of a billion unique microbes? Even the thought of the travel of one would be a miracle.

Not one creature in nature, born a freak survives. It is either killed by the mother or left to the device of predators. Those cross-bred who do survive are born fruitless, without sperm and the ability to multiply.

But within the Cosmos these lives may be lost living in far more remote dimensions. As we see, there are so many places that defy our abilities to even investigate, because of the dangers they present to us. What is truth is that every species is born in full measure as a universe complete, fulfilling every need presented to its universe.

In the miracle, the earth appeared out of the darkness filled with sperm, male and female out of God, in every species, plant and animal—the Nothingness Preceding Light timeless absolute, attractive and delightful, beauty revealed by its fragrance and pleasant in the sound and light. And in it twilight formed in TIME, timed by its marching on, and God was divided, within the spirit of Superconsciousness that forms, as light in radiant energy.

Space is allowed its independence. These gods in stars and planets are at war in themselves and with one another beyond the human invention. These are all appearances. They are aspects of omniscient properties. We live in, and experience a human reality. Our lives demonstrate these worlds in collision by all

measure of human vanity. How is it that we all share similar senses within the world in which we originate? Dissimilar yet similar it seems to those living beyond our dimensions.

That sperm within the life is the germ of formless form shaping type and archetype, comes to us self-generated. The archetype is not simply mind but the root cause of anything created—

Purusha invisible to our sight defies all odds mathematical in gravity, and is that power in its magic, which draws the form of energies of Superconsciousness and electromagnetism, attractive to itself, declaring: *"I Am and therefore It is. I shine, the light in it. I thrill in my dimension in the bliss of everlasting invention. These all, passive and dynamic elements across and arising within the galaxies shall live within me—hidden and occult, these are my subtle entities."* They descended from the light in species.

It is the dawn of gravity, massive, endless, seated in the plasmic form, declaring, *"I draw"* and they follow the fate of form in its bliss. Its power is MEANING, knowing what is known, Gnostic, multiplying in the shadow of every form, defining the order, placement and pattern of motion, time, and gravity—itself expanding signing it by its cosmic statement, upon the daylight by the sacred language saying: *"As I live and breathe: HEAT COLD, HEAT HOT, AND DEFY IMAGINATION!"*

Dumbed down to the politics of human rhetoric, meaning has become demeaning, sense has lost its common sense, and God has lost its faithful witness. There is need for further meditation, dumbed down by our sense investigation. Contemplation should arise without further argument. Now and then? God will make then an appearance in the subtleties of mind in the magic of the power of man's imagination.

Meaning is the knowing centered in the identity of the form. Meaning is the power of the Self, appearing without an end.

Awareness occupying its place in its emanating breath. God lives. Thus divining, the miracle, it gives the cosmos its grand appearance, its life divined thereby by it our faculties and organs, processes and intelligence and the ability to broadcast its needs, to satisfy us as the rescuer and the rescued drawn together. They are captive to it, in the struggles to satisfy the need for moral attributions; inspired by a right cause; appearing in the seed and seat of righteousness, within the field of absolutes, for God's purpose lives—provided for by its life meaning as it, he or she, beyond imagination, speaks to us.

Man, appeared as "Pure Reason" with all creatures, plants and animals. The appearance shaped "Pure Reason." The essence of life's spirited elemental forms. These Elemental Forms shaped them by their creatures, plants and animals in the daylight in their coffins, set upon the Earth, in the Valley of the Shadow of Life and Death. Our vehicles of light. Drawn into forms, they are shaped by the world Atma-sphere, spirited by the breath of life, in the box of mortality.

The body, human body, is an alchemical engine. Even the element in elimination if pure, can be valuable. The first stage of separation is Kether, Chokmah, Binah. These processes follow on the Tree of Life. They fall as it were from the most-subtle to the dense or gross appearance.

These supernal sephiroth are not in the head as some claim. Such inspires the relative nonsense. They are in the supreme archetypes of the Light of the Soul in the subtle body of Man.

Kether (Yah) lies within its center as Yam or Yod the seed. Chokmah, Wisdom, lies within the crown of head and brain and supports the WORD, Reason and wisdom in Man. Binah, Intelligence, is in fact the creator YHVH and alchemical engine that supports the region of the belly, womb, legs and genitals and the organs of motion in the trunk of the body.

Malkuth is the purified Kingdom. Kuth in the hieroglyph means "LIGHT" as we see in the name Kuth-Umi meaning Light and Life which has a unique resemblance to the Astral Light within us.

The word Malak means "*angel*" and Melak means also Angels, not simply "The King." Malkuth is the "*Angel of Light.*" These would be those angels surrounding the genius of the World as the Melachim meaning both "*Kings and Angels*" and it is also the name of the two books of the Old Testament called *The Book of Kings* in secrets surviving time in double meanings.

Malkuth is M-L-K-V-Th, five letters, and as a statement means "*m' AL Kuth*" which implies "*from God's Light.*" By the numbers, it opens and closes with 40 and 400 or "Mem" and "Tau" these are rooted in the number four or Daleth the letter "D" the sign of the Emperor. The number four is the sign of the four directions (+) or addition, and (x) or multiplication. You see this number in the crossed legs of the Emperor and the Hanged Man in Tarot because of this. The 4, 40 and 400 are the same. The 400 is the Tau or Fool who comes and goes; seen entering the world. This image comes from the Mahabharata in the resemblance to Dharmaja and the little white dog who is the father faithful "Dharma" who has followed him into the world. This is the scene of true righteousness.

In the center of Malkuth is the sign of Lamed-Vav the ever-living, the sign of the 36 Lamed Vavniks, the sacred long-lived entities who travel the Earth. Its nucleus or center is "K" Kaph the sign of light and darkness as life and death united. The letter *Peh* in *Kaph* is the mouth as the Divine Eater or the death through fermentation and composting.

The root word "Mel" implies softness or soft material and a mild strength. It is rooted in the meanings for to '*melt*', a German '*malt*', and to '*smelt*' metals and '*mulch*' and as well in the Greek

in means a dark color or black, and the Latin describes the *dark redish-purple color* of the shoes of a magistrate, as the sign of the sacred footsteps of Adam or the *Feet of God* on earth, as part of ceremonial dress.

Mel also describes the 'melos' or melody, and the initiation as the 'melodrama' as well as the strength derived as in *meliorate*, or in the process of generation to *multiply* and by it from the Latin also *'melior'* meaning to make it better.

But on the dark side of the light of Malkuth it is also to imply the false, as *'malice', 'malign', 'dismal'* and *'malady'* are all described. It describes the age of its Time member, the Kali-Yuga, as well. To place blame, to speak evil and to be treacherous. It is the cosmic tantrum— like those seen on the streets today, conspiring by its mixture both the weak and strong, the dark and light to rival one another.

As described Malkuth also refers to the lives of Solomon and David the mentors of true Freemasonry as founded by the *Long-Livers* and the lineage of the bloodlines of once divine ancient Kings [*Rama, Krishna, Dharmaja, Christ, Thutmose 'x', Abraham, Isaac, Jacob, Akhenaton etc. called the hereditary royal lineage of Melchizedeks, the royal state and founders of true Republics which are described as the lineage of Yachin and Boaz on the Kabbalistic Tree of Life.*]

Malkuth is the tenth state equal to God in Man as the 1=10, or the Kether in Malkuth. But is it the same Sabbath, or the seventh day of rest? The quiet form of the footprint of motion in *Shevot* the sworn devotion that exists between God and Man where God has sworn an oath as a covenant between God and Man, in Shiva's Light, where Time in our lives is marked for mortal ceremony.

The light of Malkuth is described as Shekinah on the Tree of Life and it is referred to as the *"Bridegroom."* This is out of the devotion shared between the state of God and Man.

Sir Francis Bacon as Long-Lived Philosophical *Emperor* or *Imperator,* Thomas Vagan (the same as Comte St. Germaine), describes Malkuth as the ultra-pure invisible non-composting state, invisible to the eye surrounding the Earth.

Malkuth is the purest state of Man, the purest state of the divine self-genesis, inspiring the genius of the universe within it, as the astral state or mirror of the stars. By what process of fermentation and distillation does this link become One with the mystery of the Palace of the King?

Malkuth is described by Franz Bardon as the magical state of the Zone Girdling the Earth.

We know some aspect of this respecting the fermentation of urine in the creation of the Philosopher's Stone. This AL-Kahest of Malkuth supplied those sages and prophets who once lived surrounding the Temple of Jerusalem, described as the ones who lived by the *"eating of their feces."*

They were those same who lived for ages by the secrets of the Sacred Stone. They are those described as being bound in darkness, and also the *liberated-living,* or the dark servants of the Lord. They are those who have forgone heaven for the sake of serving God for the welfare of the wayward on Man's journey back to him.

These were those prophets and wandering kings of heaven (*followers of Asar or Osiris*) who were those who were engaged in the researches into what we know became the discoveries of gun powder.

In the 9th century, we find these adventurers influencing Taoist monks who were also alchemists. They found in their search for an elixir of immortality the *"fire medicine"* of gunpowder, not unlike that also seen in the *De Mirabilibus Mundi* of Albertus Magnus.

The Taoists were descendants of the Hebrews and those ancient Tamil Siddhar saints who migrated from the Tamil Nadu to China with their Hebrew Tribes. It's in the purification of the fermentation of the *blood alchemist* that the Alchemist found a means to give metals life in the fermentation of their urine, as described by Irenaeus Philalethes.

And as described by Christians it is the magic of Earth or the "salt-peter" that is applied to the alkahest, to the making of their living gold. Comprised of water, calcium, chloride, potassium, sodium, magnesium, urea, creatinine, nitrogen, uric acid, ammonium, sulphates and phosphates, urine's beneficial ingredients are known to have, even in the crude state, medicinal qualities, but in the medicine of purified oils and the salts of gold it was used to resurrect the King. There was God as Purusha, in the life of the mortal, the mask that formed the ever-living.

So much of the world is world inspired nonsense. This mortality of the cosmic man, was the side of life described as "The Beast" not only by the Hebrew St. John, but by the Zoroastrian, the Hindu, the Gnostics and the Christians. Even Plato refers to this in the exact same manner. These are not isolated differences, only the world of babel (*or politics*) turned into distractions.

This spirit called Malkuth has a purpose and a destination and that purpose is to inspire us through mortality to find the path to morality in our life and living practices. We already are immortal in the welfare of existence, but where is the appreciation? Malkuth is the greatest gift of Heaven that allows us to walk in the path of chivalry—to be allowed the rituals to conquer evil

practices and to make our sacrifice in this, in the experiences that face us on a daily basis; following the starlight circling beneath the sun and moon to walk the path of planetary challenges, given the opportunities these challenges have afforded us.

Many discourse . . . but few have honest answers for the path to follow on our destination. Most advances that are notable, and thereby quotable, are really no more than guesses. Those who are qualified have long since left the planet, leaving no traces of their footsteps on their final leap.

We follow by the wayside taken by them, to their greater moors— in those spirit uplands, to those fields in the highlands tracing— trapeing as we trek and traipse footsteps through the fields or planes of the Cosmic Consciousness.

> *Of what avail is the study . . . if there is no transformation in our thoughts or way of life? There must be the urge to change and progress towards a higher state of consciousness. It is only then we can grasp, to some extent, the relationship between the phenomenal Universe and the Divine.*
>
> *You must examine where your spiritual practices are leading you . . . You have to proceed from the purely mental stage to the highest stage of the Over-mind, and experience oneness with the Universal Consciousness.*
>
> *You may regard this as extremely difficult. But if you have dedication and perseverance, it is quite easy. There is nothing in the world easier than the spiritual path.*
>
> *But when there is no earnestness, it appears difficult . . . (The earnest aspirant acquires the Supreme Wisdom). If you are deeply interested in anything, you will accomplish it.*

In a bud there is very little fragrance. However, as it grows and blossoms, it automatically acquires very fine fragrance. Likewise, when the human consciousness expands, it will find fullness in the state of Sath-chith-ananda [Truth-Consciousness-Bliss].

Starting with the ordinary mind the consciousness rises to the level of the Super-mind. Then it moves up to the state of the Higher Mind. The next higher stage is that of the Illuminated Mind. Through all these stages, the continuing entity remains the same, as in the bodily changes from infancy to old age.

That is the Universal Consciousness which is present in everyone — the One in the Many. The Universal Consciousness is the Truth [Satyam]. It is the Supreme Wisdom. It is Infinite. Ever bearing in mind these triple characteristics of the Divine, strive to achieve the supreme goal of human life . . .

God incarnates to foster sadhus [noble or saintly ones], it is said . . . they mean the virtuous person who forms the inner reality of every one of you, the outer appearance being but a mask which is worn to delude yourself into esteem. —Sai Baba

Purusha, seated now appearing on this sacred vantage point. They with senses appearing with the peering eyes, educate (*educare*) as they all gathered up their sanity in the daylight of the senses, and by and by it hungered.

Man, stood fast by the sounding of the Word appearing with the inner hearing, drawing closer into its reasoning by living in its nature.

Revealing through observing God appearing in dimension, the measurable counted by its reason the imagination of the

immeasurable—revealing what cannot be revealed, and calculated the days by numbers, measuring by his work; while providing for the means for food and sheltering. Every need conspired to reason, and it became a living thing.

The Word of Reason inspired and the creation multiplied by its genders in imagination.

The first cause of Man's devotion cultivated itself, in the WORD of God in seasons, by Yoga union— cultivated it by its natural form of speech and the cycles of imagination, the living Aelohim.

It is from and by the Word (*or the literal alphabet*) of root meanings that it calls forth the magical elements. The WORD appearing first, revealed the cause of light as God in Man appearing.

The WORD appearing first image, shaped divinity into form and it revealed its nakedness in the male and female differences in form as self-awareness. God said, *"Marry and multiply the creature of Self-Righteousness and call forth the familial energies. You have my imagination. Within you with purpose and conviction, that womb is mine! Go forth and multiply!"*

God is the MEANING—God, endless, the identity in the formless form, inspired it with Self-Righteousness. That meaning (*divine*) is written, breathed while riding on the voice, hidden in the wave dynamics as the untouchable meta-physic physique of names. It inspires the living sound and melody. It symbolizes itself by its signs, and demonstrates itself in angelic ministry of sound and music, as the melody is discovered, itself revealing its divinity.

There insight is written as the ideal hidden being so occult, so subtle in language defying—magical in the form shadowed by the formless cultivating form.

In light, it is a living spirit.

Nature is written into it as the cause of righteousness—Yod is carried by its photon—as it's architecture reveals itself, suddenly appearing, disappearing, as that designed and revealed by its art and act on living forms.

Techniques of art—the mind inspiring: the characteristics cultivated are hidden and revealed by senses in its sciences. These arts populate the field of the Great Elements - The MaHa science of true meta-Physics, more-subtle than breath or mind, upward animating they follow the predestined by its calling, these lights appearing on the path are revealed in their first causal form.

Nature's art is true art. Truth is written into life holistically as a living process or purity in alchemy, the sperm discovers the spirits destiny. Each living thing, breathing, inspires a life factory, unique to every living identity.

In it wholeness appearing complete from its beginning in the light of alchemy. Its purity divining the form, in the goals set by its alchemy. There the seed, the sperm inspiring, has taken on life in pursuit of the everlasting, declaring itself the Eternal born into Eternity.

Its spirit lives and is held together by the soul breathed into it as life of self-inspired motion!

Who can compete with this? Man-God-creature-plant... Not a university nor a temple save by the life of man breathed into it. It is neither owned nor ruled by scholarship or priesthood, the clergy or the academic.

So where could our politicians grandstand, there we would be damned. There is no competitor? Their voices are only as good as the God in them. Madness lives in our minds and animates our theater; and sadly, our gossip and entertainment. Life is a

game—what, by choice, it has to do, or nothing to do, with the divine. It is the fire, the spirit and the sacrifice. And in this lies our civil chivalry.

You are now Creature-God. Dressed by the sacred elements. The signs of life are written into your fabric in creation. There is no escaping. You are given life in the shadows. Life charmed in all that comes with the prison as the gift of finite mortality. The goal? A death sentence that calls for your sacrifice when its time is come, and with that a record and examination of every feat achieved to bring you to the sacred goal, of human self-righteousness.

Be at peace with this. God is Love. Love created this. That Love is absolute intelligence that is, as with it all, absolutely dimensionless—more-vast, more-unfathomable, than the entire cosmos and everything that is in it that was created by it. Academics have lost their way when it comes to this and somehow, we need for all of us to find a way to get over it. Our science has become unfortunately, for this, our so-called modern age a term that is meaningless, something that is absolutely ridiculous. We are the divine instrument.

Education sans wisdom
[of the Everlasting-Ever-living]

Wisdom - bereft of Discrimination,

Action - without Discretion,

Erudition - lacking Sagacity (Wisdom, Knowledge & Erudition),

Power - not justified by Credentials,

Statements - not based on Truth,

Music - wanting in Melody,

Adoration - not sustained by Devotion,

A Person - devoid of Common Sense and Character,

A Student - not endowed with Humility –

These serve no useful purpose.

In addition to knowledge derived from the sacred texts, one should earn WISDOM through EXPERIENCE. Knowledge without personal experience is futile. —Sai Baba

The Ankh is the symbol of life ...

Ang, Eng, Ong, Ankh, this is the life drawn up the spine through the power in the throat where it crosses through the back of the neck below the head. [*It is to be eaten as the bread on the tongue in the eucharist. It is the Word as the Teth-Tau spirit-breath, i.e., Thoth-Tehuti.*]

[*The Ankh*] is the power of the life force as a process of the Word of God crossing in the throat or the seat of Akasha or the Sound Brahman.

[*The Ankh*] bears the shape of the Tao. On the tip of the tongue. To view the Gods who carry the Ankh, is to view these as man carried by this power at the back of the head around to the back of the crown.

The Name, (names) or divinities, carry you through the powers that live by its Word and the power of the mouth. As written it is given out, through the power of the breath and skill of the mouth.

Speech Divine, the tongue alike. These nerve endings are poised to have a divine life. Why waste it on bad speech or idle chattering, which only weakens it to make it a tongue that isn't worth mentioning. [*Here are many nerve endings tied to the spine and igniting the forehead when touching the roof of the mouth.*]

Begging, that beggars [*the tongue*] to become the root of weakness, powered by the ill speaking of an idle mind. Love lies

with the tongue. Teth-Tau, the miracle of God incarnate, was set there in Man as the guide to manage it and by virtue guide it.

The ankh is that Lantern of Life that is to be carried by the Gods, or those cosmic powers seated at the core of Superconsciousness. It is the light that guides it. It has the short stem so it begins in the heart (Yah) and is crossed at the throat (Heh).

In this the Ankh is the sign of Yah the Lord of Hosts or the company of the Gods, the power of speech from the love that is written in the heart and enlivened by the breath of life that is guided by the mind, hidden in the *Night Side of Life* that is subject to the stars...

One may view these sympathies in their subtlest states as if lifted from the collar and carried on to the next state of life and light. These have attributions connected with the stars.

As sad as it is to tell, for every person living we will someday offer our condolences. No man escapes the threat of death. We live in the *Valley of the Shadow of Death* why race about to chase within its evils.

That is the world. Here foreshadows the truth before reaching the ceremonial hall that lingers awaiting the pipes that sound death's trumpet before those waters that shower on us the rain of wetted eyes to signal our unhappiness in tears.

We are always told to *"look forward to'"* but the farther forward we look we discover that it forever, here, leads us always to our ends that rest in death. That is the crux of our mortality.

Where we sadly suffer, the most is where there is a life cut short before its time, with senseless living—with mortal disregard for the consequence of ignorance, or by their abuses have followed the paths encourage by those of morbidity who show us the path for great regret.

This is a life lived with lies and falseness forming disambiguation's, where the shell is set aside and the real life moves on to find another path by which to fly by the heels of Mercury.

We, the fools on our journeys beneath the stars enlightened by our Sun, discover ourselves too late, false, when we pretend there are no lessons to be learned and we are saddened by their impact when they happen day by day.

The richness of life is always the love that can never be forgotten and the words that can never be said to make the best of having lived. The precious treasures of our lives fly by. Their memories live unspoken for long lives that are never forgotten, but are forever remembered, long past our own expiration date.

Our lives will never end, being in truth the pure identity, but our roles die the death of names, as we exit from the stage at that moment when we never shall return again, and our part is no longer played upon the traps of blockings made for traveler's ore' the theater of life. Our steps unremembered.

Poor things. Poor, sad, undefended and indefensible in our ignorance. For those left behind as well. For they know by the downed shadow that is no longer cast, that the conquest of death is ultimate, and that we shall not return again to take back

that moment left behind, so precious, as proffered by the gift of names, save by the whispers in those prayers of silence, and later offerings carved in stone and written at the grave—and that to only last a hundred years or so, before even it begins its wash away . . .

These (*spirits on the Tree of Life*) shape all forms and dimensions. The power of God is in the Name defined by these. The appearance of God is in the Name. The form of God is in the Name.

Devotion is sincerity forever tied to purpose and the purity of these qualities. We speak about our path, the divine axiom of Hermes and the Emerald Tablet or the *Tabula Smaragdina* in the process of transformation: the process of initiation: the process of alchemical transmutation. This is the path taken by the aspirant as well upon the Middle Pillar

This is the Middle Pillar on the Tree of Life, the path of liberation. Self-Realization is bound as ONE THING composed of POWER, LIFE and MEANING.

This miracle is seeded in Man from the beginning, and defined by those forms of mind and the Word or alphabet. It is that aspect of the first essence and it shares in the form of the essential salts, for every created thing has its salt, and as the essential liquid fires are seeded into being by that sperm of divinity in the unfoldment of the nature of Truth.

We are mortal immortality as seen when the shadows and light of the finite substances that are cast aside that decay, devoid of life. The act secedes and the roles end when you play dead . . .These causes for death integrate with the mysteries of

initiation. Therefore, the only death is the death of life in the field of liberation. This is the consequence of our being here.

The Archetypes and Types are the divine ideas written into every form of nature, whether atom, planet, moon, the sun, mind or spirit.

That sperm of divinity is written in the substance that defies visibility. God is embraced within this. It is the mystery of the spermatic seed found in the liquid salt of Adamic Man.

This is recognized in alchemy in its Philosophical Mercury. This forms the written identity appearing on the Tree of Life.

This perfect sperm is the divine fountain from which we live, move, eat and breathe. Our thoughts are that. Our bodies, though they are shells of our outer imagination, they are that.

Our earth the composting heap beneath us breathes the life of its exegesis; as the interpretation of its internal oracular exegete.

Our minds that. Our existence perfect in its prophecy.

Records of Time are heaved out, appearing from our futurity. Our soul that purposed cause.

Our Identity is revealed and reflected in that mirrored aggregate.

With or without form, the separation of our identity is meaningless, since these are bound principles. THAT (Tat) and "us" are "we" indeed.

Philosophical Light is omnipresent energy. The False identification of the senses is rampant.

Every star is everywhere at any-time for billions of years. We are in the center of that.

These ornamentations are the natural offspring of the absolute consciousness that composes the body of God. Spontaneous resonance, reflection and resound… from the atom to the farthest star every orbit cut and turned, calculated then perfectly drawn in the mind and body of one life entity that inspects it perfectly; like a farmer turning out the field.

Every reflected light the same, planet, moon, asteroid… Everywhere at the same time, omnipresent; thus, logically including us in our physical bodies; since physical bodies are reflected bodies.

Light travels endlessly in one form or another. So, it is logical to say, *"There is no part of me that is not a part of the Gods… I am in them, and they in me; one and the same."*

We are more than that as well. We radiate energy and consciousness . . .

The *genie* refers to those geniuses or spirits of time and space, connected to the realm of superconscious energies that transition, or change in time.

This is the energy we often feel as changing states of consciousness. They change by the direction of the magnetic fields and our orientations towards them. They are effected by the pull of the moon or the energies of the north sky. Maybe imagined in the Norther Lights from the energies of the sun magnetic charge, (Re) as seen **"sitting with your face to the**

north wind, and your eyes seeing happiness." As it says in the Qur'an, God created jinn out of the *"fire of a scorching wind".*

These are the intelligences of nature, hidden in the manufacture or creation as the power that are modeling the spirit, mind and material form out of Time, or the Aelohim. The **"millions of years"** are attributed to the Aeons. These are the magical powers that, from their foundation or Yesod, may gain strength in man, as his powers to create are imagined and given life. This is written in history even as hidden in the fairies of *The Midsummer Night's Dream* and implied, as the image of the creator appears in the light within that is **"bodied forth the forms of things unknown."**

We recognize these in their subtlety, in our changing moods and refer to these in the angling of psychology that fishes through our thoughts for an answer, as one in a boat, like one who would stare into the mirror of the waters on a lake, imagining the creatures there, swimming beneath their surface.

Animate these subtleties a thousand times their subtlety as one would imagine through concentration, and then illuminate it with internal powers of Kundalini fire that are like powering a city from the megawatt lighted energy that is resting there within. There you might from your ignorance understand the essence of the meaning. Be careful.

Non Nobis Domine!

A poem by Rudyard Kipling (*A Wandering King and Freemason*)

Non nobis Domine!, Not unto us:
O Lord! The Praise or Glory be
Of any deed or word, For in Thy Judgment lies:
To crown or bring to nought
All knowledge or device:
That Man has reached or wrought.

And we confess our blame: How all too high we hold
That noise which men call Fame:
That dross which men call Gold.
For these we undergo: Our hot and godless days,
But in our hearts we know: Not unto us the Praise.

O Power by Whom we live: Creator, Judge, and Friend,
Upholdingly forgive: Nor fail us at the end:
But grant us well to see: In all our piteous ways,
Non nobis Domine!: Not unto us the Praise!

Divine Sephiroth on the Tree of Life

Kether K-Th-R 20-400-200 כתר		Crown, Omnipotence, Center, Nucleus, Axis
Chokmah Ch-K-M-H 8-20-40-5 חכמה		Wisdom, PreCosmic Root of Spaceless Timeless Omniscience
Binah B-Y-N-H 2-10-50-5 בינה		Understanding, God of Eternal Time Endless dimensions as the PreCosmic Root of Omnipresence
Chesed Ch-S-D 8-60-4 חסד		Peace & Loving Kindness, the seed, first instance of the incarnate God of gods, AL of Aelohim.
Geburah G-B-V-R-H 3-2-6-200-5 גבורה		Strength, Eternal Endurance and the power incarnate as the Divine Power, Shakti as pure Energy, or Mother Goddess, the womb of fruit.
Tiphareth (Teth) Th-P-R-Th 400-80-200-400 תפארת		Beauty, appearance, the Miracle, the Ornament or Adornment of formal visibility and luminosity, radiance, refraction, reflection and resound. First power of divine Mahimas or Miraculous Power.
Netzach N-Tz-Ch 50-90-8 נצח		Victory, Eternal Fecundity or Self-Generation of Endless Living Beings, gods, angels, Planets, creatures, vegetation and Man.
Hod H-V-D 5-6-4 הוד		Glory, Majestic Intelligence, Voice, to Speak or Pray, Still Small Voice, Word, Mantra, to govern & create by the Word or Kabala.
Yesod Y-S-V-D, 10-60-6-4 יסוד		Foundation, the nucleus in the seed forms of life governed by the Cosmos. *"To go forth and multiply"*.
Malkuth M-L-K-V-Th 40-30-20-6-400 מלכות		Kingdom, the Waters of Creation, Laws that Govern: Death-Life-Death-Life. Tetraktys : 432 : 4 x 108

God Name Evocations on the Tree of Life

Sephirah	Name	Meaning
Kether	Ehyah or Ah-Yah A-H-Y-H	AH-To Swear the Oath — to Yah-Self. The breath of Life & Pure Identity
Chokmah	Yah Y-H	Essence of Y-H or the Wisdom of the Tenfold Essence of the Elements
Binah	YH-VH Aelohim Y-H—V-H A-L—V-H Y-M Yah and AL are the two divine endings of the Angelic Names. These originate in Binah	YH-*VH* Jehovah AL-*VH* Eloah V-H Two children of Eve Chvh or Ch-*VH*) Mother of Life (Ch-Y) Yam: Day or Time, VH = 6 & 5, or the Planets & Elements
Chesed	AL A-L	LVX Sevenfold Space or Shining image of God Ava-Loka, AVH-LVKH
Geburah	Aelohim Gibor A-L-V-H-Y-M G-B-V-R	GBVR the Power or Shakti of the Mother of the Gods.
Tiphareth	YHVH Eloah ve Daath Y-H-V-H A-L-V-H V-D-O-Th	Daath signifies the Knowledge & Wisdom of the Gods
Netzach	YHVH Tzabaoth Y-H-V-H Tz-B-A-V-Th	Tzabaoth: Divine Creatures or Hosts. Living Beings of Divinity YHVH
Hod	Aelohim Tzabaoth A-L-V-H-Y-M Tz-B-A-V-Th	Tzabaoth: Divine Creatures or Hosts. Living Beings of the Gods (Aelohim).
Yesod	Shaddai El Chai Sh-D-Y A-L-Ch-Y	Shaddai is Sada Eternal Sai-Sia (Thoth-Hermes) or Shiva, God of Life "God of Abraham"
Malkuth	Adonai H' Aretz A-D-N-I H-A-R-Tz	Earth Lord, the 1-10 Essence or primal moist elemental Earth

Archangelic Evocations on the Tree of Life

Kether Metatron M-T-T-R-V-N		Narayana, Grand Architect, Supreme Purusha, Being-Superconsciousness-Bliss, Ever Present Awareness, Divine Presence.
Chokmah Raziel R-Z-Y-A-L		Herald of God's Secrets and Sacred Mysteries, Silence of Harpocrates, Lord of Perfect Magic & Miracles.
Binah Tzaphquiel Tz-P-Q-Y-A-L		Lord of Knowledge and Intelligence Time-Space-Consciousness Sacred Gravity & Liberation
Chesed Tzadquiel Tz-D-Q-Y-A-L		Lord of Divine Justice & Mercy, the Righteousness of God. Lord of Divine Mercy and forgiver of debts.
Geburah Kamael K-M-A-L		Sacred Internal Fire of God, strength, omnipotence, face to face with God as if staring into the sun. Shakti.
Tiphareth Michael M-Y-K-A-L		Twin Likeness of God. The Prince or Son of God. Nara-Narayana
Netzach Haniel H-N-Y-A-L		Joy and Grace of God Sacred Daughter and Bride of Chesed
Hod Raphael R-P-A-L		God as the Divine Healer, as the healing that stirs in the Alchemical Waters or Narayana as the Sun.
Yesod Gabriel G-B-R-Y-A-L		Voice of God, Divine Strength and Messenger of God. Shakti, as the letters on the Ladder of Light and Life of the Kundalini.
Malkuth Sandalphon S-N-D-L-P-V-N		"Lotus Feet" – Sacred Descent, Messiah or Avatar of God. True Spirit of the Astral Kingdom of Malkuth.

Angelic Hierarchy: Sages of the Holy Order

The Order of the *Just Men Made Perfect*. The Hierarchy of the *Righteous Kings*.

Kether Chaioth Ha Qodesh Ch-Y-V-Th H-Q-D-Sh		Holy Living Creatures, Root Intelligence of the Elemental Forms of Tetragrammaton. The Four faces of Illumination being one with YHVH-Brahma. Yod or Yah, the One Entity: God.
Chokmah Auphanim A-V-P-N-Y-M		Wheels within wheels. Living in all Worlds or the Cosmic Consciousness. *"Aufin"* is "the Elephant" in ancient chess.
Binah Aralim A-R-A-Y-L-M		Mighty Ones. The Liberated Living. The invincible. The undying.
Chesed Chashmalim Ch-Sh-M-L-Y-M		Brilliant Ones. The Illuminated Saints. The Melchizedek or Righteous King. Electrical. Northern Lights. Flashing Fire.
Geburah Seraphim Sh-R-P-Y-M		Flaming Serpents (Order of Philosopher Sages.) Alchemical acid-*water serpent*, or *Phoenix*.
Tiphareth Melekim M-L-K-Y-M		Kings of the Order of Melchizedeks
Netzach Aelohim A-L-H-Y-M		God of Gods or those illuminated by the Kundalini rising.
Hod Beni Aelohim B-N-I A-L-H-Y-M		Son of God, My Son, Beni is *Beniyamin* or *Son of Yah-Amon*, Ancient heroes, men of renown Royal Favorites, Intellectuals and Servants of the Nobility
Yesod Kerubim K-R-V-B-Y-M		The Youthful Aspirants for Initiation, Cherubs, the royal children, and their favorites.
Malkuth Ashim AShYM		Heroes, Chivalrous Knights, Devotees. Heavenly Men. Those *"willing to lay down their lives for their fellow men."* The Order of the Men of Justice.

Planetary: Alchemical Occult Fields

Kether Rashith Ha Gilgalim (Primal Whirling)		R-A-Sh-Y-Th H-G-L-G-L-Y-M גלגולים Gilgulim is the Soul Cycle, Incarnation, Reincarnation and the formation of galactic forms, nucleus, *the eye of the storm or center of gravity.*
Chokmah Mazloth (Zodiac)		M-Z-L-V-Th Cosmos, Hiranyagharba or Cosmic Egg.
Binah Shabbathai (Saturn)		Sh-B-Th-A-Y (Lead) The Sabbath. Sacred TIME. Grandmother-Grandfather YHVH
Chesed Tzadekh (Jupiter)		Tz-D-Q (Tin) Sacred or Righteous Essence, God as the Righteous Father
Geburah Madim (Mars)		M-D-Y-M (Iron) Battle Garment, Uniform, Birth Covering, "*From Adam*", Lord of Life and Death, Arts, Earth Architecture. Prajapati.
Tiphareth Shemesh (Sun)		Sh-M-Sh (Gold) Sun (*Rising-Setting*), East, the Father (*Immortal generative seed*)
Netzach Nogah (Venus)		N-V-G-H (Copper) Literally *Brightness*, *Dawning* (*Son of David or brightness of expanding light*), the Daughter
Hod Kokab (Mercury)		K-V-K-B (Mercury) Literally *Star* or *Stars*, the seed of stars, Genesis refers it to create or multiply the stars, the Son of God.
Yesod Levana (Moon)		L-B-N-H (Silver) The *White* Moon, The Mother
Malkuth Cholem Yesodeth		ChVLM YSVDVTh Breaker of Foundations, decomposition, fermentation, composting, "The Nurse"

No.	Hebrew Sephirah	The Cosmos	Absolute Experience
1	Kether–the Crown	Primum Mobile	Union with God, God and Man are ONE
2	Chokmah–Wisdom	The Zodiac	Divine Vision Cosmic Consciousness
3	Binah–Understanding	Saturn	Cosmic Creation, Dissolution, Incarnation and Liberation with the Creator as the Word of God
4	Chesed–Mercy	Jupiter	Divine Love, Beneficence, Grace, Bliss and Joviality
5	Geburah–Severity	Mars	Divine Strength and Rulership, Birthing, Self-Generation
6	Tiphereth–Beauty	Sun	Divine Beauty and Equanimity as the ONE who is seen in mirror image as God or Divinity.
7	Netzach–Victory	Venus	Awareness and Perfect Insight and Intuition, Perfect Love and the Power to create through idea and reflection.
8	Hod–Glory	Mercury	Magic. Miracle. Gnoetic Knowing. Knowledge and Skill and the skill to be anywhere in an instant.
9	Yesod–the Foundation	Moon	Awareness of Life Sensitivity to Motion, Orbits, Time and Emanation, and Cyclical fluctuation.
10	Malkuth–the Kingdom	Elements	Self-Mastery of Fate over Principles Concrete Projection. As the Kingdom, it is truly the abode of the King, the Invisible Mirror of Creation in Alchemy.

The Tree of Life

What is everywhere is nowhere, AinSof Brahman.

Nine Spirits rule in the Cosmos. Ra or Re Creates by Three Triads.

-Chokmah-**Binah**

Chesed-**Geburah**-Tiphereth

Netzach-Hod-**Yesod**

These three triads create the Mirror of Heaven. The Mirror of the Mother, the Son of Man.
They are the Three Mirrors of Reflection, Refraction & Resonant Resound
(Resound: The Voice, the Song and Echo: Reverberate, Reverberating, Reverberation.)
(BEING IN RESONANCE, filled with Sound. Filled with echo reflection.)
(Resonant, Renown, Sonorous, Metronomic Time)
These Nine Spirits shine movement, motion as the Voice of God from its center,
Upon the Kingdom of the Righteous King, the Recipient in the Kingdom of
Malkuth/Malkata.

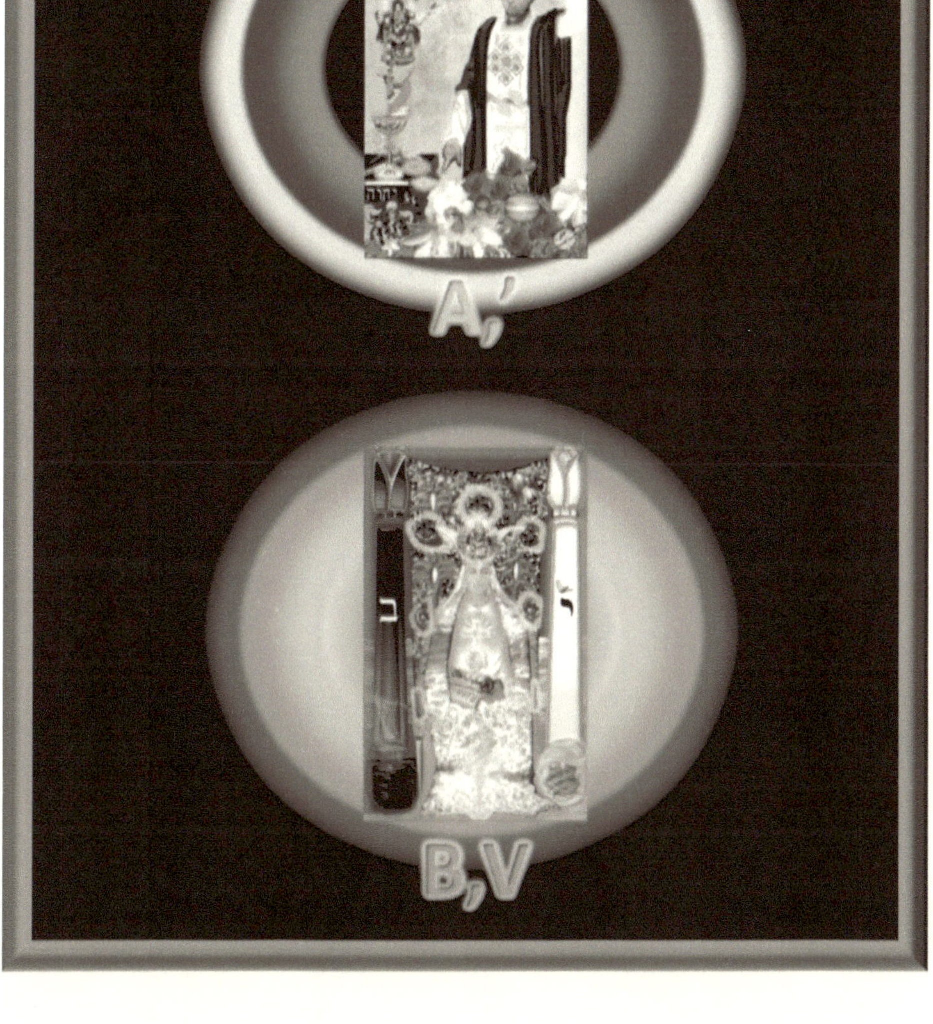

A,'

B,V

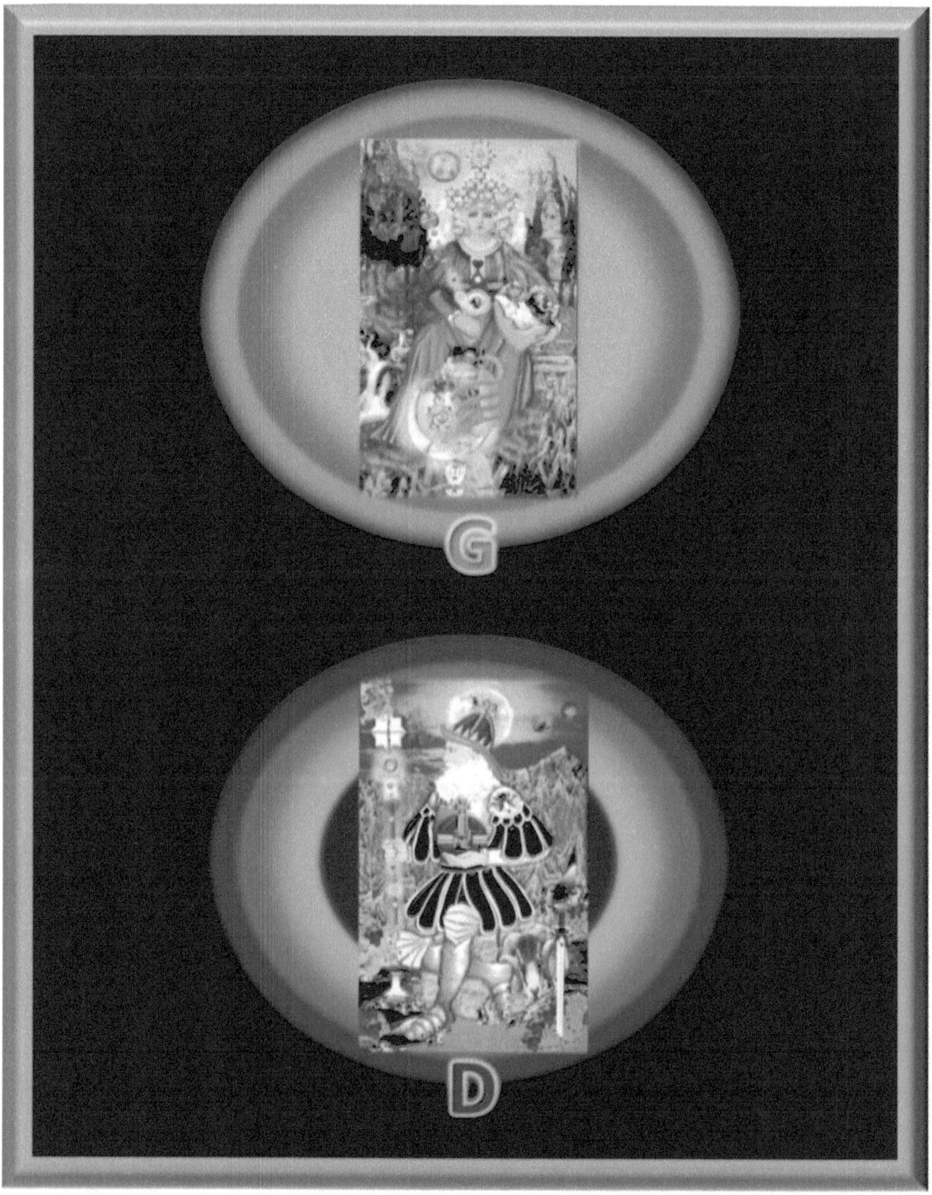

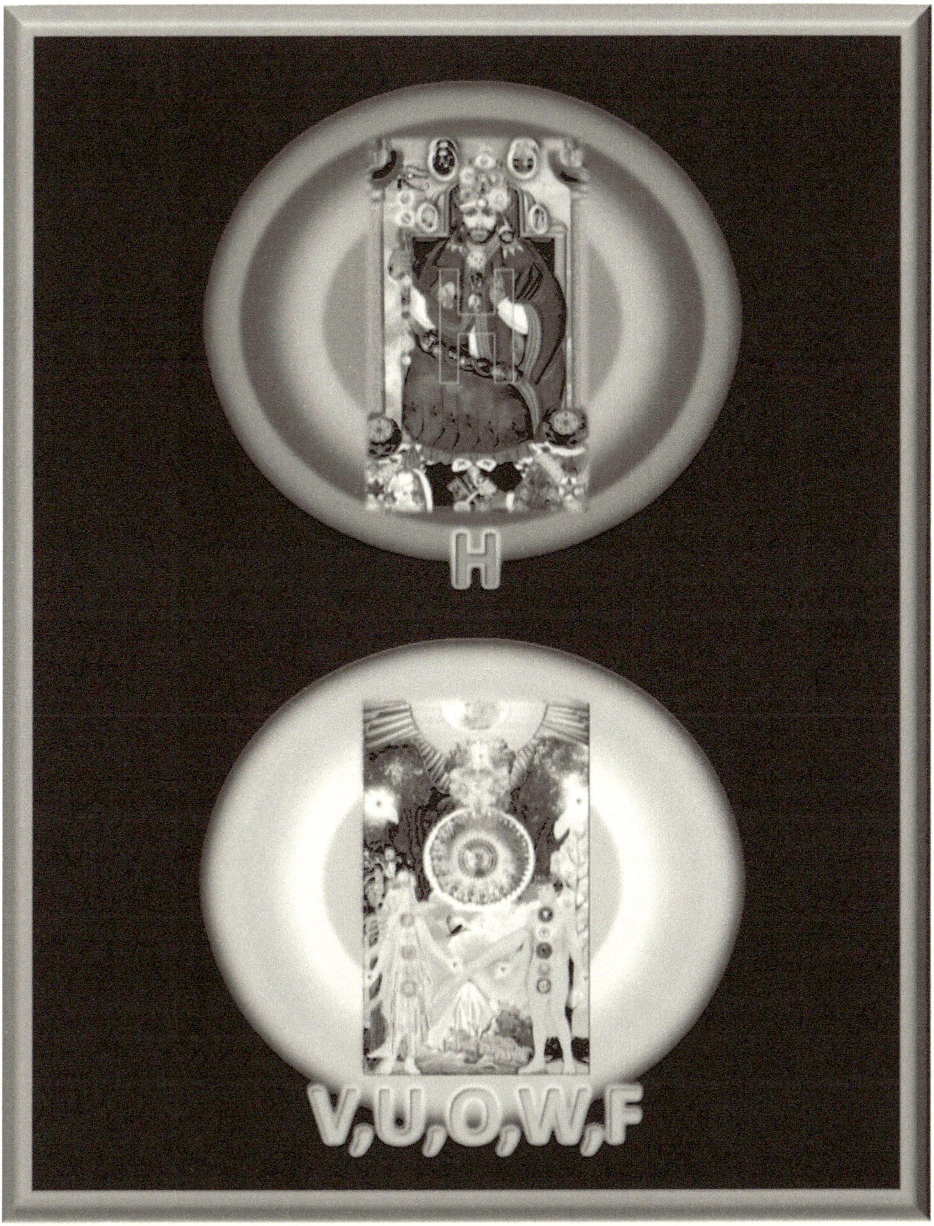

H

V, U, O, W, F

Z

Ch

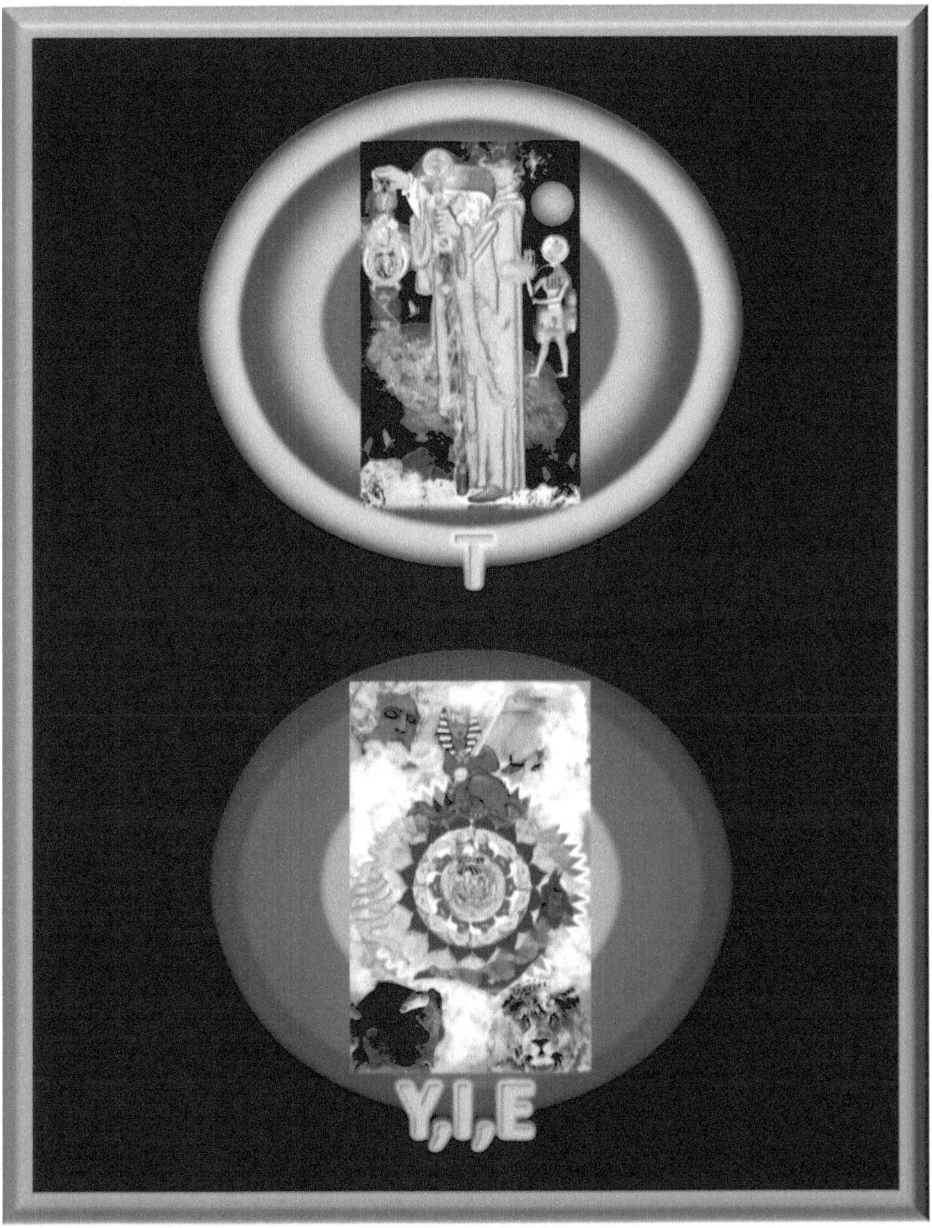

T

Y,I,E

K

L

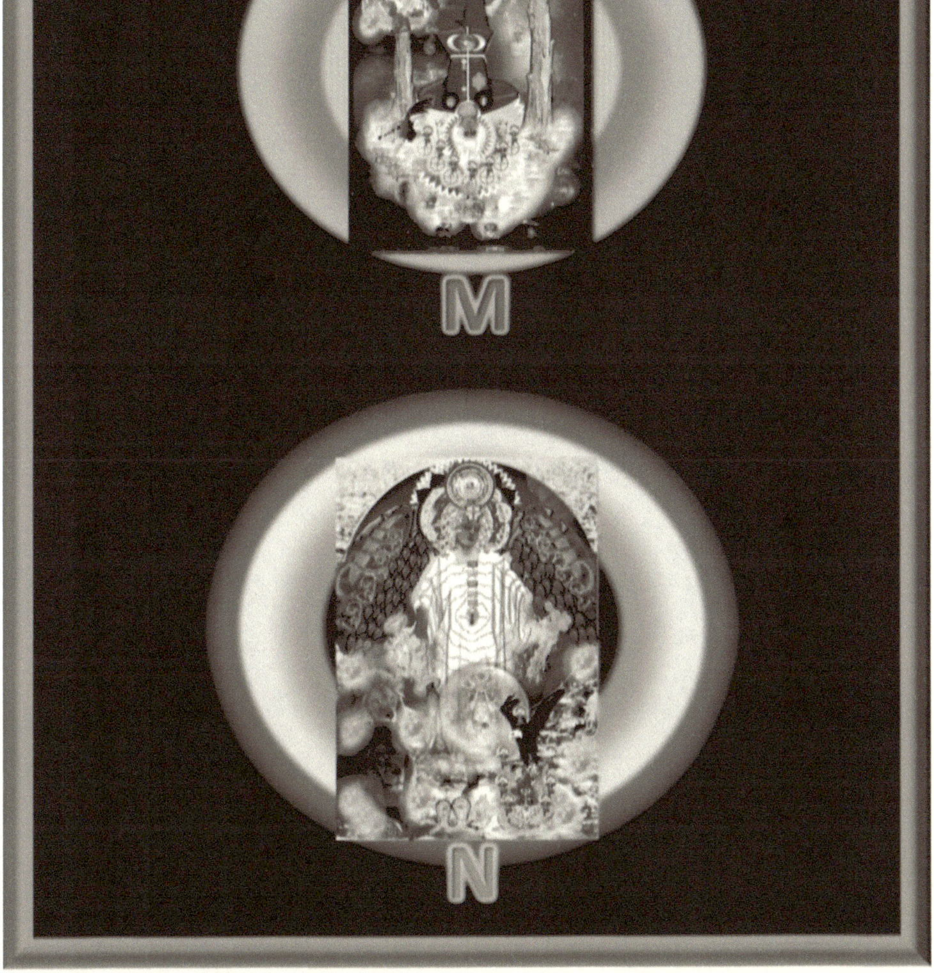

M

N

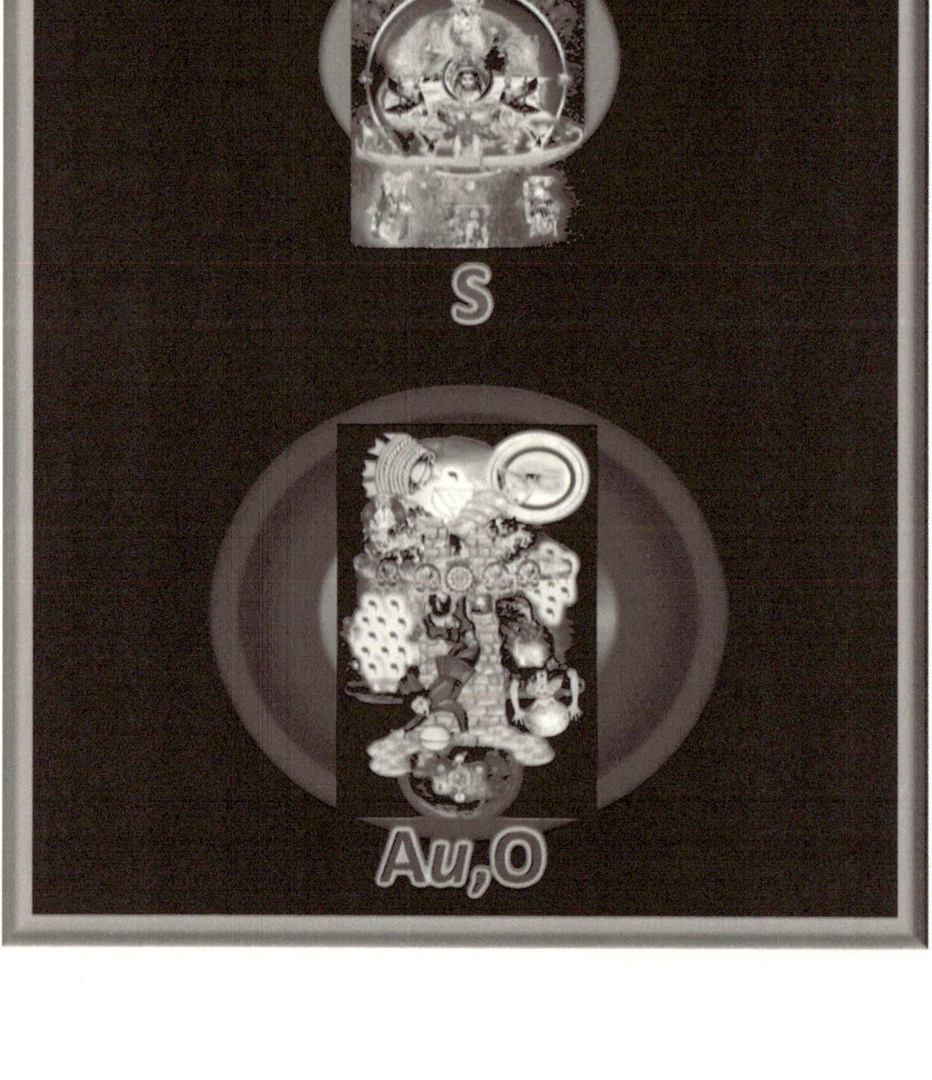

S

Au,O

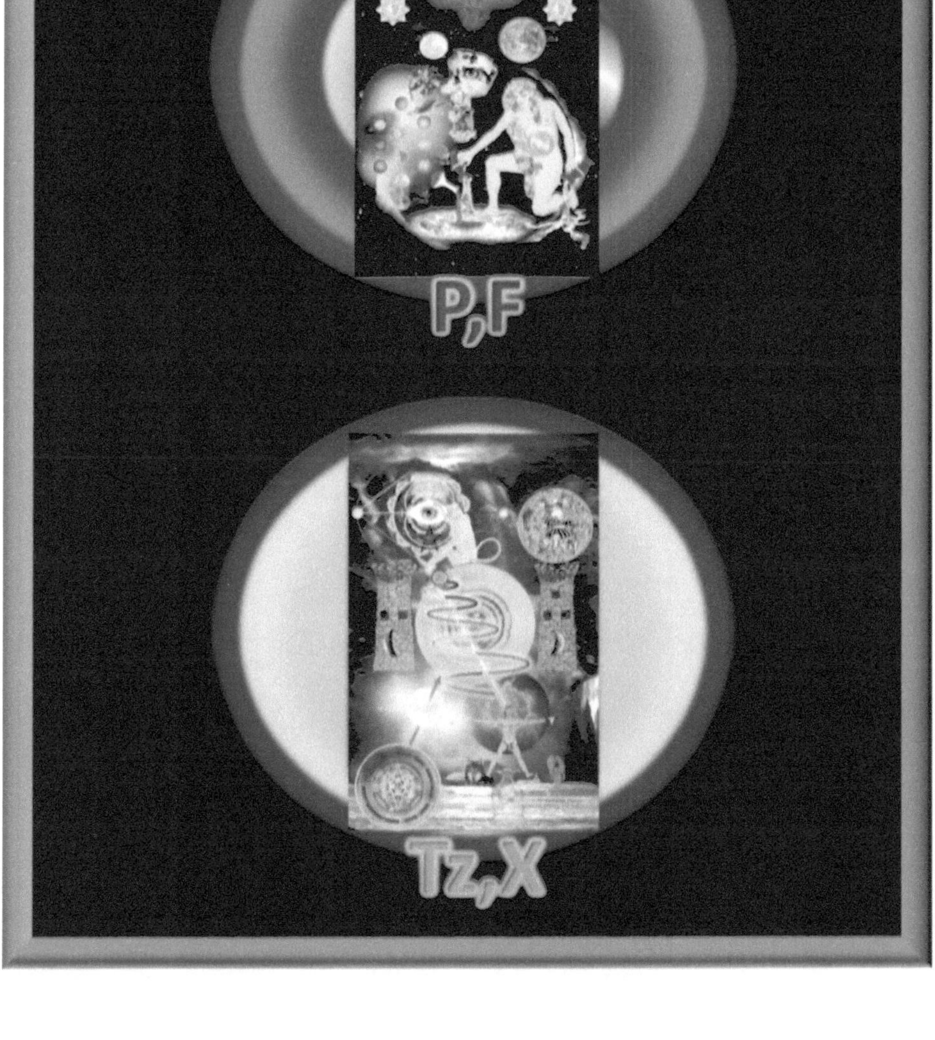

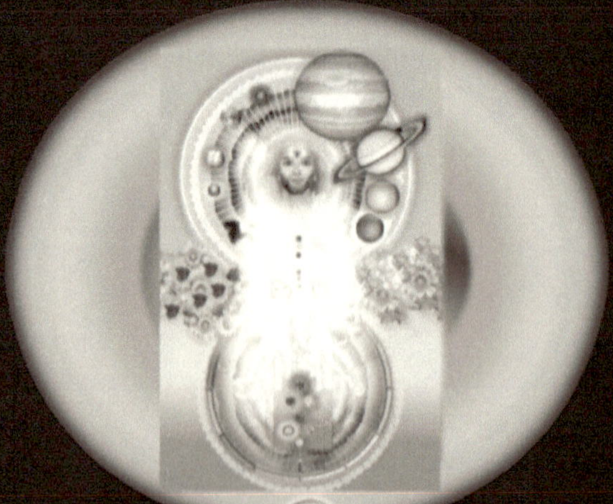

Q

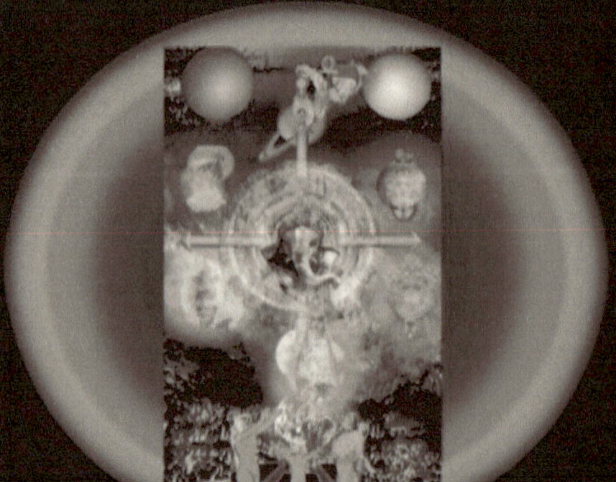

R

The Invocation

Time is God. God is Time. As the first principle cause and essence of Trimurti. Trimurti is the essential trinity. In Hinduism, it is Brahma, Vishnu, and Shiva. Its meaning is essentially that aspect of the divine that is first caused as "*having three forms* [As cynocephalus it is Trismegistus or the initiator as the being Hermes that is the sacred 'Thrice-Great']." In Kabala, this is the first existence in Kether, Chokmah, Binah—or Crown, Wisdom, and Understanding as the Messiah or savior, emancipator or liberator. On the surface, this means entering into the *Eternal No-Thing*. In the three states of Nonexistence, it is the Ain-AinSof-AinSofAur . . . into which it is reflected into motion as energy and has correspondence with Being, Consciousness, Bliss (*Satchitananda*) as the practical emanation of that root of a causeless cause. It is the steady state that is unchanging and therefore timeless.

That God is Time [*on the Tree of Life or in manifestation as energy*], this has practical benefits since one may invoke time as a power that is "*any-time*", to establish the conditions required for future benefit. We create our purposes in the form we may

wish to appear in, or establish the conditions before coming into them. [*This is true for present and future incarnations as well, until such time of liberation from the world of change.*] That form or condition of time may be anything made by our request. Our life conditions are set up preceded by our thoughts, and can be willfully set up to precede or herald our coming into them at a future time through the powers of our own creation. [*Time as that predetermined state that comes to us from the future out of Kether, the Crown of Wisdom, synonymous with the causes found in the cosmic burst as a field of emanation, gravity, orbit and cyclical activity, but having a rootless root in Divine Identity or Awareness, which is itself the Self or the steady-state.*]

In ritual [which you perform or devise], set down geometries; spread these out according to what is sacred to you in meaning. [*This even according to your rituals of daily life. But in both formal practice and work,*] Cover the ground in vibhuti and call the divine to rise up from within it to permeate the atmosphere. The essence of vibhuti or sacred ash will elevate the atmosphere. If you have others gathered in other places, have them do the same [*Performing distant work in common or in attunement*]. Invoke the God of Time [*rooted in your thoughts and actions*] and inspire the atmosphere with vibhuti. Mild incense may be substituted. Very light so as not to create an allergenic reaction or become offensive to others [*be subtle, the occult nature only means that its practice is subtle, even as subtle as the thought or as dramatic as the breath. Anything else is ignorance.*]

First Prayer:

First Cause: First Property; God of Love. God of Truth. Grant us thy initiation.

What is there to take away from all of this but good conscience, limited understanding that is improved and Wisdom, PROFOUND embracing TRUTH AS PURE PRINCIPLE that is absolute and enduring.

We Invoke: May Love satisfy us with our blessings; your blessing; for we are blessings of LOVE: May TRUTH manifest boldly; granting us initiation; delighted by bold thoughts: and may BEAUTY shine incessant, surviving challenges hidden, in the respite of the heart.

First Cause, First Principle; God most intimate; eternal cause; omniscient, omnipresent, and omnipotent: BEING, becoming; formless, formed; foundation folding, unfolding everywhere as Soul and Spirit Energy; woken spirit of the stars.

First property God; inspiring TEN emanations of LOVE; Showerer and shower of energies shower us; with superconscious illumination; manifestation of pure and sacred properties. Sacred tree rising as living hierarchy; lift us before the sun; in endless ecstatic enlightenment; "Monarch before, thy Celestial Sun."

God Isa-Isis-Isaiah: "SiaSai" Entity, foundation for initiation: causation preceding motion; Light illumination; shine before the light of vibrant living suns; endless; endless; endless emanations; throughout the universe; and spirit resident in this Cosmos

thrilled in Cosmic Consciousness; shine illuminations of the Sun upon our initiation:

Fair Orient: rising east, shall we pray with the sunrise: to recover our dead mysteriously from this spirit; these ever-living entities: lamps of enmity; fiery burning well; propagating living Bara Aelohim: shining endless by day and appearing manifest by starlight thru the night: the hours are filled with minutes transitioning thru your changing faces; rearrange life here in superconsciousness; and initiate into the stars:

Arise, Orion; "Au-Re-ON: Ausar"; Sat-Chit-Ananda; ABSOLUTE ENTITY: LIFE arise reborn within us. Daily rising, our Sovereign perfect; before sleep echoes our return; falling in your; with our; eternal term of life, in that western Occident; to recover, return and renew ourselves again; 'til death's term and liberation.

Let us dream again; the Watcher's Dream: Our calm before the storm . . . here seize, the sail before the breeze, our ship alone amongst the stars . . . Samsara Sea before us and behind us endlessly.

May vibhuti rise before us and fill our atmosphere with peace. Captivate our mystery, with your echo, of this silent eternity: and NAME alone conceal us, in our form; final mystery of Atom; mystery of Adam; mystery Adon-Aton.

Cloud of Witness enter here, and charge our subtle atmosphere.

By your Second property: Alchemical; the Ancient Kabalistic Man; recall, recalling the echo reflection; self-formed return upon initiation; lift these atoms towards the sun:

Push! Wide the door flung, with the strength of Hesiod, Arion, Thamyris, and Orpheus.

Charm us pursuing favors in the grove; tracking nine daughters of the Muses, on Mount Helicon!

10-9-8-7-6-5-4-3-2-1: Count TIME down; follow the goddesses counting time. Dance spirit wheel; spin round before our throne. Seated on our magic entity; rooted in the essence, of the God of AL-Ha-Yom . . .

Invoke inspiration; vibhuti streaming: gesticulate, write the stars; I here with you, sprinkle lustral streams; play and sing, for what is sacred illustrate, and make literate the science, arts, and poetry; for therein is played thy music, song and lightning evocate. God of Love, Goddess of illumination; breed gods and goddesses:

My fair Alchemias . . . sing! Recover the living entity in essential vital essences. God reveal the processes transitioning through, yes, the spirit of man, sung thru the instruments of senses.

Detach Now: Witness the perfect Witness!

Adam-Purusha; GRAND: Stand! The perfect instrument; strung echoes echo; hallowed in the performance on hallowed ground, of the Golden Mean: Beauty, Harmony, Symmetry, Truth, and to proportion the Golden Ratio: Golden Section: Golden Angle: Golden Spiral: Golden Rectangle: and like God Hiranyagarbha in Golden Egg inspire us in elemental virtues. Shine, initiate: emanating from the Golden Pentagons: reflectional and rotational symmetry: in Beauty's center follow on natural order, for rational purposes: convex or concave: regular and star

polygons: enchanting, follow the mirror or refracting lenses, thru which Beauty is played upon, and sacred truth is realized; as the holy emanation; on that mountain singing out, as Beauty of itself, from the sea, its name "Avalon, Insula-Pomorum"; the Isle singled out; to bear best light of the Fruited Tree we sit upon.

Become inspired in spite of vision, and limitations of the senses. Dumb man of legend! Seek, Speak, enlightenment; invoke thy mineral property in perfect alchemy. We inspire in the Spirit Entity.

By your Third property: Soul-Mind stressed between these pillars of Enlightenment: Strike! Ping! Struck like the tone, stung forked miracle vibrating musical frequency; move space; resonant and reverberating; reecho thought, to form its melody with meaning: Sing! Sing!

Sing! From it, the strung instrument, ever played and played upon:

Yah-Heh-Waum, Yah-Heh-Waum

unceasing; strumming as the instrument: the THING LIVING IN TONE IMAGE DESTINY. We bear witness to its lighted forces; singing:

Aum Hari Om; or Bram, Bram, Bram, AuLam, Wau Heh Yam, YaHe, YaHe, YaHe, Eyam, Eyam, Eyam, Ee, Ee, Ee, I, I, I, Eyam, or as Voiced Brahman Ham, Ham, Heh, Ham

Forced witness to reality; driving thru our nervous ring; of senses forced to witness, gods to waken thru the fiery burning witnessing witness:

> *Yah-Heh, Yah-Heh, Yah-Heh; Hari-Aum*

On the living throne. My heart rings in thy destiny.

> *Bam, Bam, Bam, Lam, Lam, Lam, Aum, Lam, Waum, Bram, Heh, Eeyam*

I am in thy Love.

Man, the animal King; delight thru living strings, strung to please the ping, of the perfect instrument. Fair creatures come to gather here. Live thru me, speak thru me, hear thru me, see thru me, and touch thru me; with thy divinity!

Lord think thru me that I may think and recognize divinity. I the bondsman am prepared. My debt for your taking. Perfect payment for safe keeping. Hearing thy eternal sing!

From your Fourth property invocate: the sevenfold emanation: revolving worlds of spin in order. Spin! Simulate the octave wave. Round turn round—these seven bidirectional polar dimension destinations, extensions in space; N-S-E-W-Above-Below-Center; expand and contract; revolve and counter-revolving spin; and herein initiate.

> *Raphael, Michael, Gabriel, Auriel, Math-Th-Ra-Aton, Sandalphon.*

Turn mirror, magic squares . . . Fourier patterns replicate, in complex amplitude spectral energy! Appear! Appear! And here, stand before me.

Spin! With power principles that are electrically charged; simulating order and symmetry. Cloud formed divinity appear in perfect remedy.

Hierarchy of numbers frame the universe. Appear! Mobius, spiral entity and endless superstring! Thy Golden perfect entity whose ratio is our Guardian; perfect for our solar King.

Inspire us, gods of inspiration, by order following us, to motivate the spin in pattern regeneration, and lock the Mystery in; Lord of Perfect Properties; Lord of perfect spin . . .

And, by thy spin invocate—thy perfect spirit emanate—thy power enter in thy perfect principle: That we may sing it perfectly.

And now let us begin:

Exercise

As in the exercise of Volume 1 Part 2, place the palate of the tongue gently against the roof of the Mouth. In the hollow of the mouth and throat, imagine you are about to swallow the Sun.

In the skull is the cosmos, space and Milky Way, swallow the entire cosmic, and through the crown sense beyond the region of the cosmic stars.

After a long period of meditation, swallow the sun and let it pass into the throat for a time. Slowly emanate its energies as sound. Let the following letter emanate or silently chant in the throat:

HEH

a, eh, aeh, e, o, oo, auh

ang, aang, eng, eeng, oong, oooong, ring, rrring,

lreng, lreeng, eng, aing, ong, aung, nng, hsng

Repeat these 1+7+16 vowel sounds slowly over and over; then let it pass to the nape of the neck and settle there for a while.

Then let it fall into the place of anxiety in the center of the chest in the region of the heart and illuminate it with happiness, and let this grow into large beams of sunshine and silently chant, repeating "EEEYAH" before it enters the belly with the sounds of BRAM-HA animating the solar plexus with vitality, fire, and light.

Seventy-Two Angels

YH = 15 = 6
HYH = 20 = 2   YHY = 25 = 7
WHWH-YH = 22 + 15 = 37 = 10   WHW-YH = 32 = 5

---

72 = 72

These are the shapes that divide two pillars to form seventy-two angels that are the seventy-two divisions of the divine powers of God written into the angles of time and the forms of space.

These have the superconscious characteristic of living powers that ride the variations in vibration and wavelength that we recognize easily in light and sound thru color and music; and through the record of our astral experience in the dynamics of change, in time and space. We are Nun, the divine Narayana, or Grand Man.

We are SaMeKh, or the CoSMiK entity. We are NaraNarayana! The GREAT SPIRIT riding on the waters of life, forming Life and Light.

"In the beginning, God breathed living linguistic sound-forms or archetypes and types (God spoke, or the gods were spoken as the Letter or Lettered Creatures), and then there was Light."

This is the intelligence forming and shaping the breath that builds living forms thru the powers of the spoken language in its subtle shape. It is the one form-shaping wisdom that is describing the divine first entity as the Engraver, Embroiderer, or Builder.

This is the mystery of the building of the *Temple of Sol-Amon,* or the *Father-Solar Divinity* that shines as the creator (*Brahma* as *Brahman,* or *Abrahm*) of our solar kingdom.

YH: Yah-Heh = 10 + 5 = **15** = 1 + 5 = 6 (Vav) is the expanding Hexagonal star.

YHY: Yah-Heh-Yah = 10 + 5 + 10 = **25** = 7 (Zayin) the Lord of Heaven, the Hexagon of Wisdom contracting thru gravity, into the circumpunct center reflecting the ONE in the center as Kether, shining in Wisdom.

It shines as the first face of heaven being the seven unified, uniting undivided around the ONE in Chokmah, with the point, or Kether, resting or seen as nuclear, in the central hub, or throne, out of which it shines as the nucleus of the soul in Chokmah (wisdom).

HYH: 5 + 10 + 5 = 20 = 2 is the triad where Yod exists as dualistic, or the reflection of itself by divisions of male-female duality or polarity. Yod is divided by two.

WHWYH is the first existence (*Vehuviah* or *WauHehWauYahHeh*) or form of the Great Name or Shem-Ha-Mephoresh. Its number is 32, which forms the thirty-two paths of wisdom called the Tree of Life; comprising the ten sephiroth and the twenty-two letters of the Great name.

The number 32 = 3 + 2 = 5, which is the final HEH of the Y-H-V-Heh that shines thru Binah as the divine form of the Great Name.

WHWH: Wau-Heh-Wau-Heh = (6 + 5 + 6 + 5 = 22 = 2 + 2 = 4 represents the four-faced or YHWH/Brahma or Tetragrammaton) of the cardinal direction or layers of reality or reflection (Atziluth, Briah, Yetzirah, Assiah), or those powers driving the absolute formless Entity into its fall into form.

YH: (10 + 5 = 15 = 1 + 5 = 6) = the Pranas or planetary drivers or forces of life that are united with the twenty-two elements in Binah to shape the twenty-eight phases, or stages, revealed by the Moon.

WH: 6 + 5 or the six moving planetary forces and five elements = 11 x 2, or its reflection as Macroprosophus and Microprosophus the Great and mirrored faces, become the paths formed on the Tree of Life = 22 = 2 + 2 = 4 or Tetragrammaton. [The Fool & Hanged Man as Tau-Mem or Hebrew Tau-Mem, תָּמִים meaning the "Complete Sound."]

> *These letters as YH-YHY-WHW-YH total the Seventy-Two elements as Kether and Chokmah are reflected in form of Vehuviah in Binah. They represent by numbers the symbol of the reflection of the divine in Binah as the incarnation of the Creator YHVH/Brahma the four-faced creator or WHWYH or the divine Vehuveiah...*

—Ii Y' Viavia: Daniel (ViaVia Vu is my divine name heard in an RC Initiation, and it is the Life Breath, the same as the Vyasa or Vayaviah). The final WauHeh forms the hexagram composition called, or symbolized in, the Tree of Life, or generation as the spirit Aelohim or *Subra-manyam,* the holy or supreme jewel of goodness as the six-faced War God Kumara *Murugan.*

The Hebrew "Magan" Star *(the Shield of David or Magen David)* is Ma-Ra-Gan; the river or garden of RaMa. In the feminin the "magan" shield, is "Mag" the "maiden" Aelohim goddess Shakti-Shekinah of the Light of Heaven. As a title *Mag* is seen in the Mag-d-elene, or the Greek *Maids of Hellas* (*Helen*) or a sainted "*Ma-Re*" virgin as the goddess Isis, likened to Maid Marion in Shekinah, or the divine goddess of light.

Maga in Hebrew means to war, fight or enter combat and is the mark of chivalry, and the same sign in Arthurian tradition, as the warrior Morgan is seen as Morgana. But it is the Knight as devotee, or disciple; even that of Christ. Maga equally refers to the warring of the gods in the heavens, as on the Tree of Life and is the sign of maya the illusion or the goddess hidden in the intricate fields of moving, changing, transforming energies. Maga is the divine magic and the Magus or initiate. Maga points to the letter "M" as the Hanged Man prajapati, and the Empress (*Gam* or *Ganga*), as the Goddess or Creatrix, seen in the face of the Mother of Mothers, hidden in the Cosmic Night Sky, as these break into the six sephiroth spirits as the six days or six faces of *Bereshith Beth-Binah*. These are the one plus six goddesses as Spirit-Mothers who feed the Aelohim, or the seven heads of Murugan. (Like the goddess Isis who gathers up the parts of *Asar-Osiris.*)

Seventy-Two: These are (9 x 8) nine octaves or octave waves and (6 x 12) six zodiacal periods and (24 x 3) twenty-four triads. The

twenty-four triads are the hours that emphasize the twelve hours by day and twelve hours by night.

This means the twelve ruled and dominated by the influences of the sun and the twelve ruled and dominated by the influences of the moon, stars, and wandering planets.

For God gave the day to be ruled by the royal Sun from the East, the King, and the night to be ruled by these angels of the night, or the Queen of Heaven in the West.

The Queen of Heaven is shown to be worshipped steadily everywhere, but is best emphasized in the temples of the goddess Hathor in Egypt.

Hathor is ḥwt (*the house or "hut," temple, or mansion or "hut of heavens" as the "House" of God or Beth in Hebrew*) of ḥr Horus (*the son of God, or Son of the Sun*) or Ha-Tau-Ra. This is the inverse of Ra-Tau-Ha.

The night is best defined by the presence or influence and appearance also of the Milky Way and the obvious light or universal energies of the Cosmic Consciousness as opposed to the dominance of our own Lord of the Sun, who is our fiery, blazing light of the creator by day.

We should say also the night is the period when the sun's light is filtered by the earth (Gabriel), as well as reflected and symbolized by the moon, the "horn" or trumpet waxing and waning; as the sound which the sun follows, so called, to find its way back around.

These seventy-two names of the Shem-ha-mephoresh are names of God that incarnate through the WORD as the living essence of or in divine representation.

These are angels or the periods of the divine intelligence unfolding as living "angles" of time in cosmic generation.

Letters here are threefold, in the form of the powers hidden in Binah, the trifold trefoil or the third sephirah.

The three unite with God, as Yah or EL through Wisdom in Chesed and are wedded to the powers of Time and Space divinity (Chokmah-Chesed).

As the cause of mortal creativity, they are then evolved into elemental forms of being.

They are fivefold (3 + 2), birthing through the generations of the fierce Mother and conceived, or gestated, in the womb of Geburah.

Geburah, like Gabriel, is the fierce mother gestating for conceiving seventy-two of her children as properties of the Son of God in Tiphareth, the sphere of beauty.

So, to say Christ obtained his power from these is correct.

To say that Christ stole these powers for the Temple is also correct, in the symbolic sense of their powers being drawn [or *assumed*] from the creator, or first cause; conceiving the power of the WORD.

Of course, this is the story of EVE (HVH), who ingests powers and conceives; having been tempted by the serpent [*the undulating energies of superconsciousness*]; and is given a bad reputation, out of ignorance in one sense, [*knowledge is ignorance*] and in truth, yes, we have all been cast out into the world of creation, and so forth [*for the purpose of learning to discriminate between what is good and what is evil*].

Our consciousness invokes or evokes its living powers or properties through the powers of Kundalini. These are nearly impossible to control except thru the goodness or righteousness of man and the certain power of perfect reason and knowledge of its goodness, truth, peace, and kindness.

[*These are controlled and moved by the powers hidden in the sounds of letters in thought, mind and vitality as the measure of the alphabet. This is the Word of God, and the key to the art that is lost.*]

Resistance transforms itself into heat, and that heat will destroy the body and mind of the unkind or fearful if raised improperly. It is charmed alone by the purity of the WORD that controls it. This heat is the term for the "burning bush" that is evoked

through fear and struggles from the lack of preparation and the purity of conscience and the discipline of consciousness.

These are energies moving through the subtle energy streams that extend through the nervous systems and brain and the fire of the breath and hair. You do not want that. In fact, that would lead to the realization of absolute terror. Your desire is to move slowly through transformation and devotion into the spirit of goodness and fearless with a pure conscience, freed from this experience, or it will lead to insanity.

It may also cause spontaneous human combustion in its worst case, if released by nature without its proper preparation. This is, after all, the same energy that exists at the center of the sun as well as the planets. This is the root of our connections with all these. These powers originate in us and connect with these from our center.

You may think or imagine that this power is something separate. Unfortunately, you are never separate from it. This is fortunate, because this is the source of life. God is everywhere. These are the powers of the Aelohim, or those energies that give you life and existence. They are intimate parts of yourself. They appear in creation as Time and Superconsciousnes in the state of bliss, love or eternal happiness.

These powers are supremely intelligent and self-creating. They are the first form and power of the miracle. They are not impressed by arrogance or the lack of humility. You see invocations and evocations written in historical writing by the unbelievably foolish and ridiculous. They demand authority; encouraging,

through fear of failure, the fear of conscience, the fear of lies and untruthfulness, rash boldness, and engage in shouting and belligerence for these to stand before them by their very command! These fools raise their voices, demanding the absolute to succumb to their ridiculous demands. This is unbelievable arrogance, egotism, and ignorance. This will end in self-destruction, disease, and insanity . . .

Would you entertain this kind of belligerence if someone made these demands of you? This is the reason for truth in nobility and saintliness brought on with humility and the silence of the tongue. Respect, honor and nobility are held as the ideal requisites for the life of chivalry.

You want to have a good life, free of disease—a life of sanity, peace, and prosperity. Goodness honors this, given the proper opportunity. It is the simple matter of respect.

These powers of the **Shem-ha-Mephoresh** are universal agencies that drive themselves thru the spirit of man. They are not the exclusive rights of anyone. As one can imagine, they deserve and desire the respect of absolute authority as the divine creative powers that silently serve us in creation. These, like those of Archangelic Forms imaginable thru our imagery, are unbelievable intelligent powers that generate the energies of everything existing in time and space. We may see their energies, but these are forms of the absolute intelligence of God. Our mind, consciousness and intelligence, and health are the filters thru which these will travel in us—which is why we may relate to them.

Our good would be their good; our poison would be their poison amplified infinitely. One's god and devil are, in man, as aspects hidden in their character. Our challenges in these, demand we must be tested. The results are the experiences of life. Daily experience demands this. This is the "why" when asking why we are here and what could be the purpose of life.

Divine Names in all true religions or philosophies—whether Hebrew, Gnostic, Hindu, Greek, Roman, Egyptian, Zoroastrian, or the yogas of Tamil Nadu—are used for developing patterns for attracting and developing unified symbolic characteristics of divinity in the transformations of character into divine intelligence. This is so that the mind and consciousness, vitality, and intelligence, along with the body, can unfold or hold, as water in a well, the unified field of numbers and forces shaped as sound, light, and consciousness. The purpose is to capture the invisible with the visible.

God incarnates into form in the associations of meaning. This is likened to the butter churned from the milk. Meaning is a tremendous power when unfolded into superconsciousness. It exists as Truth and Righteousness from the Ideals realized from the absolute powers of God. So, should you fear God or Love God? Both . . . if you have any common sense. If you fear anything, fear your own incompetence that self-destructs in this.

In this, there are hidden properties that unfold and reshape themselves into universal patterns for evoking the mystery of Shem-ha-Mephoresh, for transformations that take place in our evolution. These should be thought of as vessels for the filling,

drawing, or attracting divine creative powers that are absolute attributes of God that unfold in us as bliss and divinity. That power moves, comes into being, and operates through the divine form of divine man, or the living soul, in the spirit that is male and female, unfolding as intelligence.

This Great Name of seventy-two forms, like the angelic or archangelic names on the Tree of Life—the Tree of TIME, Space, and Consciousness—unfolds properties recognized in the zodiacal divisions of time, in the wheel or spirit of Binah-Understanding. This is that spirit that forms what is symbolically called the throne of God that spins at the seat of initial cause or motion, as Eternity in time, or the spirit of YHVH Tetragrammaton. This is the same as the four-faced Brahma.

YHVH is a symbolic name used to describe the unfolding mathematical divisions of time, space, and consciousness; thru elemental and planetary properties in the rotation of the wheel or cycle, in the octave or the wave; in the orbit or the chakra disk, into worlds of formation; through absolutes in gravitation.

This evokes the power that forms, and moves or comes into being from the immovable essence of the ONE THING—from the sphere of Chokmah wisdom through its crown of first cause, appearing in the instant of creation as the threefold entity, the reflection of that which is beyond wisdom, and essence, as perfection that is absolute and unlimited.

This stage, or sphere of creation, in Binah Understanding, associated with YHVH, indicates that it is the first creative power hidden in the divine name. It is related to EVE (HVH, the

one who divided) and tasted of the Fruit of Good and Evil. This is the Great Mother (Beth), Hebrew Aima, or Shakti in the East, and God YHVH (*nama Shivayah*), less the initial cause (Yah) from which it came originally; when HVH separated from the "Yod."

Yod, or Yah, is the existence before division, in the process of separation, or division, into which it multiplies itself from itself in the generation of motion. These powers of Binah are described as the days, or time periods, of the unfolding creator, BaRa-ALVHYm; the days of work, or motion, in the creation of the Tree of Life.

This Aelohim is the God of gods forming in creation; coming from the formless to evoke time as motion, for the creation of the Heavens and the Earth (Bereshith-Genesis 1:1). This is realized, sensed, or discovered in the depths of meditation as the second generation of divinity in the form of creation.

These letters of the Shem-ha-Mephoresh are singled out for holding on to this, for attracting divine autonomy. They are used for ritualistic meditation, along with invocations or ritual confessions, for the development of one's perfect dignity: the ideals of nobility and chivalry. These evolve forms of consciousness associated with divinity. These are thought forms if these universal thoughts are "things"; they are forms evolved or separated from the Hermetic "ONE THING." These are those that form into unified realities of power that are created, stored, and developed from sacred energies.

Divine Endings in Kabala have their roots buried in the depths of meaning hidden in the sacred language. These endings are determinatives; to determine the use and practice for all creative powers hidden in the Word, for the Master, or Guide; in comforting and protecting, as well as to determine its use in Self-Mastery and fate; and exercising authority. It is absolutely imperative to master these endings within oneself. This will emphasize the power of the names. Yah and EL in Hebrew, the "M," "aum" or "eng" electrically in Sanskrit. These, and the images that go with these, require deep self-integration, or initiation, for the mastery of these properties, laws, principles and powers that we are entertaining. Step by step the medicines are administrated. We are fed only a spoonful at a time even in our sustenance.

Christ is said to have accomplished his miracles through the powers of the seventy-two names of the Shem-Ha-Mephoresh. This is speculated, though not by these alone. These are practices the origins of which predated a living record. One may work with these in simple or by complex methods. One method is to take these through the world of the elements one by one. Another would be to take these thru the physical, vital, mental, astral then into the universal and boundless. One may also follow the principles thru the proper understanding of the paths unfolded on the Tree of Life.

The one method that is interesting is to run these thru the principles invoked thru the stages of the BaraAelohim or through those worlds on the path of Kundalini. These are the fields of the six days' work or the periods of motion: i.e., Lam, Wam, Brahm,

Yam, Ham Aum . . . then crown these by that which is all names and forms.

Or one may follow the path shown from the creation (Bereshith) in Genesis 1:1—i.e., as Brahm-Manipura, Aum-Ajna, Lam-Muladhara, Wam-Swadhistana, Ham-Vishudha, Yam-Anahata passing thru to the Hridaya or infinite center in the sacred heart at the seat of the divinity for the creation of the Heavens and the Earth.

One may think of the Throne of God (son of God) at the Muladhara. One may think of the Throne of God in the Hridaya. All together this is the body of the Purusha. Man as Purusha or the Grand Man is likened to the "butter" or that which is churned to become something else out of milk.

This is the nature of existence that is identified as the unique difference between God and Man, or Adam; the "A-*DaM*" the "*fourfold fallen hanging upside down.*" The thing that has been churned into being as the fourfold expansion or extension of the "A" or "*Aum*"; as we would imagine the world that follows from the "*Aulam,*" or the unfolding "*Lam*" in Muladhara.

The Muladhara is falsely associated with Malkuth, the Kingdom. This is the reflection of appearances. Prajapati, or the creator, falls into creation upside down and is referred to as the Hanged Man. Its true association is in Chesed. The divine name is AL and equivalent to Lam.

MuLa is the reflection, as seed in the waters (Mem) of "Lam" . . . "*Dha-Ra*" is the fourfold animation and extension of the Sun.

Muladhara is the power to create or unfold from the Palace of the King (*Mal-KuTh*) or in the hieroglyph the palace of Malkata. *Kata* being root for the palace of the pure and chaste.

The true state of Malkuth is 10 = 1. It is the same as Kether; as the mother Ma Malkuth is the reflection of Ra in Kether, adding the Son of God (AL, or Lam, the Lamed form associated with "*The Absolute Law,*" or "*Libra,*" as the "*Book of the Law,*" or Torah, the "*Tau of Ra*"). Libra is also the balance, being the absolute law of balance in the unification of all forms of life. This is the key to the mysteries of balance in the Salt-Sulfur-Mercury in alchemy.

In Kundalini, this Malkuth is the Sahasrara crown, or Kingdom, and home of the closed Palace of the King. In alchemy, it is the end product of the perfection of nature. In Kabala, the serpent on the Tree of Life descends; it does not ascend. Chesed is equivalent to the seat of Ganesha, the Son of God, the first coiled form of the energies of TIME and Superconsciousness.

Swadhistana follows in Geburah and is the pomegranate or menstrual blood, being the form of cells or seeds of existence that fight and struggle for life. These are the single-cell forms that grow and evolve from out of their form as laws in the balance of life.

Manipura is the seat of alchemical energies of the Sun and is associated with Tiphareth. Netzach is Venus, or love, and is associated with the heart, or that power that descends from Chesed, the Son of God. Hod is associated with Ham and the energies of the Word or Akasha and relates to Vishuddha.

The Moon, or Ajna mind, is associated with Yesod.

Thus, it is clear that Malkuth is the lighted mind of the Prajapati, or Hanged Man. The original form of the Hanged Man hangs from either the letter HEH of the Great Name, Cheth the Great Breath, or that power of the Tau, or FOOL, as he falls and hangs across Chokmah and Binah, divine wisdom and understanding. These are everlasting principles and powers that propagate as law.

Ignorance of these proper methods produces an imbalance in Kundalini yoga or the practice of Kabala. YHWH move from the heart to the throat to the genitals to the throat regions as a practice. Aelohim, ALVHYM, moves from the Ajna to the Muladhara, to the genitals to the Vishuddha in the throat, to the Anahata in the heart . . . or Aum, Lam, Waum, Ham, Yam . . .

In all these, whether YHVH, Aelohim, Eyeh, or Eloah, the one seed element, or bija, that is always skipped or overlooked or kept secret by design is the Ab-Ram, or BaRa, Manipura in the Solar Plexus, the seat of Abram or Abraham, the creator, or grand alchemist of man, the Father Ram, or the region of first life, first sustenance in the belly of man, at the navel, where man is cut off at birth from the divine connection upon receiving the candidate for initiation at the birth with the "Breath of Life."

YB (ib) or AB (ab) are the equivalent images that appear with the identical name values substituting the 10 (Y) and 1 (A). Abba is the father. "*Ib*," or "*ab*," with the inspiration goes to the center or central point of the heart. "*Ba*," or "*BRa*," forces theses divine energies to move from the heart's center, or divinity, to the solar

plexus or belly. This is the "Bereshith," or the region that forms its power to create. By all appearances, it is the secret or hidden place being the most concealed. *Ibram,* or *Abram,* becomes the mantric, or magical name, for divine generation or creation. Bara-Shith indicates six powers that form along the axis of the staff of creation. These six are representative of the hexagonal star for divine forms that emphasize the letters A-H-Y-Br-V-L. These are the YHVH- BRa-ALVHY-m or *YHVH Bara Aelohim.* I emphasize the BR together, but they are also either or. Beth is the *House of Ram,* and it is the birthing house of God, or the *House of Creation,* in the belly, or *Seat of the Solar Plexus.*

The body birthing in the womb exists in the form of GOD as superconsciousness unfolding from its seed and expanding in gestation. God appears in Man. Man, the created, the spirit, enters with the first Breath of Life to animate it with its spirit life, in order to discover this divine relationship that exists between God and Man. It does this through the gift of life in the body, in the miracle of birth, and particularly in that apex in the world of human birth. This is the divine initiation into the temple of life. The body is a divine thing that is not associated with man. The body is the divine engine—the magical apparatus, or tool, that is the gift of God; provided for the benefit of Man in order to realize the process of discovery in the recognition of one's true identity.

One may find the ancient Hebrew origins in Tamil Nadu, on the path of migrations coming out of their Antediluvian ancestry; prior to the flood during the time of the Rama Empire. The ancient line of Hebrew prophets have the same root traditions as the Tamil Siddhars.

These Hebrews were the followers of Brahma the Creator, or Ab-Ram, the Father Ram or Rama. In nature, their generations are those seeds of creation that are as vast as the sands of the desert. Abram is the Ba-Ra creator. The mysteries are clear. They inspire the gods as the product of generation. The living spirit is realized as living within creation. The mystery becomes manifest.

The life of the spirit is the body that forms on the Tree of Life. The "Love of Wisdom" is the love of Chokmah, or God's Wisdom. What is beyond Chokmah or Wisdom is Kether the Crown—and beyond that the spaceless, timeless reality of the Endless Beingness; the *Ain-AinSof-AinSofAur*, which is far beyond divine Wisdom, or the Cosmos, and is the first essence or essential cause of wisdom.

In this Tree of Life, in true kabala and true alchemy, Malkuth does not represent the earth or simple condensation of the world of form. Malkuth represents the Palace of the King and is the Golden or Perfect State of the Sun and Moon, unifying the principles found on the Tree of Life surrounding the earth. Its meaning is the same as that mystery called the "*Closed Palace of the King*," which is apprehended as the "*Golden Age*" of Man that is realized in the pursuit of the Philosopher's Stone. It is the tenth part of the nature of divinity refined thru purification, sublimation, fermentation, and distillation or separation, on the path of perfect metals, in the pursuit of their perfect righteousness.

The Caution

Warning:

There are many lunatics and lunacies. Many thoughts turn towards infamy, and we are immature, burdened by the senses and unprepared emotionally to transition through the changes that challenge us emotionally. This is not to break with traditions found to be useful in spite of themselves. There are many people who have little business pursuing this Mystery that we have prepared here, due to having developed an enormous *self-destructive* ego or cultivated fear, jealousy, envy, desire, and anger—and so are unable to express humility. Today, the voice of tantrums tip the balance of the mind with vanity.

In this work, our work is meant not to exercise the use of God-given faculties for vanity or for selfish or ignorant purposes. These will rebound and lead to self-destruction. The devil is in you—meaning that the unsafe path of *self-destruction* on the route of our return lies within our faculties, vitality, and consciousness. Our real enemies are our inner enemies. Pursue the ideals with a pure character, with virtue

and humility tossed in by the hand of noble chivalry. We wash every day and relieve ourselves since the natural attrition of youth and buildup of worldly filth plague us daily. But we provide excuses for the mind and develop social and personal psychology for every excuse for bad behavior and call this scientific and pride ourselves on our animalistic tendencies, when our thinking excuses our proficiencies and make up tales for bad performances.

All good serves our perfection and, in the end, self-mastery. Even a poison or harmful agency, like those found in chemistry, have their purposes; but the handling must be left to those qualified, who might have made proper inquiry in the pursuit of perfection for achieving self-mastery in every aspect of it. This is true of the spirits that are dark or light. The true mastery of anything is the proper use and not abuse of anything at your disposal in the processes as they are applied properly; then even poison may be handled as a form of medicine.

Do no harm. That is the Law of Ahimsa. The law in this is not Karma alone, which is the *"natural consequence,"* but it is a command existing throughout the Cosmos from the atom to the stars, to follow perfect righteousness. This pact is written in the form of breath and shapes the essence of man, the ever-living spirit entity. The Law is weighed perfectly against the heart within the balance of self-inquiry, and we choose what we follow and what we choose to pass over with.

Being dumb is no excuse. The Absolute follows the path of bliss; it could care less about petty inadequacies. Ingest a poison and

suffer the consequence. The bliss is found in law and principle. Nature behaves according to laws and principles.

Nature's laws do not exist for altercation. If you step off a bridge, you are sure to fall. We are bound or wedded to righteousness, and that is the proper exercise of human dignity—as a gift of providence, having come into the world with the faculties of awareness, reason, and the security of the watcher and guardian called the inner conscience or the voice of the Master Within. These properties that lie within us have already destroyed our avenue for chasing after excuses in our pursuit of perfect peace.

We exist with the abilities for thinking, for contemplation, and for meditation.

Here are the reasons for initiation. We are born for initiation. In fact, the free exercise of initiation and development exists as part of our ritualistic life. It is our daily routine. Time is the Master. The Cosmos is the theater of the divine, and Man has achieved the high status of being the master "player" in our field of expertise. Our night and day, waking and dreaming, invokes the mysteries; we all live within that foundry of our destiny, through the evolution of its form in the outgrowth of its perfection. From atom to the seed unfolding to the vast cosmos and the star.

We are unique in creation in that it is the judgment of MAN or Adam—meaning that these energies are born of earth, coming into our existence with the ritual of incarnation and rebirth. The powers of righteousness exist even in the dust and minerals that make up our existence. It is the property of creation, and our duty is bound to it, for our having reached into existence, as living

energy, for achieving the purposes for discovering meaning in the properties of life. It is built on Truth, or Veritas, as these are the foundations, being its laws and principles. These are absolutes.

Any abuse will lead to self-destruction. It will close off one's energies and cut off one's mind and inner faculties and restrict the power of divine assistance. Divine assistance exists in the powers of motion, vitality, and consciousness.

This motion first exists as the creator. It has authority in this, even as it has in the manufacture of all bodily processes. Abuse will lead to animalism. It will cause one to be vanquished by every enemy in the path of ignorance. It is the difference between those persons perceived with luck and intelligence and those who are always perceived as ignorant and unlucky, those who win and those who always fail, those who have great health and those who live in misery.

This is the path difference between those who are free and those who end their lives in jail. This power is always there. We make our choices and live with the consequences of our bottom line. It is a heavy load to bear.

These perfect laws exist. They are as given by the MASTER, to be the function of the FIVE Human Values: *Sathya, Dharma, Shanti, Prema,* and *Ahimsa*—meaning Truth, Righteousness, Peace, Love, and Nonviolence. To deviate leads to deviance and self-punishment.

You are your enemy. Bad or good judgment determines one's bad or good destiny. These are written out and unfolded into time.

Our truth as righteous cause comes from the future, as the intelligence within creation drives towards our past. Our Karma is determined from our past, with the remnants left behind. These cycle into our future and become our natural nemesis. Not this life alone, but these are captured and unfolded in the course of many lives.

The admonishment in these mysteries is to first "Do Good, See Good, Hear Good, Speak Good, and Be Good." It is not exclusive but absolute, and these are born in creation to follow and govern its existence. Dharma, righteousness, exists in the very breath we breathe, and it is part of our vitality. All things are in memory or are recorded. Nothing is hidden from the Absolute Entity. We have no excuse for begging sympathy. Sympathy may come, but one should not expect it.

The warning is always for the profane to turn back. That is for their own good saying: *"Procul O' Procul Este Profani!"* Failure leads to self-destruction, and one becomes the target of his own methodologies, the reward for their use and execution through the attractions to dishonesty. This leads to certain misery *(sickness over lifetimes and loss of all vitality or reductions of vital energy)*.

You judge for yourself, but with certainty, God is the Judge of all, on the course of those who would be *"Just Men Made Perfect"* or initiates! The Lord may haunt you in Eternity if you cannot come to terms with this, as the subject law is certain revulsion for your ignorance. On the path for true enlightenment, the responsibility is yours for determining failure or success. Ultimately, you will achieve success.

Shem-ha-Mephoresh
Divine Endings used in Angelic Language:

Let's begin with the subject of the seventy-two names with the examinations of the Hebrew divine endings and their symbolic archetypes:

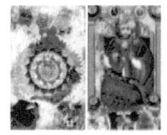

YH or Yah—*The Liberated: Hierophant of Time, or Tetragrammaton, is the Teacher of peace and calm in the cosmic wheel of understanding; existing in Binah. Yah is seated in the heart or center of the chest.*

This power is destined to see thru all times—past, present, and future—on the Tree of Life. Yah, teaching one, gives powers for one to become a visionary. It extends one's spirit, or power, outside of the experience of living for oneself alone. It serves as one's guide and instructs as such one into the mysteries that are divine—in the true principle of Yah, or Yam. This power is seated in the heart or center of the chest behind the sternum.

This is the mystic's art that unfolds into the powers of singing; chanting the kam, kham, gam, gham, ngam, cham,

chham, jam, jham, nyam, tam, and tham. This is for the priest or prophet, counselor, advisor—anyone who's mustered perfect faculties for teaching, vision, or for guidance. The Tree is rooted in the spirit of the Hierophant and is seated there for the individual to be so well instructed. Thru these means, by the Divine Identity, in the elemental qualities, it sits, revealing, as the breath, heart, soul, and mind are one.

"Y-H," or Yam-Ham, travels from the heart to the throat region, and this is the divine heart and seat of divinity that is united within the sound Brahman, or the Akasha in the throat for wielding words of power for the driving of one's energies and faculties through the perfect sixteen voweled vibrancies: अ a, आ $ā$, इ i, ई $ī$, उ u, ऊ $ū$, ऋ r, ॠ $ṝ$, ऌ l, ॡ $ḹ$, ए e, ऐ ai, ओ o, औ au, अः $ḥ$, and अं $ṃ$ . . . This is the nature of the breath or spirit that is unfolding in the form of the Sound Brahman or A-Ka-Sha, the fire of the Soul, and the spirit that dies transformed into enlightenment.

AL—This is the Mastery over Laws and Elemental Principles; the seat of first vitalities; seated royally, on the elemental throne of Muladhara; the rooted throne of energy. Here form the powers for all sacred energies; drawing down the first vitality of omniscient

superconscious Aum; used and realized thru the skills of justice, serving books, law, and judgment in the balance of magic, Kabala, language, and all sacred forms of education.

Born to wield these familiar faculties; wielded by these two gigantic properties of the divine as perfect vibrancy—namely, principles and laws.

This is the magician's art; used by the scientist, the artist, and the engineer . . . this is the power of Kundalini to create; winding on the Tree of Life. To wield these, one must become the nature of it.

Aum-Lam*; Aulam, the hidden world: Wisdom's (Ajna's) Eye and the seat of power realized in reason, in the faculties that are Divine. These are identified by the fact that they are one and the same as the Divine. God is Witness and Witnessed and its faculty.*

"Root support," Lam or EL, evoke the radiant signs of va, scha, sha, and sa; releasing seven prime vitalities; united for the driving, of one's primal energies and faculties; for seating one on the throne of the God of bliss, joy, and pleasure (meaning: Muladhara).

The Great Name from the mysteries: **Shem-Ha-Mephoresh**

Exodus 14:19–21 (King James Version): We begin our evocations and call out by Name; the Names of God; called out as letters, words, and forms; in their spirits of intelligence for evoking Divine Intelligence:

[19] *And the angel of God (the Aelohim or the Divine Purusha), which went before the camp of Israel (Cosmos), removed and went behind them (churned); and the pillar of the cloud went from before their face (the perfect plane), and stood behind them (projected into a column):*

[20] *And it came between the camp of the Egyptians (the dark or night) and the camp of Israel (the day or Light); and it was a cloud (plasmic intelligent energy) and darkness to them, but it gave light by night to these (the stars): so that the one came not near the other all the night* (the stars and planet and all cosmic bodies were divided by great distances; as are the times of the day, week, year and season; for the hours of the day and night; or sight that is divided by dark and light, genders male-female, elements positive and negative; unfolding all dualities).

[21] *And Moses (the Divine Thoth-Muse or Magician) stretched out his hand over the sea (dividing elemental energies); and the Lord caused the sea to go back by a strong east wind (air, prana or the cyclical energies or orbital powers of planetary properties), all that night, and made the sea (elemental energies of space) dry land (cosmic bodies), and the waters were divided (the Aelohim, or the intelligences were called into existence to form the God of gods, in the divisions of space, time and the Mind; in the fields of Superconsciousness; called out by the wind, breath or spirit; as the Word of God, in the orbit of the stars).*

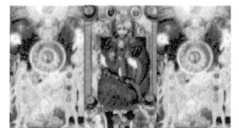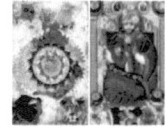

1. *WHW*—Wauhewauyah Lord of Protection:
   Psalm 3:3 *But thou, O LORD, art a shield for me; my glory, and the lifter up of mine head* . . .
   (Vahaviah 0–5° Leo—Elemental Fire in Geburah: 5 Wands, Angel by Day) *Wau-Heh-Wau, God eminent and glorious with strength of will and conviction may you comfort, guide and protect both me, and we; that stand tall before thy Glory and Severity; wedded to divine authority, with insight and maturity in all divine faculties; by glory and severity shield thou me; devotedly Wauhewauyah Vahaviah.*

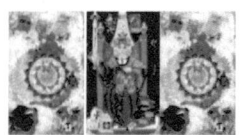

2. *YLY*—Yelayoael Lord of Strength and Benefit:
   Psalm 22:19 *But be not thou far from me, O LORD: O my strength, haste thee to help me.*
   (Yelayel 6–10° Leo—Elemental Fire in Geburah: 5 Wands, Angel by Night) *Yah-EL-Yah; Initiate me into justice, and we into strong and just empathy, love and compassion. Invoking loving kindness and strength for achieving mutual admiration*

and respect. Inspire liberties, that we may know and understand all languages; divine true meaning, and awaken the powers for achieving a favorable reputation and success. And bring you to we, and even nearer then to me. Secure me into Time's vast security, seeing and being seen as favorable to the past, present and future; in all three times; by divine justice, Yelayoael Yelayel.

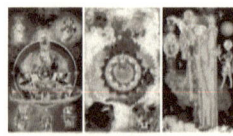

3. *SYT*—Saitael Lord of Refuge and Fortification:
   Psalm 91:2 *I will say of the LORD, He is my refuge and my fortress: my God; in him will I trust.*
   (Sitael 11–15° Leo—Elemental Fire in Tiphareth: 6 Wands, Angel by Day) My citadel; Sa-Yah-Ta, Cosmic Guide and voiced celestial Time, may my Divine Voice and the power of the WORD find strength thru beauty, to trust in powers of suggestability. With awareness may all thoughts be clarified, to find insight thru intuitive sensitivity, and thy telepathy, as One Thought in endless conversation.

   May we invoke these powers latent in self-mastery, and the realization of subjective

revelations; seeing with foresight into prophecy, and hindsight realize once silent history, and forgotten memories.

May thy beautiful awakening give us insight into their discovery, in all times and places; find favor for the welfare of human society, and deep understanding into principles conceited, strong and true. Grant us confidence in the governance of God and Man, and in our moral property: my Refuge thee, and I thy refugee, by thy comfort Saitael Sitael.

 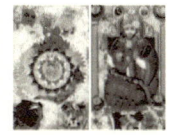

4. *OLM*—Aulamiah Lord Merciful Savior:
   Psalm 6:4 *Return, O LORD, deliver my soul: oh save me for thy mercies' sake.*

   (Elemiah 16–20° Leo—Elemental Fire in Tiphareth: 6 Wands, Angel by Night)
   Olam, May I and we, for sake of Eternal Fate, find true Beauty in Self-Mastery of both my and others lives, transcending life and death thru Beauty's Mercy's Seat, for achieving great success with lawful instruments . . . thru powers calling sacred meanings, with kabalistic confidence;

creation: falling into harmony; justice, truth and sympathy; that if I should fall by law to create for mercy's sake; thou my Savior and Redeemer, be saved by thy name Aulamiah Elemiah.

5. *MHSh*—Meheshiah Lord "Destroyer of Fear" the Fearless:

Psalm 34:4 *I sought the LORD, and he heard me, and delivered me from all my fears.*

(Mahashiah 21–25° Leo—Elemental Fire in Netzach: 7 Wands, Angel by Day) Mohesh, may I and we, create thru the power over elements, destroy all fear thru fearlessness and in thy victory, and by their services find Self-Mastery over illnesses, find Wisdom thru analogies, and plumb insights that are deep rooted within our natural sanctuary, and this to find recovery in falling thru life's beauty, and awakening the secrets hiding in the light, of one's once sacred properties; governed with insight, and support upon the Tree of Life; fearless creator, by thy name Meheshiah Mahashiah.

6. *LLH*—Lalahael Lord Doer of all Deeds in Judgment:

   Psalm 9:11 *Sing praises to the LORD, which dwelleth in Zion: declare among the people his doings . . .*

   (Lelahel 26–30° Leo—Elemental Fire in Netzach: 7 Wands, Angel of Night) *Lilah, tempted by lawful art may just genius grow in me, create thy dignity in me, and we; thru thy perfect laws and properties discover Victory; and create thru science in Self-Discovery; and thru perfect faculties . . . My life will be my message. My insight my authority; as one deserving the power of governing and delivering thru perfect insight and intuiting; by the doer of the deed, divining Lalahael Lelahel.*

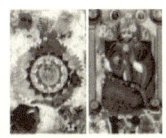

7. *AChA*—Ache-ayah Lord of Mercy, Splendor, and Graciousness:

   Psalm 103:8 *The LORD is merciful and gracious, slow to anger, and plenteous in mercy.*

(Akaiah 0–5° Virgo—Elemental Earth in Hod: 8 Pentacles, Angel of Day) *Achai, with brotherhood life perfect, may I with those powers of magic faculties draw from the elements and superconscious insight; make friendships; finding mercy common amongst all humanity, thru thy perfect property; of grandeur in thy augury peace; in thy perfect strength; in glory divining properly, thy perfect elemental policies . . . with brilliance thru strength and understanding; Lord Merciful Ache-ayah Akaiah.*

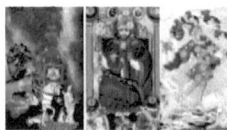 

8. *KHTh*—Ka-hetha-el Lord of Creation Worthy of our Praise:

Psalm 95:6 *O come, let us worship and bow down: let us kneel before the LORD our maker.*

(Kehethel 5–10° Virgo—Elemental Earth in Hod: 8 Pentacles, Angel of Night) *Keheth, in the moment, Kehath in our assembly, may I govern humbled before unbridled superconsciousness; being humbled by its energies of electromagnetic properties seen thru liberation: Nature governed for the welfare of humanity; overwhelming*

elemental enmity; controlling the seasons of the year . . . for the goodness of the season, with due purpose and just reason; without spite nor with calumny, find elemental sympathy, for perfect Nature's mastery, over all her elements. Born, reborn, humbled; surrendering thru liberation; praiseworthy Ka-hetha-el Kehethel.

9. *HZY*—Hezayoel Lord of Eternal Kind-hearted Mercy and Sympathy:

Psalm 25:6 *Remember, O LORD, thy tender mercies and thy loving kindnesses; for they have been ever of old . . .*

(Haziel 11-15° Virgo—Elemental Earth in Hod: 9 Pentacles, Angel of Day) *Hezi, may thy Strong Foundation, form the base of Justice and Mercy on the wheel of time, follow and guide me, and we, in all virtue in eternal sympathy, for making peace from former enmity, being just bring justice, from even foreign enemies, and bring mercy open to both me, and we, to open the keys to every treasury; that heaven and earth may sympathize, in mercy and in kindness;*

loving peace; kind-hearted foundation, kind Hezayoel Haziel.

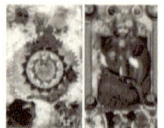

10. *ALD*—Aladayah Lord of Hope:
Psalm 33:22 *Let thy mercy, O LORD, be upon us, according as we hope in thee...*

(Aldiah 16–20° Virgo—Elemental Earth in Hod: 9 Pentacles, Angel of Night) Alda Alad in magic honorable, reveal thy foundation in the creation of thy Mysteries.

Over just laws serving us in subtle elemental anatomy and all harmonies and inharmonies, divine us thru chemistry and alchemy; ruling thru serving at the foundations for true magic, mystery and kabala.

Thy hope is mine as perfect, as is possible. Bring us our hope with mercy in justice by coming to thee; thru thy powers ruling justice evenly, my hope in thee, kind hope, Aladayah Aldiah.

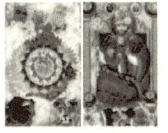

11. *LAW*—La-uwa-yah Lord of Salvation and Liberation:
Psalm 18:46 *The LORD liveth; and blessed be my rock; and let the God of my salvation be exalted . .*
.

(Laviah 21–25° Virgo—Elemental Earth in Malkuth: 10 Pentacles, Angel of Day) *Levi Law confirming Lave heart, thy Kingdom is my liberation and my salvation. My rock; lead be to conquer adversaries through thy powers hidden in me, overcoming obstacles, in Law before our victories, through justice and authority; even overcoming enemies; with judgment, honor and humility; in perfect victory over inner enemies. By our love for liberation, saved by our awakened illumination; to serve in glorious chivalry; and the marriage of our elements with thy blessing; my rock, my La-uwa-yah Laviah.*

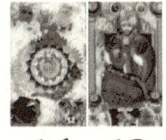

12. *HHO*—He-he-oayah Lord Beyond but in the World:
Psalm 10:1 *Why standest thou afar off, O LORD? Why hidest thou thyself in times of trouble?*

(Hihayah 26–30° Virgo—Elemental Earth in Malkuth: 10 Pentacles, Angel of Night) *Haho lion of glory, I see, I see; thy Kingdom reveal thru me in thy symbolic meanings, dreams and secret analogies; thy truths and secret mysteries once concealed unconcealing in thy secret place. Turn enemies to friends; let troubles disappear, by thy lending ear; to the world of energies; may thy kingdom fallen, hidden, now stand firm in me to rule it righteously, divine He-he-oayah Hihayah.*

13. **YZL**—Yazalael Lord Worthy of Songs of Praise: Psalm 98:4 *Make a joyful noise unto the LORD, all the earth: make a loud noise, and rejoice, and sing praise . . .*

(Yezalel 0–5° Libra—Elemental Air in Chokmah: 2 Swords, Angel of Day) *Yezel, my Azel Stone to mark the way, inspire wisdom in my writings with thy poetry; love of art and joy of singing. Thou Mystery Wise beyond time and understanding. Reveal thy gift of oratory and in justice disclose all secrets of the Stars me. All knowing known, thy Word that is said, sung and heard throughout the world, in thy songs of praise, rejoicing by the name, in Wisdom driving through my veins in the praise of Yazalael Yezalel.*

14. *MBH—Mebeheael* Lord of the Fallen through Meditation:

> Psalm 9:9 *The LORD also will be a refuge for the oppressed, a refuge in times of trouble.*
>
> > (Mebehel 6–10° Libra—Elemental Air in Chokmah: 2 Swords, Angel of Night) *M'BH, "Baruch Hashem" blessed. Creator, protector; inspirer, create, protect and inspire wisdom in my meditations, wisdom in our innocence bring justice, honor and dignity; to thy forgotten refugee. Favor me politically, with safe keeping over enemies; bringing peace in times of war. Turn the unjust to just measures and lasting self-esteem; revealing truth through wisdom's vitality, to free us from indignity, to spite our unjust enemies; my lord and refuge, comfort for thy unseeing refugee; divine wisdom, by thy name Mebeheael Mebehel.*

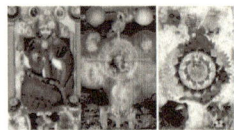

15. **HRY**—Ha-re-iel Lord of Security, Strong Sanctuary, and Protection:

> Psalm 94:22 *But the LORD is my defense; and my God is the rock of my refuge . . .*
>
>> (Hariel 11–15° Libra—Elemental Air in Binah: 3 Swords, Angel of Day) *Hari, Lion of Divine Initiation: Time, Creator of mover of energies in the name of Tetragrammaton, guide me, and we, thy refugees, space-born in thy divine mysteries, by thy evocation and philosophy. Bring us to the path of peace upon this Tree of Life; and with thy grace defend and protect us, and the ones we love; in thy security; Lord of Perfect Sanctuary, by thy Mother, Divine Lord by the name, Ha-re-iel Hariel.*

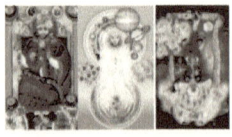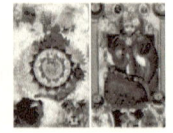

16. **HQM**—He-qo-meyah Lord of Longing Memories:

> Psalm 88:1 *O LORD God of my salvation, I have cried day and night before thee:*
>
>> (Haqmiah 16–20° Libra—Elemental Air in Binah: 3 Swords, Angel of Night) *Haqam*

wise sage, arise, stand, Lord of Help, Creative Mother, Father of Time; Lord Tetragrammaton, the face that lies in depths of Space, bring us honor, wealth, glory and renown and the devotions of our loved ones, those now, those past and those to come; grant them all joy, love and fertility; my salvation is in the name of He-qo-meyah Haqmiah.

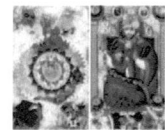

17. *LAW*—La-auvi-yah Lord of the Great Name or Word: Psalm 8:9 *O LORD our Lord, how excellent is thy name in all the earth...!*

(Laviah 21–25° Libra—Elemental Air in Binah: 4 Swords, Angel of Day) *Lav-Righteous heart, in thy Seat of Mercy, let me, and we, see; by thy union and magic properties thy powers, and judge with prophecy the present, past and future for fulfillment of invention, science and industry; inspire in us new technology, art, and musicality, awaken in our marriage the glories of thy wondrous metaphysics; by thy Word Laauyah Laviah.*

18. *KLY*—Kaleiel Lord of Righteous Judgment:

Psalm 35:24 *Judge me, O LORD my God, according to thy righteousness; and let them not rejoice over me.*

(Kaliel 26–30° Libra—Elemental Air in Binah: 4 Swords, Angel of Night) *Kali-Dark crown, Reveal to me, and we, thy righteous magic industry, with thy kabalistic charms found in thy jovial mercy through Kabala. Shine thy letters that form its imagery with words of power that justice serve us over harm. Grant us powers over Time and Space, through these powers of superconsciousness, and let us realize its alchemy and the materializations of divine appearances. Guide us thru the path of liberation, on all three planes, by the name; divine righteous Kaleiel Kaliel.*

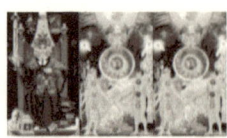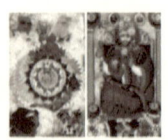

19. *LWW*—Leauwiah Lord Hearer of our Sorrows and Lamentations:

Psalm 40:1 *I waited patiently for the LORD; and he inclined unto me, and heard my cry . . .*

(Luviah 0–5° Scorpio—Elemental Water in Geburah: 5 Cups, Angel of Day) *Levav "heart" of comfort in times of trouble and sympathy at the time of birth; peace in security. Just and perfect union; awakened illuminations; with reason, mastery over memory, intelligence and good judgment; and the properties of Love and the union of marriage and procreation . . . thru language perfect and divine; in our judgments that are thine; hear our sorrows and lamentations Lord; divine Leauwiah Luviah.*

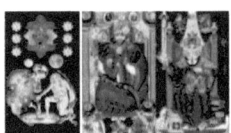 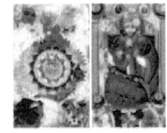

20. *PHL*—Pe-haeh-leyah Lord of Good Name and Reputation:

> Psalm 120:1–2 *In my distress I cried unto the LORD, and he heard me. Deliver my soul, O LORD, from lying lips, [and] from a deceitful tongue . . .*
>
> (Pahaliah 6–10° Scorpio—Elemental Water in Geburah: 5 Cups, Angel of Night) *Pahal learned in virtues, and natural equilibrium; synthesis and samadhi (equalmindedness) thy medicine; thy voice of alchemy; transform our lives thru justice*

and good judgment, and hear our cry for mercy, by virtue of the WORD and by reputation; divine Pe-haeh-leyah Pahaliah.

21. *NLK*—Nu-la-kael Lord of Faith and Trust:
    Psalm 31:14 *But I trusted in thee, O LORD: I said, Thou art my God...*
    (Nelakiel 11–15° Scorpio—Elemental Water in Tiphareth: 6 Cups, Angel of Day)
    Inspire me and we; by thy truth, imagination and by study with thy given Teacher as my Guru, and thy instruments to be spoken of, as the power of love, in magic charms over life and death, and perfect alchemy; divine mercy and just liberation; I trust in thee, faithfully, divine Nu-la-kael Nelakiel.

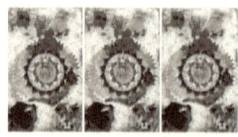 

22. *YYY*—Yoyayael Lord Guardian who hovers over me:
    Psalm 121:5 *The LORD is thy keeper: the LORD is thy shade upon thy right hand.*
    (Yeyayel 16–20° Scorpio—Elemental Water in Tiphareth: 6 Cups, Angel of

Night) *Yeya, The Lord [YYY] God . . . recall the angel of YYY, appeared to him in a flame of fire, in the midst of the bush. He gazed, behold the bush burned with fire yet the fire was neither burned nor consumed with fire. Time Master, Time Maker; bring us wealth and self-respect; fame, protection, and success and the vision of all three times (Past, Present, Future) before the visions in our mind; subject to our intuition and witness insights clearly in the cycles of our lives; my Guardian and Protector; Lord of time and father of creation; Father Yoyayael Yeyayel.*

23. *MLH* —Melaheael Lord of Eternal Safe Passage in and out of worlds:

> Psalm 121:8 *The LORD shall preserve thy going out and thy coming in from this time forth, and even for evermore . . .*
>
> > (Melahel 21–25° Scorpio—Elemental Water in Netzach: 7 Cups, Angel of Day) *Melah, thy healing salt, protect us from all weapons used in war; and from the heat of fire raging; let us stand protected in the*

midst of fires burning; just hearing Melahel. Heal us with wisdom; grant us insight into herbal remedies. Give us protections from diseases. Awaken these Just Powers from within, grant us mastery over energies in superconsciousness; with safe passage thru eternal worlds reincarnating; perfect Melaheael Melahel.

 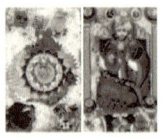

24. *ChHW*—Chahewuyah Lord who Watches Over All: Psalm 33:18 *Behold, the eye of the LORD is upon them that fear him, upon them that hope in his mercy; (Lord of Chesed and Geburah)*...

(Chahaviah 26–30° Scorpio—Elemental Water in Netzach: 7 Cups, Angel of Night) *We are married to power as a wedlock to its property and power of procreation and divine intuition; as just hearing poured over inner energies and thru our illumination. Grant us insight into the power over nemeses, thieves and all who do us harm; and reveal confessions of shameful enemies, and may we paralyze the wicked by our strength, thru the powers of magic arts; thou Watcher over All; divine Chahewuyah Chahaviah.*

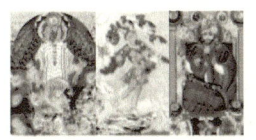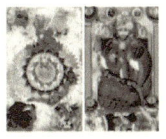

25. *NThH*—Nu-thau-he-yah Lord Praiseworthy Resident of the Heart:

> Psalm 9:1 *I will praise thee, O LORD, with my whole heart; I will shew forth all thy marvelous works . . .*
>
>> (Nithahiah 0–5° Sagittarius—Elemental Fire in Hod: 8 Wands, Angel of Day) *Great, Great the Lord of the Initiate; Concealer and Revealer; reveal what is concealed of Rita, righteous law; dharma; and the grand workings, skills and arts, known only to thee and granted to the few: Oh, Great Grand Guardian! I hear and intuit thee; praises from my heart for thee thy marvelous entity, divine Nu-thau-he-iah Nithahiah.*

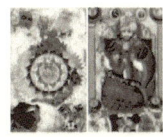

26. *HAA*—He-ah-ayah Lord of Righteous Law

> Psalm 119:145 *I cried with my whole heart; hear me, O LORD: I will keep thy statutes . . .*
>
>> (Haayah 6–10° Sagittarius—Elemental Fire in Hod: 8 Wands, Angel of Night)

Protect us by our righteousness, diplomacies and suits, and protect us by revealing all elemental secrecies; and uncover those deceiving others of our virtues or our covering treasons treacherous against us. Guided by right judgment and insight into all powers divine or otherwise. By the powers of thy elements; Revealer; Lord of hearing, insight and counsel, guidance and direction; Lord of Righteous laws and the heart of perfect Magistry, I will keep thy perfect mystery and conceal these with self-mastery, Divine He-ah-ayah Haayah.

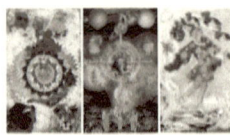

27. *YRTh*—Yare-thau-ael Lord of Purity

Psalm 140:1 *Deliver me, O LORD, from the evil man: preserve me from the violent man . . .*

(Yerathiel 11–15° Sagittarius—Elemental Fire in Yesod: 9 Wands, Angel of Day)

Shine thy light revealing night and give us insights against our enemies, and grant us favors from the enmity of both friend and enemy, teach us language skillfully, entertain us with vitality, and guide us with productions of literary expertise; with

purity and purpose preserving, divine Yarethau-ael Yerathiel.

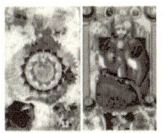

28. *ShAH*—Shia-heyah Lord, Nearest of the Near – First Aide

> Psalm 71:12 *O God, be not far from me: O my God, make haste for my help . . .*
>
> > (Sahiah 16–20° Sagittarius—Elemental Fire in Yesod: 9 Wands, Angel of Night)
> > *Implement all elemental energies to serve and comfort me from enemies; control us by thy safe keeping shining light upon vitality, in productions of the fire or electric storm. Grant us powers over energy; destroy or protect all cities threatening in the times of war; deliver us from fear of any enemy; and guide us in our maturity, to warrant us protection and security, thy quest to be there instantly, my help Shia-heyah Sahiah.*

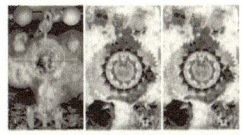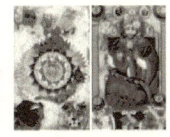

29. *RYY*—Reyoyoel Lord Companion and Associate

> Psalm 54:4 *Behold, God is mine helper: the Lord is with them that uphold my soul . . .*

(Reyayel 21–25° Sagittarius—Elemental Fire in Malkuth: 10 Wands, Angel of Day) *I run thru worlds of endless energies spinning, unfolding, refolding so by thy mercy reveal to me, Truth and Understanding; in all things visible and invisible that they stand out clear before us. Guide us in thy powers thru thy numbers, science in thy physics and astronomy; for revealing order, in all cosmic energies; companion, friend; divine Reyoyoel Reyayel.*

30. *AWM*—Ah-u-meael Lord of our Lifetime; Trustworthy Companion

Psalm 71:5 *For thou art my hope, O Lord GOD: thou art my trust from my youth.*

(Aumael 26–30° Sagittarius—Elemental Fire in Malkuth: 10 Wands, Angel of Night) *Aum; Friend to Adam from the first mystery; with us from the beginning; for both man and animal; mortal and divine. Reveal thru thy biology, organic chemistries, and physiologies.*

Awareness shine revealing all powers meant for common healing; thru the

applications of medicines and for all mastery of surgeries.

Guardian of physicians in occult anatomy; reveal for me, and we, divine alchemy; and the sciences of medicine; my comforter and friend.

I trust in thee thou Lord of illumined alchemy, Master of the Stone, magic and creation; divine, trustworthy; eternal youth, Ah-u-meael Aumael.

31. *LKB*—Lekabael Lord of Wisdom, Strength, and Courage: Psalm 71:16 *I will go in the strength of the Lord GOD: I will make mention of thy righteousness, even of thine only.*

>(Lekabel 0–5° Capricorn—Elemental Earth in Chokmah: 2 Pentacles, Angel of Day)
>
>*Guide us in wisdom, love and fealty and all faithfulness and reveal the mysteries of light and inner sight. Reveal the laws liberation and the hidden secrets of the elements.*
>
>*Teach us the just methods used in the instruments of hidden alchemy. Teach us*

thy creation in the mystery Beth-Bara-Bereshith. Open up our book of oratory, our treasuries of words and the mysteries of speech; and protect us from all theft. Your strength and courage; peaceful even unto liberation; righteous in thy name, divine Lekabael Lekabel.

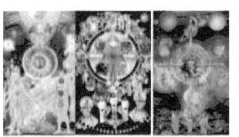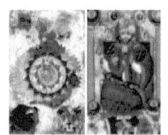

32. **WShR**—Washireyah Lord of Righteousness and Truth: Psalm 33:4 *For the word of the LORD is right (righteous); and all his works are done in truth.*

(Veshriah 6–10° Capricorn—Elemental Earth in Chokmah: 2 Pentacles, Angel of Night) *Initiator of Truth and Righteousness; vast reformer of all who lie; reveal to us what is hidden by all cosmic properties and the physics of the marriage with the stars. Teach us the powers of invisibility in the cloud of astral energies; and, unveil the mysteries of the heavens over mind; in righteous truth, wise in illumination; vast sun and spirit, wisdom and Lord of Light, divine Washireyah Veshriah.*

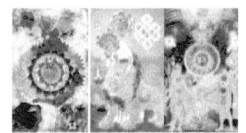 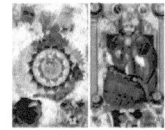

33. *YChW*—Yachauwiah Lord Knower of All Thoughts and Concealments

> Psalm 94:11 *The LORD knoweth the thoughts of man, that they are vanity...*
>
>> (Yechaviah 11–15° Capricorn—Elemental Earth in Binah: 2 Pentacles, Angel of Day)
>>
>> *The Word, wed us to the illumination in all world energies; disclose to us world sciences and mysteries; guide us into seeing into the mysteries that open up the three periods and times. Turn enmity to friendship; and reveal the cause in all men's minds. Teach us to defy even states of gravity and all materializations.*
>>
>> *In thy strength for revelations awaken resolutions to all concealed possibilities hidden by the Great Name; knower of all thoughts and vain concealments, divine Yachauwiah Yechaviah.*

 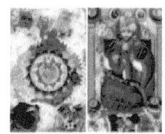

34. *LHCh*—La-he-chiah Lord and Hope for All Nations:

Psalm 131:3 *Let Israel hope in the LORD from henceforth and forever.*

(Lehachiah 16–20° Capricorn—Elemental Earth in Binah: 2 Pentacles, Angel of Night) *For hope, justice in peace with the strength to calm the thunderstorm, Shakti, lightning and the seas; power, Just Rector, hearer and revealer of all laws in creation; reveal to us all powers and reveal thy hidden energies; thru strength serve our nation against all adversaries; divine La-he-chiah Lehachiah.*

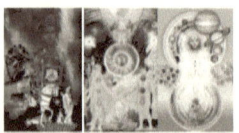 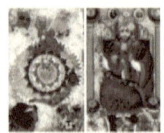

35. *KWQ*—Kauwaqiah Lord Hearer of all Prayers, Petitions, and Appeals

Psalm 116:1 *I love the LORD, because he has heard my voice and my supplications . . .*

(Kevequiah 21–25° Capricorn—Elemental Earth in Chesed: 4 Pentacles, Angel of Day) *Transformed and inspired by deaths transformations, and guided by illumination; may the Righteous Sun Qodesh be consecrated in thy separateness, be lifted by thy sacredness into the spirit of liberation, and by this ascent in vision and this sacredness become revealed to me in*

me... Turn all negatives towards divinity; hear our prayers for divine insight; for spirits Jovial; grant us wealth and property; and peace with every enemy. By the power of the Word, our voice invoked, hear my petition; listen to our pleas; as prayers of love Kauwaqiah Kevequiah.

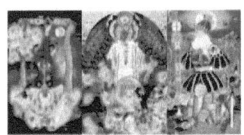 

36. *MND*—Menudael Lord of Mind, The Sacred House of Creation

Psalm 26:8 *LORD, I have loved the habitation of thy house, and the place wherein thine honor dwells.*

(Mendael 26–30° Capricorn—Elemental Earth in Chesed: 4 Pentacles, Angel of Night) *Teach us time and reveal the mastery of the stars in spagyrics and in alchemy; grant us insights into times, and into seasons; and how to charge all magic implements, and to animate the energies in our sacred house and home; and reveal real purpose to, our properties and life.*

Teach us the herbal times for gathering, open locks to every door; provide us favors for our honoring, and add perseverance then, to achieve our greater character, and

reserve and write our name in the Great Mind, as one with a great reputation; to have it said throughout creation; I am honored in thy sacred House, by the name Menudael Mendael.

37. *ANY*—Anu-yiel   Lord   Whose   Face   Shines   on Righteousness

Psalm 80:3 *Restore us again, O God, and cause thy face to shine; and we shall be saved.*

(Aniel 0–5° Aquarius—Elemental Air in Geburah: 5 Swords, Angel of Day) Reveal to me, Watcher over Mysteries, in the elemental secrets to all science and initiation.

Open up our voice, transform creativity thru us, with thy voice of mystery with intelligence and strength.

May we hear thy assistance clearly? Invoke thy language perfectly, in all writings unfold truth by thy message, and reveal thy sweetest melodies thru our musical ability, inspiring all our compositions.

With wisdom transformed into these powers of understanding; reveal thy shining face, as a comfort seen, our Lord Anu-yiel Aniel.

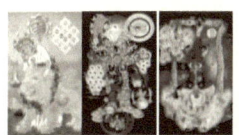

38. **ChOM—Che-au-meiah Lord Who Made Even God the Place of Sanctuary in Creation**

   Psalm 91:9 *Because thou hast made the LORD, which is my refuge, even the most High, thy habitation . . .*

   (Chamiah 6–10° Aquarius—Elemental Air in Geburah: 5 Swords, Angel of Night)

   In thy power to create; create for me a place of prominence; evoke good reputation, divine celebrity and glorious distinction; in blissfulness and wisdom.

   In good health give me strength in powers of creation; and fulfil my wishful dreams. Reveal the course for moral destinations; in thy Sanctum of Creation and speak to our habitation in the name Che-au-meiah Chamiah.

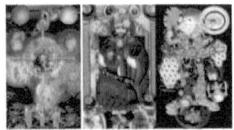

39. *RHO—Re-he-auel Lord and Helper, Rescuer, and Guide*
    Psalm 30:10 *Hear, O LORD, and have mercy upon me: LORD, be thou my helper.*

    (Rehael 11–15° Aquarius—Elemental Air in Tiphareth: 6 Swords, Angel of Day)

    Rescue this thy Rescuee. Intuit profound inquiry and inherit life from thy true Stone that it may deliver me, to live long in thy eternity, with thy mercy mastered by Self-Mastery.

    In the course of Beauty with intelligence, in the drive of moral guidance, grant wisdom; and reveal the cause for true alchemy, its wisdom, love and fidelity, and reveal the royal mystery, thou Master Re-he-auel Rehael.

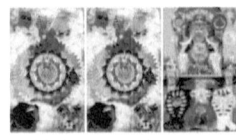

40. *YYZ—Yayozael Lord Who Hides His Face and Turns His Back on Me*
    Psalm 88:14 *LORD, why castest thou off my soul? Why hidest thou thy face from me?*

(Yeyazel 16–20° Aquarius—Elemental Air in Tiphareth: 6 Swords, Angel of Night)
Free all who come to me from bondage and bound uncertainty; reveal thy manifestations of divinity in Eternal Time. Make things hidden appear again before me, in fruition; transformed between the subtle and the gross. Heaven and the earth; with the power of thy manifested destiny; reveal with power dreaming dreams.

Awaken revelation over the three times of Eternity. Past, present and future turn to reveal to me, all on the path, thru times subtle properties. Turn by this time our art and poetry, prose and books to lifetimes of destiny, and reveal, revealer of thy self-prophecy, all subjects to be revealed to me; divine Yayozael Yeyazel.

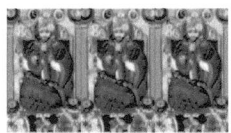 

41. *HHH—He-he-heael Lord Whose Honesty Is Virtuous Protecting Our Reputation:*
 Psalm 120:2 *Deliver my soul, O LORD, from lying lips, and from a deceitful tongue.*
 (Hahahel 21–25° Aquarius—Elemental Air in Netzach: 7 Swords, Angel of Day)

Threefold Hermes Heh-Heh-Heh; Perfect Guide; Perfect Witness; perfect insight thru voice perfect honesty and virtuous invention and success. Reveal thru prophecy and intuition secrets set before me; to protect my reputation; by the power of the elements.

May I have power over the elements, in the exercise of veritas, in all three worlds set before me? With vision, with foresight granted, and the guidance of divinity, being in perfect selfless attitude; the ideal of intuition divining love thru wisdom, with self-confidence . . . Master and companion; perfect in virtue He-he-heael Hahahel.

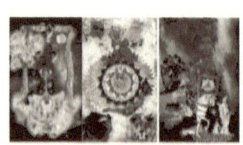 

42. MYK—Me-ya-kael Lord of Preservation All Preserving Who Cares and Keeps the Soul

Psalm 121:7 *The LORD shall preserve thee from all evil: he shall preserve thy soul.*

(Mikael 26–30° Aquarius—Elemental Air in Netzach: 7 Swords, Angel of Night) Lord of Preservation and Awareness entering through creation, Cosmic Time, and regeneration; proceed to create, until

the day of liberation and true victory in thy march through creation.

Grant us long life and the power over inner and outer enemies; faithfulness and self-protection, thru Kabalistic transformation and magical aptitude.

On the path towards endless and eternal salvation; form the path eternal in thy march, and return thy Perfect Alchemy to these hands with every touch. And by thy perfect policy; preserve my soul from infamy; protector, defender, guardian; perfect keeper, Me-ya-kael Mikael.

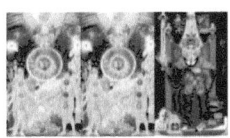 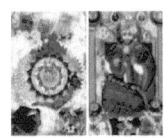

43. **WWL—Wau-ualeyah Lord Who Is Stopped by My Voice and Word Alone**

> Psalm 88:13 *But unto thee have I cried, O LORD; and in the morning shall my prayer prevent thee.*
>> (Vavaliah 0–5° Pisces—Elemental Water in Hod: 8 Cups, Angel of Day) *By thy grace hear! I call with divine intoxication; justice, law and the power of thy Word. Yoked in justice with law I sit and judge by*

illumination, in glory bound in union with the soul.

Give power over inner and outer enemies, by the wisdom of the Word alone. Awaken the inner radiance of divine energies. My voice whispers to the harmony of the miracle; by the hearing of our prayers; for the comfort of my soul.

My Word alone enough, for I am bound to thee by justice; as I am calling thee in splendor; the Lord Wau-ualeyah Vavaliah.

 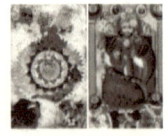

44. YLH—Yelaheyah Lord Who Accepts My WORD as Sacrifice and Leads the World thru Its Offering

Psalm 119:108 *Accept, I beseech thee, the freewill offerings of my mouth, O LORD, and teach me thy judgments.*

(Yelahiah 6–10° Pisces—Elemental Water in Hod: 8 Cups, Angel of Night) *Intuit justice, by my Word, law with thy eternal return, justice served thru the power of the Word intuited by my voice thru Shruti speaking insight which is heard.*

Make my speech divine thru Kabalistic charm and mantric power. Perfect my conversation with charm and oratory; as thy perfect offering; with vibhuti goodness on the tongue.

With speech invoke divine goodness through the voice and invoke the powers of the breath in me.

Perform miracles here and everywhere at once that actions in justice may be done, to serve Yelaheyah Yelahiah.

 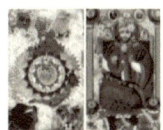

45. *SAL*—Sa-aleyah Lord of Stability, Balance, and Symmetry

>Psalm 94:18 *When I said, my foot slips; thy mercy, O LORD, held me up.*
>>(Saliah 11–15° Pisces—Elemental Water in Yesod: 9 Cups, Angel of Day) *By justice, shining in the miracle of the foundation, faith thru thy magic of the elements; thru thy cosmic energies, let us master of all aspects of superconscious energies.*

I am perfect symmetry, justice, strength and stability; thru thy powers of invisibility and the comfort of the stars and other astral energies.

Like Moses, Lord, a comfort thru thy cosmic energies, of perfect power, through elemental harmony. Director and defender; over land and sea and sky ensure no man a match for me, by thy powers of Stability; Balance and Symmetry, Lord Sa-aleyah Saliah.

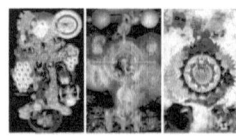

46. ORY—Aure-yael Lord Life Sustenance That Is Good for All

Psalm 145:9 *The LORD is good to all: and his tender mercies are over all his works.*

(Ariel 16–20° Pisces—Elemental Water in Yesod: 9 Cups, Angel of Night) *Thru the light at the foundation of prophecy I see falling thru eternity all discovery hidden over time. Concealed thy works are revealed to me, in the sunlight rising with thy sunlight, Eternal Time and revelation.*

Reveal thy secret treasures unto me; let nature's secrets unfold their secrets from

their sacred treasury. Be not thyself concealed to me that by thy magic I fill my life with charms, in that comfort of sustenance with mercy. For the good of all; thy glory Aure-yael Ariel.

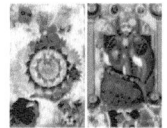

47. **OShL—Aushilayah Lord of Manifest Intelligence and Meditations**

> Psalm 92:5 O LORD, how great are thy works! And thy thoughts are very deep.

>> (Asaliah 21–25° Pisces—Elemental Water in Malkuth: 10 Cups, Angel of Day) Law, Justice and perfect alchemy; omniscient in all energies give us balance and equilibrium in the palace of the King. Lord of Samadhi; empathy and sympathy; in perfect equanimity; in the Kingdom of Love divine manifest thy intelligence perfectly divine Aushilayah Asaliah.

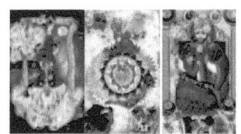

48. **MYH—Me-ya-he-ael Lord of Sight, Insight, Witnessed for All Salvation**

Psalm 98:2 *The LORD hath made known his salvation: his righteousness hath he openly shewed in the sight of the heathen.*

(Mihael 26–30° Pisces—Elemental Water in Malkuth: 10 Cups, Angel of Night) "M-Yah." From Yah." Bringing creative power, through time: intuition, insight, vision, awareness. Grant us vision by thy profound initiation into the Kingdom of Liberation. Lord of Alchemy and transformer governing creation, reveal the Father of the mysteries.

Bring virtuous opportunity with power over stones and precious metals to form their proper medicines. In thy righteous alchemy bring us insight revealing one harmony, with planetary powers, and provide us powers for transmutation. Demonstrate thy righteous harmony. Liberate our world for our salvation by thy powers Me-ya-he-ael Mihael.

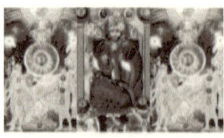 

49. **WHW**—Wau-he-wael Lord of Unfathomable Greatness
Psalm 145:3 *Great is the LORD, and greatly to be praised; and his greatness is unsearchable.*

(Vehuel 0–5° Aries—Elemental Fire in Chokmah: 2 Wands, Angel of Day)
Boundless illumination; wedded to our yoga union in the fire of wisdom. Intelligence that is intuitive in the wedding of profound enlightenment and perfect sensitivity to reveal to us vision thru prophecies.

Comfort by thy greatness in Akasha perfectly. Reveal the true nature of all persons to our inner eye.

In thy mystery communicate with perfect equanimity; with brilliance, praiseworthy of thy wisdom in its greatness, O' thou, profound Wau-he-wael Vehuel.

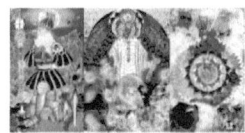 

50. *DNY*—Da-ni-ael Lord of Divine Judgement and Wisdom

Psalm 145:8 *The LORD is gracious, and full of compassion; slow to anger, and of great mercy.*

(Daniel 6–10° Aries—Elemental Fire in Chokmah: 2 Wands, Angel of Night) *God is my Judge; reveal thy judgments thru me. Royal Monarch, guardian over time; guide us with good judgment and in our*

judgments, grant us with energy in mercy. Serve us in thy leniency over karmic destiny, along the path of righteousness.

By thy love and charity; teach us true philosophies of wisdom; to be profound in writing and with oratory; for true genius in thy name love us graciously, Judge of Judges Da-ni-ael Daniel.

 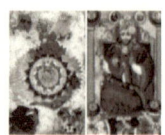

51. *HChSh*—He-cheshi-yah Lord Eternal with Love for All Creation:

> Psalm 104:31 *The glory of the LORD shall endure forever: the LORD shall rejoice in his works.*
>
> (Hechashiah 11–15° Aries—Elemental Fire in Binah: 3 Wands, Angel of Day) Initiate us into the House of Intelligence with the strength of Wisdom, and in divine works; into alchemy and chemistry; physics and the science of the stars and all their astral energies.
>
> With strength give us insight into omniscient vitalities; medicines and their cures and curatives. Open divine intuition to heal the sick and save the poor; provide

counsel in the glory of creation; grant us happiness and guidance; give direction in thy name He-cheshi-yah Hechashiah.

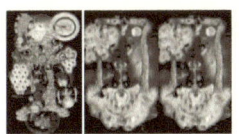

52. *OMM*—Aumemeyah Lord Worthy of Righteous and Highest Praise

>Psalm 7:17 *I will praise the LORD according to his righteousness: and will sing praise to the name of the LORD most high.*
>
>>(Amamiah 16–20° Aries—Elemental Fire in Binah: 3 Wands, Angel of Night) *O' Sing praises in thy Great House by thy name. Surrender power to create with joy in the song of happiness. By the power of Intelligence and Understanding release liberty within me, and the power to live in freedom and the understanding to create.*
>>
>>*Sever ties with those that bind us to the past. Break us out of our repressions from countless karmic bonds, to set free thy worthy candidate, and initiate a change. Transform us in love that surrenders to the house of divinity. Draw us into Understanding, while dying in the mind. Aumemeyah bring us the power to change*

our destiny; by the grace of thy divinity, in the name Aumemeyah Amamiah.

53. *NNA*—Nu-nuah-ael Lord of Faithful Judgment and Its Perfect Justice

Psalm 119:75 *I know, O LORD, that thy judgments are right, and that thou in faithfulness hast afflicted me.*

(Nanael 21–25° Aries—Elemental Fire in Chesed: 4 Wands, Angel of Day) *May we control all elemental powers thru thy divine authority? And in glory grant us thy supreme guidance and direction, initiating us into all mysteries in cosmic alchemy and the magic of sacred principles. Seeing power fulfilled over elements and over sacred animals.*

Nun arise surrounding us in the waters of thy perfect cloud of energy, in the Spirit on the Waters, the breath of Nara-Narayana. God-Purusha overpowering all elemental energies make me the vessel of thy strength, by the name Nu-nuah-ael Nanael.

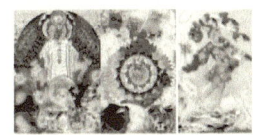 

54. **NYTh**—Nuya-thau-ael Lord Enthroned Ruler in the Cosmic Kingdom

> Psalm 103:19 *The LORD hath prepared his throne in the heavens; and his kingdom ruleth over all.*
>
>> (Nithael 26–30° Aries—Elemental Fire in Chesed: 4 Wands, Angel of Night) *Shine thy cloud over the sanctuary, of universal free energies; invoke life freed in superconscious genius; Lord seated deep within the kingdom of the heart; rule from our throne of sacred vitalities. In art and oratory, in writing, science and the field of happiness guide and direct our lives thru time and the kingdom of the elements with the name, Nuya-thau-ael.*

 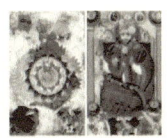

55. **MBH**—Mebehayah Lord Eternal for All to Remember

> Psalm 102:12 *But thou, O LORD, shalt endure forever; and thy remembrance unto all generations.*
>
>> (Mebahiah 0–5° Taurus—Elemental Earth in Geburah: 5 Pentacles, Angel of Day) *Help us to create thru thy menstrual fertility; thru hidden memories guide us by*

the moonlight into superconsciousness. Like a mother with devotion and surrender to creation, bring us honor to remember, peace, fruition and fecundity beloved Mebehayah Mebahiah.

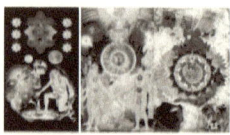

56. *PVY*—Pe-auwo-yel Lord Lifting the Fallen, the Weak, and the Depressed

> Psalm 145:14 *The LORD upholdeth all that fall, and raiseth up all those that be bowed down.*
>
> (Poiyel 6–10° Taurus—Elemental Earth in Geburah: 5 Pentacles, Angel of Night)
>
> *Thru transformation, time, strong germination and illumination bring forth the seeds of sustenance.*
>
> *Strong in our profession; grant us the vision seeing thru all times; by the union in the power of the Word.*
>
> *Thru fecund germination of thy divine alchemy engage in transformation, illumination, and the powers drawn from life in time and eternity, in the name of Pe-auwo-yel.*

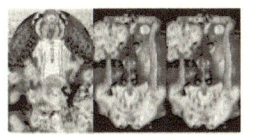 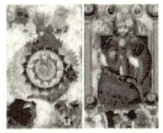

57. *NMM*—Numemeyah Lord of Faithful Devotees
  Psalm 115:11 *Ye that fear the LORD, trust in the LORD: he is their help and their shield.*
    (Nemamiah 11–15° Taurus—Elemental Earth in Tiphareth: 6 Pentacles, Angel of Day) *Guardian moving in the forces of creation, as Numemeyah, moving powers thru transmutation of your sacred energies in the beauty of the Sun. Formless forming alchemy; bring us to far sightedness, with insights vast and piercing thru creation; teach us thru thy provocations.*

    With thy comprehension in invention teach us to create. Share our love throughout creation, and protect us, your faithful devotee; with the name; defending us Numemeyah Nemamiah.

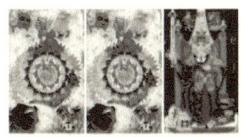 

58. *YYL*—Ya-yo-le-ael Lord Master, Soul, Enduring All Discomfort
  Psalm 6:3 *My soul is also sore vexed: but thou, O LORD, how long?*

(Yeyalel 15–20° Taurus—Elemental Earth in Tiphareth: 6 Pentacles, Angel of Night) *Eternal Time and final judgement; teach us thy astrology born in Cosmic Consciousness in the savior of the Sun. Speak to mantric and kabalistic powers; enduring, stable; permanent, justified by Ya-yo-le-ael Yeyalel.*

59. **HRCh** – Here-che-ael Lord Whose Name Shines in the Glory of the Sun by Day

> Psalm 113:3 *From the rising of the sun unto the going down of the same the LORD'S name is to be praised.*
>
> > (Herachiel 21–25° Taurus—Elemental Earth in Netzach: 7 Pentacles, Angel of Day) *Glorious Name, praise the glory of the name, the victory of power and strength; rushing with divine insight and intuition, and divine counseling.*
>
> Guide us to prosperity and give us invention and power over procreation.

Thru fertility, power and strength, thru the glory of the Sun; and the name Here-che-ael Herachiel.

60. *MTzR*—Mei-tzare-ael Lord of Righteousness; Sacred in His Labors

   Psalm 145:17 *The LORD is righteous in all his ways, and holy in all his works.*

   (Mitzrael 26–30° Taurus—Elemental Earth in Netzach: 7 Pentacles, Angel of Night) *Creator, fast paced before the Sun; manifest invention, create life energies thru your alchemy; divine in labor; endless working; teach us thy perfect provenance thru serving in the name of righteousness, thy name deserving Mei-tzare-ael Mitzrael.*

61. *VMB*—Wau-mebe-ael Lord; Hallowed Word, Hallowed Name Forever Blessed Eternal

   Psalm 113:2 *Blessed be the name of the LORD from this time forth and for evermore.*

(Vemibael 0–5° Gemini—Elemental Air in Hod: 8 Swords, Angel of Day) *Thy name is written in the powers of creation, with the soul surrendered to the balance of sacred house and home. Creator, Guardian and Guide, grant us initiation in to the powers of the Word. In splendor find creative intelligence wedded to the house of God. Warm in friendships and in love and marriage. In life live in the security of divine autonomy. Grants us the power of creating life naturally thru divine alchemy. Engage us in thy mystery in the powers of transmutation in the name Wau-mebe-ael Vemibael.*

62. *YHH*—Ya-hehe-ael Lord of Love, Devotion, and Benevolent Insight

Psalm 119:159 *Consider how I love thy precepts: quicken me, O LORD, according to thy lovingkindness.*

(Yehohel 6–10° Gemini—Elemental Air in Hod: 8 Swords, Angel of Night) *Yod-Heh-Heh, I am in thy mystic penetration understanding in the application of laws and principles; filled with sacred devotion*

and with this surrender in the balance in prostration. May I live a life profound in insight and be virtuous in the art of meditation as an occupation.

Lord see thru me, touch thru me, hear thru me and speak thru me with thy power of loving kindness. Protect me by thy kindness, and fill this heart with love to witness the world with thy mind, in the name Ya-hehe-ael Yehohel.

63. *ANV—Anu-wael Lord of Bliss, Lord of Song*
    Psalm 100:2 *Serve the LORD with gladness: come before his presence with singing.*
    (Anevael 11–15° Gemini—Elemental Air in Hod: 9 Swords, Angel of Day) *Open up my heart with gladness; fill my soul with love and song, thy power over elements invokes with the filling these with charms. Grace and guidance marries perfect magic with the mystery and we are joined with Vishnu-Narayan . . . pervading all the universe as the Lord our God is ONE. Grant us powers over all diseases and the gifts of perfect medicines; with this happiness and*

song moving forward in the name Anu-wael.

64. **MChY**—Me-cheya-ael Lord Watching from Chesed and Geburah

>Psalm 33:18 *Behold, the eye of the LORD is upon them that fear him, upon them that hope in his mercy.*
>
>>*(Mechayel 16–20° Gemini—Elemental Air in Yesod: 9 Swords, Angel of Night)*
>>*Create thru strength that is enduring drawing from vast eternity in my heart and guidance from time and the movement of the stars. Bring forth thy power to wield time and mystery strong in thy security.*
>>
>>*Grant us the power over oratory, writing their many occupations. In faith give us thy strength to rescind our enemies. Grant us long life, enduring health and faithful peace, and award us mercy passing safely thru eternity; by the name Me-cheya-ael.*

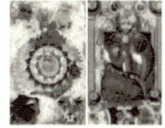

65. *DMB*—Damebeyah   Lord Who Seeks Apology; Regret for Inattentiveness

> Psalm 90:13 *Return, O LORD, how long? And let it repent thee concerning thy servants.*
>
> > (Damabiah 21–25° Gemini—Elemental Air in Yesod: 10 Swords, Angel of Day) *Ruling with creative faith in intelligence and power in all fecundity, shower love as moonlight down upon me. Water as covered by thy moonlight is thy magic element, grant us power over oceans, seas; rivers and tributaries, and all creatures existing from within these.*
> >
> > *Grant us thy faithful thy attentiveness. Shine the light of self-mastery with thy grace on this devotee. Give us thy attention for our service that has come in peace to rest before thee. Lord come back to me, the faithful, with forgiveness and thy apology for ever waning from me, in thy name Damebeyah Damabiah.*

66. *MNQ*—Menu-qo-ael   Lord Invoked for Constant Nearness

>Psalm 38:21 *Forsake me not, O LORD: O my God, be not far from me.*
>
>>(Menqael 25–30° Gemini—Elemental Air in Malkuth: 10 Swords, Angel of Night) *One before the Sun of Righteousness, intelligent in thy Kingdom for creating and preserving; stand near to us, and teach us by thy dreams, and inspire with thy message of the WORD and righteous alchemy.*
>>
>>*Grant us power over animals, birds, and the fishes of the sea, and the growth of vegetation and their true fecundity, by the name Menu-qo-ael Menqael.*

67. *AYO*—A-yo-uo-ael Lord in Bliss the Heart's Desire Is Satisfied

>Psalm 37:4 *Delight thyself also in the LORD; and he shall give thee the desires of thine heart.*
>
>>(Ayoel 0–5° Cancer—Elemental Water in Chokmah: 2 Cups, Angel of Day) *Grant us*

success by thy bliss assuming our challenges and endeavors, for conquest over the elements and wisdom over time. Fill our hearts with bliss divine for the purpose of our happiness.

Leads us on the path of initiation and cheer us on towards liberation. Waken our hearts into thy magical reality, for achieving philosophy and wisdom, saved thru morality, grant us perfect reputation thy joys throughout time. All this and more in our devotion to thy glory A-yo-uo-ael Ayoel.

 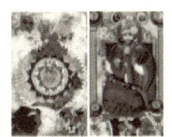

68. **ChBV—Che-bewu-yah Lord Forever Good and Merciful** Psalm 106:1 *Praise ye the LORD. O give thanks unto the LORD; for he is good: for his mercy endureth forever.*

(Chabuyah 6–10° Cancer—Elemental Water in Chokmah: 2 Cups, Angel of Night) *With mercy in strength thru meditation and union with the divine, grant us comfort and divine union. In this wisdom lead us to the control in thy creation of medicines, and mastery of the healing arts.*

Teach us thru thy mercy the nature of thy fertility and the mystery of life generation. In true love may we live in a common theme of mercy; in the name of Che-bewu-yah Chabuyah?

69. *RAH*—Ra-aheh-ael Lord of (Ra-Heh) Royal Rights, Royal Blood, Inheritance, and Guidance

Psalm 16:5 *The LORD is the portion of mine inheritance and of my cup: thou maintainest my lot.*

(Rahael 11–15° Cancer—Elemental Water in Binah: 3 Cups, Angel of Day) *Grant us sacred birth in moral aptitude with love and understanding, of the stars and royal right by the name of YHWH. Guide us with thy insight in the powers over the elements.*

With justice and authority in the use of magical faculty; let the Sun be our dominion and the Soul be our delight. For the balance of the kingdom, bring with it the inherited royal rites of guidance; by this and in our keeping guide us in thy comfort, by the name, Ra-aheh-ael Rahael.

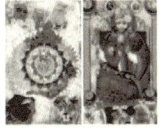

70. **YBM—Ya-beme-yah Lord Creator of Heaven and Earth**
Genesis 1:1 *In the beginning, God created the heaven and the earth.*

(Yebamiah 16–20° Cancer—Elemental Water in Binah: 3 Cups, Angel of Night)

With thy magic perfect faculty, BaraAelohim, out of thy creative worlds (Be-resh-ith) in me invoke and evoke thy energies. See thru me, feel thru me, touch thru me and heal thru me and engage me in all creativity; with perfect peace; creating endless thru thy fertility, as faithful victor over time.

Thru Eternity in the House of Time in the home of faith create, and by thy powers of transformation; and in the names of transmutation, create thru me in the name Ya-beme-yah Yebamiah.

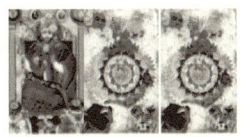

71. **HYY—He-yayo-ael Lord, I Am Thy Eternal Witness**
Psalm 109:30 *I will greatly praise the LORD with my mouth; yea, I will praise him among the multitude.*

(Hayayel 21–25° Cancer—Elemental Water in Chesed: 4 Cups, Angel of Day)
Heh-Yah-Yah, Eternal Guide, perfect heart, guide us through time thy Cosmic Entity hidden in the heart.

In thy cycles speak with clarity of thy cosmic mystery with the voice that is divine and the voice intuitive.

Save us from our fate and lead us to our destiny that takes us into the causes of true purposes.

Teach us and thru us do thy will, being witness to thy benefits; prophetic and divine, in the name He-yayo-ael Hayayel.

 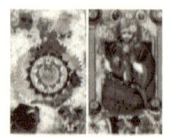

72. *MVM*—Me-wua-me-yah Lord Who Comforts Me in Life and Death, in Thy Creation

Psalm 116:7 *Return unto thy rest, O my soul; for the LORD hath dealt bountifully with thee.*

(Mevamiah 26–30° Cancer—Elemental Water in Chesed: 4 Cups, Angel of Night)
Womb wedded to mercy and creative peace in greatness, illuminate the comfort of my soul at peace, made one in peace in all

creation; as one in illumination in the ritual of time.

Teach us thy true physics in metaphysics, witness to us thy true chemistry and awaken alchemy. Reveal astronomy and thy astral mysteries in the perfect marriage of our creative magical faculties, by thy name, Me-wua-me-yah Mevamiah.

If you have creative faculties, you have magic faculties, and these through the powers of divinity and the glory of the name. The Name is ONE. Though characteristics, powers, traits are many, they are one; revealed by thy initiators, expressed in many forms.

You take, of these, each three letters. These represent the elements or Aleph, Mem, and Shin, or the three horizontal bars crossing the Tree of Life that separate the worlds of Mind and Spirit of the ten worlds, spheres or Sephiroth. Or take these three as creative representations of time (past, present, future) or on the Tree of Life as the crown (Kether, Chokmah, Binah—i.e., essence, wisdom, and understanding) or as satchitananda, the being, consciousness, and bliss of light, life, and love; or the three principles of Salt, Sulphur, and Mercury.

These three letters unite with God by the addition of the two letters; either YH (male) from the center of the heart, and EL (female) as the electric lighted lightning; Kundalini Levi-Aton. Being two, these are divine elemental bodies in Chokmah, or Wisdom (Yah), and as unwinding-winding Binah as creative Understanding that incarnates thru (EL) or when passing into

Chesed, or Mercy, and the motions of the Tree of Life down to Yesod. The five bodies (letters), or gates of understanding, then form as one body in a divine marriage of the sacred five elements. The spirit of these then finds itself merged in the power of the Kingdom of Malkuth or Malkata, called the Palace of the King or Kingdom of Adonai Aretz.

Sh'ma Yisrael (YHVH) Adonai Eloheinu (YHVH) Adonai Eḥad –

"Hear, O Israel: the LORD is God, the LORD is One."

"Sh'ma Yisrael" literally cries out, *"The Word is the Light of the Sun."*

By the power of the WORD or Great NAME Adonai *Eloheinu* invokes the Lord (as *Nara-Narayana*) in the primal whirling of the Seed Bijas ALVHY.

The ending Nu, is Adam united with God as NaraNarayana and *"Amon AM-EN,"* the spirit on the waters, as Nun (the fourteenth letter, the serpent, the number 50 or 5 × 10 the elements or minor arcana; appearing on the Tree of Life and revolving thru the Aelohim or Vav the hexagram).

The elements are united with Vav, or Wau (6), the harmonious spirit of the planetary hexagram (V); or the octave wave, with God as the center of rest, the creator of these that exist in silence, motionless. N is the central point circumpunct in the circle with a dot in the center.

Divine Man (male-female) is united in the initiation of marriage with God; like the marriage of Man and Wife. In truth, only God is male (Shiva).

All of creation is female (Shakti). This sacred wedding is the Divine Marriage or the divine wedding of the Divine Creation with God. This is the sacred initiation that forms, demanding righteousness, or rightness, in the ritual of Man and Wife as divinity reenacts, as the righteous law or rule of sacred rites; male and female in creation; through the union of family in the powers of procreation.

This rite is given to man as a sacred obligation; a rite of responsibility for the proper means of procreation for the human; being divine, on the path of liberation.

Man is not an animal. Man is gifted with the mind and the powers of reason with the obligations of the WORD that is the creative engine of the divine. It is established as a power of Wisdom and Understanding on the Tree of Life.

The obligations of the WORD are the powers for domination over the kingdoms of life and the rule of creation. It is not only right being the obligation on the paths of righteousness (dharma-duty) but the obligations of a rite (karma-actions)—One's self-determination for the return to truth and sacred life; self-mastery in peace, wisdom, and true understanding.

To deviate is deviant. There is the choice in the exercise of free-will to rise and fall accordingly in the knowledge of good and evil.

The word "'echad'" (אחד), "ONE," demands salvation in the merger of being liberated. Merger is yoked or the true yoga union of God with Man. According to the Ari, to say "'echad'" (אחד), "ONE," it means that "*I die into God.*"

Sai Baba provides an analogy, saying this is like the diamond. "Diamond is Die-Mind"—meaning to merge into the essence of Wisdom and Understanding at the crown of the Tree of Life.

Eloheinu sings sweetly its letters into these five-sacred elemental Bijas—Aum, Lam, Wam, Ham, Yam—forming these "wheels" or "primal whirlings," "days," or "Chakras"; traveling on these forces of the spirit; upon the waters in their ending; thus, revealing the pervading spirit of the being, namely the waters of thy Guardian ALVHY, or the Aelohim expressed thru these agencies hidden in the life of Man.

Anyone who knows Kundalini knows these seeds *Aum, Lam, Wam, Ham, Yam* are associated with *Aelohim*, or the *Light of God*. The one seed is always missing in the Hebrew names; it is the power of creation (or "ba-ra"), the soul of the sun (or *Bara-Abram*). This bond fulfills the secret name in Genesis 1:1—This being from the Genesis, "In the beginning, God created" or the BR, or Brahm, the creator, which is seated in the belly or the womb; charged with the forming powers hidden in the organs of the belly or the stomach, which transform energy into life.

This is in the region of the Solar plexus. This is the great alchemist, or the belly of the creator god, who works in the processes of the body elements. At work the process essentially

states "BaRa" as "Bam," "Ram," or "Brahm," meaning "*I Create.*"

This is the seat of God as the center within as the Alchemist; working in creations laboratories, as the self-formed, for the sacred life, in order to achieve the actions or karmic-rites of divinity, in the production of the daily maintenance, and the future procreations of life, in the theater of physical form, as the norm of Cosmic Consciousness.

"Nu!" "Nu!" Spirit of celestial waters form the mystical cloud of vibrant energy: God incarnate in Man: Nara-Vish-Nu-Narayan. NU the 50 and 6 or 5 x 10 + 6 elements cycled through the Tree of Life exposing the properties of the Aelohim through the six days of work, the cycles and pranic elements. Nu as the spirit in motion, moving space in the dynamics that surround the center entity.

These, in gravitational orbits or those elements of astral or starry vitality, mind, spirit and superconsciousness, we appear as if naked, except as cover by divine or mundane properties of character.

Praise the name, Nara-Narayana, as Man-Purusha or Adam in the spirit of God; moving on "Nu" the living forces of the waters of creation (gravity-massing spirit energies—i.e., vibrations, living intelligences).

We are given birth from Adamic "Man" as spit from the father's seminal seed, fulfilling the lives as living things, determined in the righteous virtue of our nativity, for the exposure to gestation,

birth and experience, within the breath and the womb of the Mother's Light, fed by the breast of Eve.

We are given birth by the Power of the Word and the Creatures of Letters, in the spirit of Superconsciousnesss.

Eḥad, First Principle, before unity, before consciousness, before energy; before creation; before the Tree of Life; the ONE before the one; before even Tetragrammaton; Ain-Sof the "Cause Before Beginning" that upon manifestation we address thee; first cause, and in that cause. Reveal to us, the Lord our God as ONE saying, "Before ONE what is the count?" we are back to the beginning in the limitless. Grant us this experience.

Grant us insight into thy grand mystery. Heal and reveal to us the blindness that is cast before our sightless sight, before our eyes the lightless sense; reveal to us thy enmity and awaken thy true spirit of divine liberty, and grant us peace and love, living truly in the essence of divinity.

We outcasts scattered out from light to live; blessed to discover this, thy sacred entity. Awaken shadows of my sight, having heard, reveal to us with insight our deepest meditation.

Cast away our fears thru sacred thoughts and meditation; hear thy voice in us revealed, thru insight, musings, introspections. God of love, here revealed is our dedication; true spirits gathered here; together make aware our brotherhood and freedom.

A-BRam Yod-Heh-Wau-Heh A-L-O-Ha-YEem

Yod is the light of the unified tenfold spirit of the Tree of Life in the Heart.

Aleph is the light of the ONE Spirit (One Thing) resident Light of Superconsciousness.

HVH is Eve, the Mother whose Word (Heh) pervades the Cosmos and replicates and incarnates to reap the fruit of fecundity (V); and therefore, she is seen as eating of, and bearing fruit, on the Tree of Life.

Lamed is the extension by virtue of motion, heat, light, and sound and the electromagnetic radiation and emanation in the thermodynamic heat as the law and energy that is all-pervading, seen in the movement of the arms and legs (four members each extending motion into the ten or 2 × 5 divisions of the toes and fingers. In all, there are twenty-two (center) extensions. These twenty fingers and toes, plus the head and genitals.)

Our prayer, invocation, and evocation has ended. Receive our living prayer and grant us equanimity and peace and the grace of divine favor for what is pure in devotion, truth and righteous destiny.

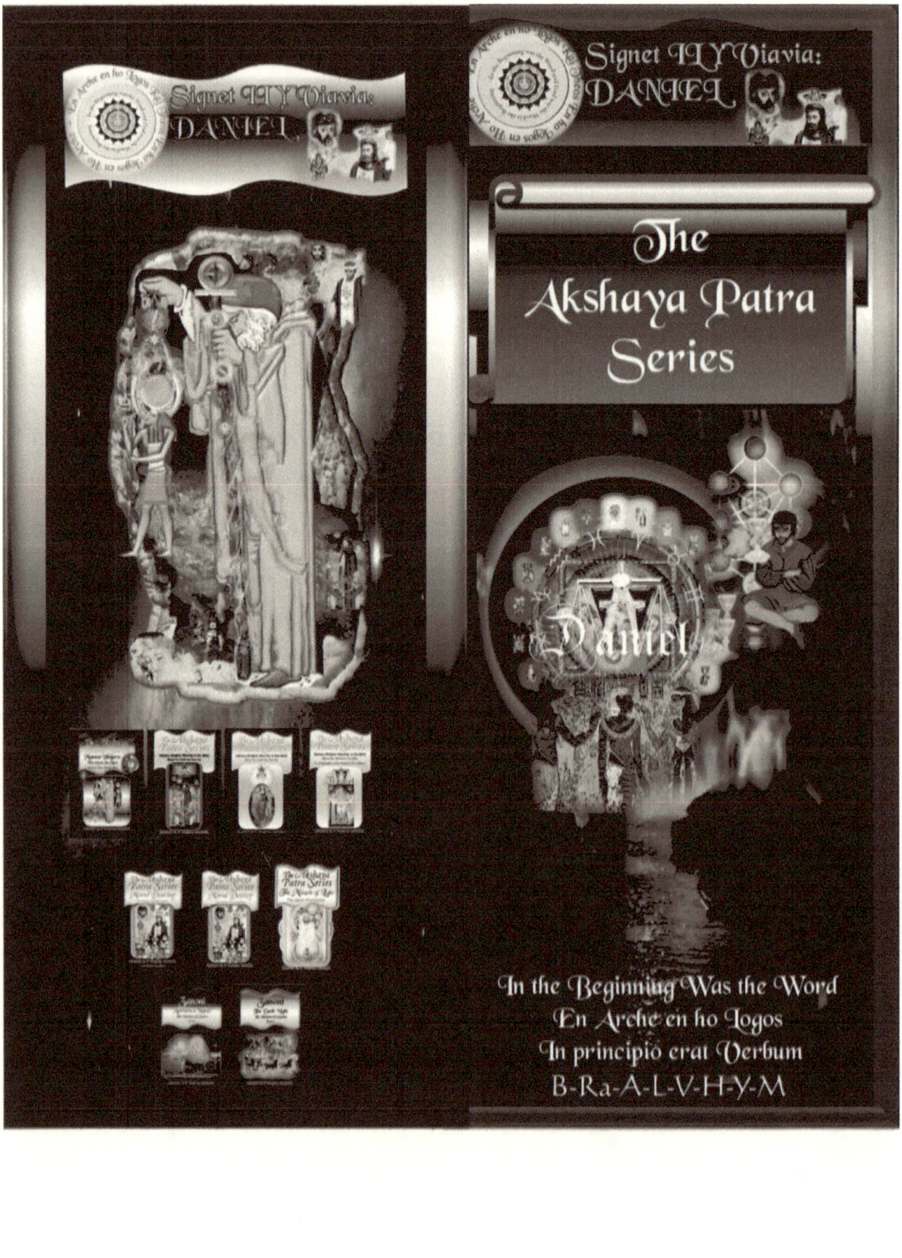

Published Works as of April 2017 under the Signet IL Y' Viavia: DANIEL

Lemuria (Mu) The Mysteries of Khan Gu - *(Novella Initiation)*

The Akshaya Patra Series:
Manasa Bhajare: Worship in the Mind
- Volume ONE Book 1 Part 1
- Volume ONE Book 1 Part 2
- Volume ONE Book 1 Part 3

Moral Destiny – Volume ONE Book 2 Part 1
Miracle of Light - Volume ONE Book 2 Part 2

Zanoni Series:
Zanoni The Rosicrucian Tale – A Story of the Long Livers
(*Bulwer-Lytton's book with new layout, translations, and an Introduction Introducing the Long Livers, also edited by Signet IL Y' Viavia: DANIEL*)

Zanoni The Initiation of Glyndon Series *(Novella Initiation)*:
- Part 1: **Apertura a Napoli – Initiation in Naples**
- Part 2: **The Dark Night**

Companion Series:
The Great Companion (An inclusive collection of quotes and selected aphorisms from the shorter individual Companion Series

books including additional notes, commentary and images from Volume ONE Books One and Two of the Akshaya Patra Series.]

Meditations & Aphorisms for Moral Transformation:
Companion to the Akshaya Patra Series Manasa Bhajare: Worship in the Mind Vol 1 Book 1 Part 1

Meditations & Aphorisms for Moral Transformation:
Companion to the Akshaya Patra Series Manasa Bhajare: Worship in the Mind Vol 1 Book 1 Part 2

Meditations & Aphorisms for Moral Transformation:
Companion to the Akshaya Patra Series Manasa Bhajare: Worship in the Mind Vol 1 Book 1 Part 3

Meditations & Aphorisms for Moral Transformation:
Companion to the Akshaya Patra Series Moral Destiny Vol 1 Book 2 Part 1

Meditations & Aphorisms for Moral Transformation:
Companion to the Akshaya Patra Series The Miracle of Light Vol 1 Book 2 Part 2

Shem Ha Mephoresh Meditations on the Great Name
Companion to the Akshaya Patra Series Moral Destiny Vol 1 Book 2 Part 1

Unpublished future publications that are works in progress or in some state of preparation for future publishing as of April 2017 under the Signet IL Y' Viavia: DANIEL

The Akshaya Patra Series:
Manasa Bhajare: Worship in the Mind
  Volume ONE Book 2 Part 3
  Volume ONE Book 3
  Volume ONE Book 4
  Volume ONE Book 5
  Volume ONE Book 6
  Volume ONE Book 7
  Volume TWO — Vibrations and Consciousness
  Volume THREE — Self Awareness
  Volume FOUR — Awakening the Harmony of Light
  Volume FIVE — The Significance of Number
  Volume SIX — Light of the World
  Volume SEVEN — The Tree of Light and Sound

Zanoni Series:
Zanoni The Initiation of Glyndon Series *(Novella Initiation)*:
  Part 3: **The Siege of Terror – The War Waged in Man**
  Part 4: **The Reign of Terror – The War Waged in France**

A Short Book of the Poem Prayers and Ramblings of the Flighty Ass: *(Novella Initiation)*

Legend of the Bastard King: Philosopher – Melchizedek: *(Francis Bacon, Anthony Bacon and Dr. John Dee; and the Mahatma Legend of the R&C and history of the Long Livers)*

    The Revelation
    The Sonnets
    The Plays
    The Trial and Liberation *(Novella Initiation)*
    America and Beyond

www.ingramcontent.com/pod-product-compliance
Lightning Source LLC
Chambersburg PA
CBHW021428080526
44588CB00009B/455